M000159308

Spoonfuls of Germany

For history, culture, and cooking - enjoy!

Nadia Hassani

The Hippocrene Cookbook Library

Afghan Food & Cookery
Alps, Cuisines of the
Aprovecho: A Mexican-American
  Border Cookbook
Argentina Cooks!, Exp. Ed.
Belarusian Cookbook, The
Bengali Five Spice Chronicles, The
Bolivian Kitchen, My Mother's
Brazil: A Culinary Journey
Cajun Cuisine, Stir the Pot:
  The History of
Calabria, Cucina di
Chile, Tasting
China's Fujian Province, Cooking from
Colombian Cooking, Secrets of
Corsican Cuisine
Croatian Cooking, Best of, Exp. Ed.
Czech Cooking, Best of, Exp. Ed.
Danish Cooking and Baking Traditions
Danube, All Along The, Exp. Ed.
Emilia-Romagna, The Cooking of
Egyptian Cuisine and Culture, Nile
  Style:
English Country Kitchen, The
Estonian Tastes and Traditions
Filipino Food, Fine
Finnish Cooking, Best of
Germany, Spoonfuls of
Greek Cooking, Regional
Haiti, Taste of
Havana Cookbook, Old (Bilingual)
Hungarian Cookbook, Exp. Ed.
India, A Culinary Journey
India, Flavorful
Indian Inspired Gluten-Free Cooking
Iraqi Family Cookbook
Jewish-Iraqi Cuisine, Mama Nazima's
Kerala Kitchen, The
Lebanese Cookbook, The
Ligurian Kitchen, A

Lithuanian Cooking, Art of
Malaysia, Flavors of
Mexican Flavor, Muy Bueno:
  Three Generations of
Middle Eastern Kitchen, The
Naples, My Love for
Nepal, Taste of
New Hampshire: from Farm to Kitchen
New Jersey Cookbook, Farms and
  Foods of the Garden State:
Ohio, Farms and Foods of
Persian Cooking, Art of
Pied Noir Cookbook: French Sephardic
  Cuisine
Piemontese, Cucina: Cooking from
  Italy's Piedmont
Polish Cooking, Best of, Exp. Ed.
Polish Country Kitchen Cookbook, The
Polish Heritage Cookery, Ill. Ed.
Polish Holiday Cookery
Polish Traditions, Old
Portuguese Encounters, Cuisines of
Punjab, Menus and Memories from
Romania, Taste of
Russian Cooking, The Best of
Scottish-Irish Pub and Hearth Cookbook
Sicilian Feasts
Slovenia, Flavors of
South Indian Cooking, Healthy
Spain, La Buena Mesa: The Regional
  Cooking of
Sri Lankan Home Cooking, Rice &
  Curry:
Trinidad and Tobago, Sweet Hands:
  Island Cooking from
Tuscan Kitchen, Tastes from a
Ukrainian Cookbook, The New
Ukrainian Cuisine, Best of, Exp. Ed.
Warsaw Cookbook, Old

Spoonfuls of Germany

German Regional Cuisine

Expanded Edition

Nadia Hassani

HIPPOCRENE BOOKS
NEW YORK

Paperback Expanded Edition, 2013

Copyright © 2004, 2013 Nadia Hassani.
All rights reserved.

Map on page 9 from *Foods and Beverages from Germany*, © German Agricultural
    Marketing Board CMA
Cover photography by Ted Rosen
Interior and author photography by Ted Rosen

Cover design by Brittany Hince
Book design by Acme Klong Design, Inc.

For more information, address:
HIPPOCRENE BOOKS, INC.
171 Madison Avenue
New York, NY 10016
www.hippocrenebooks.com

Previous edition ISBNs: ISBN-10: 0-7818-1057-4 (hc) / ISBN-13: 978-0-7818-1057-9 (hc)

Library of Congress Cataloging-in-Publication Data

Hassani, Nadia.
  Spoonfuls of Germany : German regional cuisine / Nadia Hassani. --
Expanded paperback edition.
    pages cm
  Includes indexes.
  ISBN-13: 978-0-7818-1308-2 (paperback)
  ISBN-10: 0-7818-1308-5 (paperback)
1. Cooking, German. I. Title.
TX721.H365 2013
641.5943--dc23

                                                    2013012848

Printed in the United States of America.

Contents

Foreword

Irma Rombauer's monumental *The Joy of Cooking* begins with an epigraph from Goethe's *Faust*: "That which thy fathers have bequeathed to thee, earn it anew if thou wouldst possess it." When I attended high school in Frankfurt am Main, Goethe's hometown, I studied *Faust* inside and out, but I never thought that this sentence would reveal its wisdom and truth to me through German food and by writing this cookbook.

I grew up in Germany in a bicultural family. Between my father, an immigrant from Tunisia, and my mother, a native of Westphalia, the meals we ate at home were eclectic, consisting of whatever my mother could assemble for dinner after a long day in the office. Most days we would have quick and easy meals: steak, pasta, and a salad. We never had fast food or frozen dinners. There was not much fast food available in Germany at the time. But that did not matter, because my mother deeply detests ready-made food. She still recalls with disgust the day we had just moved into a new apartment and she, as a last resort, warmed up ravioli straight from the can.

The few typical German dishes we had at home were *Grünkohl* (kale stew), which as a child I dreaded (not any more!), and *Rouladen* (beef roll-ups), which I loved (and still do). My maternal grandmother Lydia introduced me to a number of traditional German dishes when I came to her for lunch after school. She made me potato pancakes and filling bread puddings, which I preferred over the daily regimen of meat at home. At Christmas, she baked a variety of cookies, and for special family occasions she made a Black Forest cake so good no pastry shop version has ever fully satisfied me.

Except for these few goodies, I was not very fond of the traditional German foods I knew as a child. After family gatherings in my mother's native Westphalia, I complained to my parents about the old-fashioned, uncool, and bland home cooking. My mixed genes and struggle with a bicultural identity, I am sure, also contributed to my indifference towards German foods.

The summer I graduated from high school, I helped out in my mother's cousin's upscale restaurant in Caracas, Venezuela. This experience marked the beginning of my serious interest in cooking. For two decades, I explored the cuisines of many lands and cultures, but, with the exception of a few cakes and other desserts, I treated Germany as a blank spot on my culinary map.

Ironically, my emigration to the United States in 1998 brought me closer to German cooking. Moving to America meant the loss of most of my cultural references practically overnight. I felt this even more when I met my husband, and his two young children. I had not read the same books as a child, did not know their nursery rhymes, had never eaten macaroni and cheese, and had not a clue about who or what a Sloppy Joe is. I realized that catching up to the American lifestyle and culture would take forever and would always remain a patchwork since I could not turn back the clock. So I decided to turn the tables and introduce a few elements of my own culture into my new world. This, I hoped, would have the double effect of widening the horizon of my new family and fighting my occasional attacks of homesickness (which creep up on me especially during holidays).

My craving for German foods set in not long after I came to America. Before my visits to Germany, I send my mother a wish list of German dishes. I also started to do what many expatriates do: with each trip home, I bring back a few ingredients that are difficult or impossible to find in the United States. It's amazing how German food is all I can think about during the eight-hour plane trip from Newark to Frankfurt.

For the first two years after I came to the United States, I worked as an editor at Hippocrene Books. The publisher, George Blagowidow, hired me fresh-off-the-boat. Five years later, George must have been reading my mind when he asked me to write about German regional food. Writing this cookbook helped me rediscover my roots without leaving my home in America.

In this book, I take an approach different from most German regional cookbooks. The recipes are arranged into four regions: North, East, West, and South, rather than into the sixteen German federal states. While all regions have their distinctive food traditions, clear culinary borders within the regions are often difficult to draw, because many dishes have traveled around and have become popular in neighboring states, often with slight variations and under different names.

I discovered an abundance of German regional dishes, many of which were new to me. It thrilled me to learn that German cuisine has so much variety. Selecting the recipes for this book was therefore no easy task, and I realized very quickly that drawing a complete culinary map of Germany would be impossible. I primarily picked dishes that I find tasty. The 200 recipes in this book are an eclectic and personal selection that carries no claim to completeness.

My criteria for selecting recipes were driven by several considerations. I wanted to honor the food pyramid and find a reasonable balance between dishes with heavy meat content and those with little or no meat. True to its reputation, German cuisine *does* include a lot of meat dishes, especially pork. As well, I only included recipes with ingredients that are easily available in North American supermarkets and specialty food stores. Whenever possible, I provided alternatives and substitutes for typical German ingredients. I sacrificed several deserving dishes because I did not want to frustrate the cook and send her or him on a shopping odyssey.

Delving into the foods of Germany and the history and stories behind them gave me tremendous pleasure. If you enjoy these recipes half as much as I enjoyed preparing and writing them, I will be very satisfied.

A Fresh Look at German Cuisine:
a Cinderella about to be discovered?

When I originally worked on this book in 2003, new cookbooks about German cuisine in German were far and few. Today, ten years later, almost every region, era, and topic has its own cookbook: from farmhouse cooking to cooking with local ingredients, from cookbooks by celebrity chefs like Alfons Schuhbeck to food and recipe memoirs about the lost world of Eastern Prussia, and cookbooks celebrating and reinterpreting the once shunned socialist fare of the German Democratic Republic. Although one swallow (the bird, that is) does not make a summer, something of a renaissance is afoot. Diners are rediscovering German cuisine and polishing its reputation.

For the longest time, German cuisine had a bad image, as much within Germany as in the rest of the world. "German gourmet food" was viewed as an oxymoron. Either you ate gourmet food, or you ate German food, but the two did not go together.

While the French and Italians adore their cuisine and freely rave about it, the majority of Germans turn their noses up at German food. The reason for this disdain is not so much that German food really fits its stereotype of being heavy, fatty, and lacking refinement; the disdain actually runs deeper than their stomachs. The explanation lies in the history of the first half of the twentieth century, especially the twelve dark and somber years when Germany set out to dominate the world.

Over the past six decades, Germany has recovered from World War II on many levels. Although the country has been completely rebuilt, the damage to the cultural identity of the German people has yet to be fully repaired. After the war, being patriotic and proud of one's German heritage was looked down on because it was inextricably linked to the extreme nationalism of the Third Reich. The general mood included a feeling of low self-esteem. Celebrating German culinary traditions ran counter to the national psyche. Instead, in the postwar years, Germans opened their kitchens and their mouths to the cuisines of other countries. Almost every German home cook I know can make minestrone and tiramisú but most have never cooked a semolina dumpling soup or a red berry pudding from scratch. Nearly everyone in Germany has a wok but hardly anyone owns a spaetzle press.

Yet, traditional German cuisine never entirely disappeared from culinary memory. When I started to work on this book, I asked family and friends in Germany, as well as German expatriates and foreigners who had lived in Germany or frequently visited the country, about their favorite German dishes. The first reaction, especially among the native Germans, fits the well-known prejudice and antipathy towards German food. Out of dozens of people of different ages with whom I talked, the almost unanimous answer was: "German food—that's not my cup of tea." But when I insisted it couldn't be that bad, I extracted languishing confessions about the wonderful dishes that mothers and grandmothers had prepared.

The list of dishes I compiled reveals the tremendous variety German cuisine has to offer. Usually the diversity of German food and drink is acknowledged only when it comes to beer, bread, sausage, and ham, all of which boast several hundred different varieties. German cooking is far more diverse than is often acknowledged, and reducing it to pork knuckles with sauerkraut is a great injustice.

The many wars on German soil were detrimental to the development of a highly refined cuisine, according to Wolfram Siebeck, one of Germany's most beloved food writers (his column in the weekly newspaper *Die Zeit* has legendary status) and outspoken gourmets who teaches Germans how to eat well. Germany's location in the heart of Europe made it a battlefield throughout history but this situation also had culinary advantages. The country stretches from the coast of the North and Baltic Seas to the Alps and thus offers a fabulous variety of all kinds of produce, seafood, meat, game, and dairy products, all of which have shaped the specialties of each region. Additionally, Germany borders nine countries: Denmark, the Netherlands, Belgium, Luxembourg, France, Switzerland, Austria, the Czech Republic, and Poland. Each neighbor has had an important influence on German cuisine.

Until the unification of Germany in 1871, the country was divided into many different states, whose only common denominator was the German language and at times religious affiliation. After Germany became a unified state, large German communities with distinct culinary traditions remained outside the German Empire, for example the Germans of Bohemia. A country parceled up like this, some people argue, was never able to develop a distinct culinary tradition as one nation. This, however, can also be argued the opposite way—it was exactly this political fragmentation that led to the development of many different regional food traditions. One example is the distinctive cuisines of the cities and towns that belonged to the Hanseatic League, a loose but nonetheless successful trading association that included major cities like Hamburg, Lübeck, and Bremen. In those cities, housewives could buy imported foreign foods, and exotic ingredients found their way into local dishes.

For a long time, France provided the model for fine dining in Germany. The historic hostility between Germany and France was put aside when it came to food, particularly during the eighteenth century, when German high society ate French food exclusively. William II, however, the last German emperor, who abdicated at the end of World War I, ordered the court to eat only German dishes. Today it is Italy whose cuisine is at the forefront of fine dining and the new German epicurean's heaven. German politicians are no exception. Many leading social democrats recover from their public duties under the Tuscan sun, earning them the nickname "Tuscany party" (*Toskanafraktion*) in the late 1980s.

The German bourgeoisie coined its own form of cuisine, which is commonly known as *gutbürgerliche Küche*. The term, which sounds rather antiquated to modern ears, has remained in the German language to the present day. It stands for solid but slightly refined German-style comfort food with generously portioned quality ingredients. Sauerbraten with lots of gravy, potato dumplings, and red cabbage is a meal that qualifies as *gutbürgerlich*. The *gutbürgerliche Küche* is similar to our contemporary notion of a meal, consisting of appetizer, main course with side dishes, and dessert. The meals of the German farmers, however, included just one dish, usually some sort of stew or a thick, nourishing soup. On Sundays, a roast with potatoes and vegetables was served. This diet explains why recipes for distinctive side dishes are scarce, especially in rural areas.

With a short respite before the outbreak of World War I and during the 1920s, the first half of the twentieth century did not give the Germans much opportunity to dwell on their culinary traditions. The differences between rich and poor were leveled; having enough to eat was all that mattered. In her 1979 autobiography, film diva Marlene Dietrich recalls how she was the only one whose face did not turn yellow from eating rutabagas day in, day out for breakfast, lunch, and dinner, and in every possible form. Again during the depression in the 1930s, there was no room for culinary sophistication. In Nazi Germany, Germans were trained to adhere to the motto "Canons instead of butter."

In postwar Germany, when food was no longer scarce, Germans in the western part of the country could finally have their fill. This era went down in history as the *Freßwelle*, literally "the wave of pigging out." In those days, the national identity was still too shattered to even think of picking up German culinary arts. Instead, with immigrant workers arriving from other European countries, Germans started to discover the foods of other nations. Pizza is the oldest and the most successful of the immigrant foods in Germany. The first pizzeria was opened in the city of Würzburg in 1952. It took time, however, for German restaurant goers to warm to pizza. To many Würzburgers, pizza looked like a strange pancake. The first patrons were American GIs who craved the pizza they knew from home. Today, Greek foods such as gyros and tsatsiki are as common as falafel sandwiches and Chinese spring rolls.

Another food phenomenon of the postwar era is the appearance of fast food in Germany. Today the country has its share of the golden arches and other American fast-food chains, but even before they popped up, snack bars called *Imbißbuden* existed everywhere. They are individually owned businesses where the most famous of German fast foods, *Currywurst* (sausage with a ketchup and curry topping) is served, alongside another German fast-food classic, *Pommes rot-weiß* (red and white French fries served with ketchup and mayonnaise). And, of course, *Döner Kebab*, the Turkish minced lamb specialty molded around a spit and roasted and served in pita bread. The Turks are the largest immigrant group in Germany, and their fast-food outlets are becoming an integral part of the way Germans eat today. There are more than ten thousand Turkish greengrocers in Germany, with clientele from all levels of German society.

Germany was divided until 1989, a total of 44 years. The culinary scene in the East, behind the Iron Curtain, was much different from the West. The only thing the divided country had in common was that in neither the East nor the West was the celebrating of German culinary arts encouraged. Food in the East was much scarcer than in the West. The absence of a Marshall Plan, which made it possible for West Germans to quickly rebuild their country, was obvious in the East. At the top, the Communist government publicly stigmatized fine dining as bourgeois decadence. As a consequence, and also because private initiatives and businesses were not welcome, many regional foods and traditions disappeared almost completely. For example, the legendary specialty turnips, *Teltower Rübchen*, almost died out. Some regional specialties, however, such as *Baumkuchen* (cylinder cake), survived. Their production was even encouraged, if not out of culinary passion, then certainly because as exports they brought in western currencies.

The fall of the Berlin Wall in 1989 created tremendous challenges for the newly reunified Germany, especially bringing the standard of living in the East to the same level as the West. Reviving the culinary traditions that had been almost lost was certainly not at the top of the agenda during the first years. But now that the necessary infrastructure is in place—a large number of hotels and restaurants have opened or reopened in the five states of what was formerly the German Democratic Republic—a quiet culinary revolution is taking place. Many young chefs, trained in the West but with roots in the East, build their menus around local products, often with outstanding results.

Rediscovering old recipes is not limited to the East. In many other regions and micro-regions of Germany, local culinary traditions and foods are experiencing a rebirth. Grandma's forgotten recipes are in demand again. This revival goes hand in hand with the desire to use locally grown foods. Germans are known to be very health-conscious. And what foods could be better than the ones grown organically by local producers for generations? The legislation of the European Union, often scolded for its destructive effects on national agriculture, gave producers of local foods another boost, when it introduced the Protected Designation of Origin and the Protected Geographical Indication for Foodstuffs in 1992. These regulations are the reason why sausage can only be labeled *Frankfurter* if it is made in Frankfurt or its surroundings. Similarly, *Berliner Weiße* beer is only authentic if brewed in Berlin or the immediate vicinity.

In the story of Cinderella, a lot of fuss is made about her stepsisters. They get all the fancy clothing and jewels, while Cinderella stays behind in her gray apron, waiting to be discovered. Like Cinderella's beauty, some cuisines are less widely acclaimed than others. I think German food is like Cinderella still in her apron— only moments before the royal knock on the door, when her beauty and charm are finally discovered by the world.

Culinary Map of Germany

Northern Lights

The northern region of Germany is made up of the states of Schleswig-Holstein, Lower Saxony, Mecklenburg-West Pomerania, and the city-states of Hamburg and Bremen. This region includes several hundred miles of coastline along the North and Baltic Seas. Both Sweden, a littoral state on the Baltic Sea, and Denmark, Germany's neighbor on the North Sea, have influenced North German cuisine. The Scandinavian trait of combining sweet and sour ingredients, for example, has crept into many dishes.

The people of northern Germany have long been called *Fischköpfe* (fish heads). This unflattering epithet reflects a culinary truth: fish and seafood are staples of the North German cuisine. Kale stew with *Pinkel* (an odd-sounding word in German, too) sausage is another cornerstone of the northern cuisine. Northern Germany also has a plentiful repertoire of scrumptious cakes and other desserts, crowned by the ubiquitous *Rote Grütze* (red berry pudding).

Much of northern Germany is rural, including the state of Schleswig-Holstein, home to the famous Holstein cattle. What local farmers and fishermen put on their dinner plates every day is traditionally simple and hearty fare. Cities like Hamburg, Bremen, and Lübeck, on the other hand, take pride in their fine cuisine, which often incorporates exotic ingredients. There is an historical precedent for this as many of the cities in the North were part of the Hanseatic League, a medieval trade association that brought the city dwellers wealth and provided them with imports from overseas.

Shrimp Salad on Mixed Greens

Friesischer Krabbensalat

Fish and seafood are staples of the cuisine of the Frisia region, a low-lying area that borders the North Sea. Although the weather there can be rough even in the height of summer, both the North Frisian and the East Frisian Islands are popular summer resorts. There are often more people on the beach in bright yellow raincoats, nicknamed *Ostfriesennerze* (East Frisian mink coats) than in bathing suits!

The shrimp of the North Sea are tiny. The closest shrimp you can find in America are miniature shrimp, which count about 100 per pound. The smaller the size, the shorter the boiling time, so make sure you do not overcook them.

---

1 pound very small to
  miniature unshelled raw
  shrimp, or $1/2$ pound
  cooked, shelled, and
  deveined shrimp
$1/4$ cup light mayonnaise
2 teaspoons ketchup
2 teaspoons brandy
Salt and freshly milled
  black pepper
1 tablespoon finely
  chopped fresh dill
6 medium white
  mushrooms, cleaned,
  trimmed, and thinly sliced
4 to 6 red-skinned radishes,
  cleaned, trimmed, and
  thinly sliced
1 hard-boiled egg, peeled
  and sliced
4 cups (4 ounces) washed
  and dried mixed greens
  (mesclun mix), in
  bite-size pieces

4 to 6 servings

---

1. If using raw shrimp, bring a large pot of salted water to a boil. Drop the shrimp into the water, reduce the heat, and simmer for 2 to 3 minutes, or until pink. Drain, shell, devein the shrimp, and set aside.

2. Mix the mayonnaise with the ketchup and brandy. Season with salt and pepper and stir in the dill.

3. Combine the shrimp, mushrooms, radishes, and egg in a mixing bowl. Add the dressing and toss. Arrange the greens on a large serving platter and place the shrimp salad on top. Serve immediately with toasted bread or baguette slices.

Scrambled Eggs with Shrimp

Rührei mit Krabben

This is a quick and easy shrimp recipe, and makes a great brunch dish. It tastes best with a thick slice of fresh, wholesome bread.

1 pound very small to miniature unshelled raw shrimp, or 1/2 pound cooked, shelled, and deveined shrimp

8 eggs

Salt and freshly milled black pepper

2 tablespoons unsalted butter, plus additional butter for spreading

1 tablespoon snipped chives

4 slices bread

4 servings

1. If using raw shrimp, bring a large pot of salted water to a boil. Drop the shrimp into the water, reduce the heat, and simmer for 2 to 3 minutes, or until pink. Drain, shell, devein the shrimp, and set aside.

2. Crack the eggs into a bowl, add salt and pepper, and beat lightly with a fork. Melt 2 tablespoons butter in a large nonstick skillet over low heat. Increase the heat just a notch and slowly pour in the eggs. As soon as they begin to thicken, stir with a wooden spoon or spatula until the eggs are set and no liquid remains. Remove from the heat and add the chives.

3. Spread butter on the bread. Divide the shrimp and eggs into 4 equal portions and heap the eggs on one half of each slice of bread and the shrimp on the other half. Serve at once.

Blue Mussels Steamed in Wine

Miesmuscheln in Weinsud

Like in North America, blue mussels are the most common mussels in Germany, where they grow in the North Sea and the Baltic Sea. They are only harvested during the fall and winter, when they do not easily perish. The fishermen do not mind the summer break, as the mussels grow particularly well during this time and have a chance to multiply.

2 quarts fresh blue mussels
3 tablespoons unsalted butter
2 large yellow onions, peeled and chopped
1 stalk celery, trimmed and chopped
1 leek, thoroughly cleaned, trimmed, and chopped
1 carrot, peeled and chopped
Salt
$\frac{1}{2}$ teaspoon black peppercorns
1 bay leaf
$\frac{1}{2}$ cup coarsely chopped fresh flat-leaf parsley
1 cup dry white wine

4 to 6 servings

1. Clean the mussels with a brush under cold running water and remove the beards.

2. Melt the butter in a stockpot and sauté the onions until translucent. Add the celery, leek, carrot, salt, peppercorns, bay leaf, parsley, and wine. Reduce the heat, cover, and simmer for 10 minutes.

3. Increase the heat to high and add the mussels. Cook for 6 to 8 minutes, or until the mussels open. Discard any mussels that remain shut. Strain the broth and put the mussels in a large serving bowl along with the broth. Serve at once with fresh bread.

Barley Soup

Graupensuppe

Pearl barley (*Graupen*) had a tenaciously bad reputation in Germany, especially with the older generation, who remembers the large chunky barley as survival food after World War II. It was nicknamed *Kälberzähne* (calf's teeth) because that's what it looked like. Pearl barley nowadays has a much finer consistency, and makes a nutritious, nutty addition to soup. There are various types of barley soup recipes in north German cuisine. This is a light version with chicken and mixed vegetables.

*5 chicken drumsticks
(about 1½ pounds)
1 carrot, peeled and diced
1 stalk celery, trimmed
and chopped
1 medium yellow onion,
peeled and finely
chopped
1 leek, thoroughly cleaned,
trimmed, and chopped
1 small bunch flat-leaf
parsley, stems removed
and chopped
½ teaspoon dried marjoram
2 whole cloves
1 bay leaf
½ teaspoon black
peppercorns
½ cup pearl barley
2 teaspoons salt, or more
to taste*

4 servings

1. Put the drumsticks in a pot with 6 cups water. Bring to a boil and skim off the scum that forms at the top. Reduce the heat, cover, and cook for 1 hour, removing additional scum a few times.

2. Strain the broth into a heatproof bowl and return it to the pot. Add the remaining ingredients and 2 cups water and cook for 45 minutes, until the barley is soft but still has some bite.

3. While the vegetables cook, take the meat off the bones and cut it into bite-size pieces. Discard the bones and skin.

4. At the end of the cooking time, add the chicken to the soup and reheat it thoroughly. Salt to taste and remove the bay leaf and whole cloves. Serve hot.

Elderberry Soup with Farina Dumplings

Holunderbeersuppe mit Grießklößchen

Elderberries have truly benefitted from the renaissance of heirloom foods in Germany. With a bit of luck, you can now find elderberries at farmers' markets in the United States. I am thrilled I can now include my grandmother's recipe for Elderberry Soup in this book.

In Germany, the dumplings are made from farina (*Weichweizengrieß*), also known as cream of wheat. These dumplings are softer than the dumplings made from semolina (*Hartweizengrieß*), which are served with meat broth or vegetable soup.

Soup:
2 organic lemons
¼ cup plus ¾ cup sugar
2 tart apples
½ cinnamon stick
1 quart unsweetened pure elderberry juice
2 tablespoons cornstarch

Dumplings:
2 tablespoons unsalted butter
1 cup low-fat or whole milk
⅓ cup (2¾ ounces) farina
1 tablespoon sugar

4 servings

1. For the soup: With a vegetable peeler, remove a 3-inch strip of zest from one of the lemons. Squeeze the lemons. Put the lemon zest strip, half of the lemon juice, and ¼ cup of the sugar in a heavy pot.

2. Peel and core the apples and thinly slice. Add to the pot along with the cinnamon stick. Cook over medium heat until the apples are soft but not falling apart and the sugar is lightly caramelized. Remove from the heat immediately—the sugar should not turn dark brown.

3. Mix the elderberry juice with the remaining ¾ cup of sugar. If the elderberry juice is already lightly sweetened (*see box on page 17*) you might want to use up to ¼ cup less sugar. Add the sweetened juice to the apples and bring to a boil. Reduce the heat to low and cook for 5 to 8 minutes.

4. Dissolve the cornstarch in 2 tablespoons cold water. Whisk into the soup. Bring to a boil and cook until the soup thickens and turns clear again, stirring constantly. Remove from the heat.

5. For the dumplings: Bring butter and milk to a boil in a small saucepan. Whisk in the farina and return to a boil, whisking constantly. Add the sugar. Remove from the heat. Let sit until cool enough to handle. Shape into walnut-size dumplings with wet hands and add them to the soup. Remove the cinnamon stick and lemon peel. Chill or serve right away.

Elderberries

Not only the berries, but also the flowers of elderberries are edible. Elderflowers fried in beer batter (*Hollerküchle*) are a south Germany specialty. The creamy white elderflowers are also used to make fragrant jelly and elderflower syrup. Elderberries, which are packed with vitamins, are one of the last berries to ripen in the summer; they make delicious jams, jellies, and other preserves.

Elderberries grow best in swampy, moist soil near a pond or stream. The American elderberry, a native plant to the United States, is a wild species that is related to the European elderberry. Its flowers and berries can be used just like the European elderberries, but if you plan on foraging elderberries make sure you identify them properly. There are also poisonous red elderberries found in the wild.

An easy way to extract the juice from elderberries is with a steam juicer, an ingenious invention that you can use for many other fruits as well. It uses steam to extract the natural juices of soft fruits. I add ¼ cup sugar to each quart juice before pouring it in 1-quart canning jars and processing it for 20 minutes in a boiling water bath.

Potato Soup with Prunes

Tüften un Plum

Potato soup is often associated with German cuisine. There are numerous versions of potato soup, and each region has its own set of recipes. Potato soup with prunes is a less known sweet-and-savory potato soup from northern Germany. The prunes give it a hint of sweetness. For a fancy twist, you can wrap the pitted prunes individually in sliced bacon, sauté them, then add them to the hot soup.

2 tablespoons oil
2 medium yellow onions, chopped
4 medium starchy yellow potatoes (1¼ pounds), peeled and diced
2 carrots, peeled and diced
1 small stalk celery, chopped
1 quart vegetable broth
4 ounces lean bacon, diced
12 to 14 pitted prunes, coarsely chopped
Salt and freshly milled black pepper
White wine vinegar

4 servings

1. Heat the oil in a pot. Add the onions and cook until translucent, stirring. Add the potatoes, carrots, and celery, and cook for 5 minutes, stirring. Add the broth and bring to a boil. Reduce heat and cover. Cook for 20 to 25 minutes, until the vegetables are soft.

2. While the soup is cooking, place the bacon in a cold large skillet and sauté over medium heat until crisp and all the fat has been drawn out. Remove the bacon bits with a slotted spoon and degrease on paper towels.

3. Pour off most of the bacon fat from the skillet and discard. Briefly sauté the chopped prunes in the remaining fat, then degrease on paper towels.

4. Puree the soup. Add the bacon bits and prunes and reheat thoroughly. Season with salt, pepper, and a dash of vinegar. Serve hot.

Potato Soup with Shrimp

Kartoffelsuppe mit Krabben

It is not unusual to find ginger in old German recipes as it has been traded in Germany for many centuries. One important port of entry for ginger was the major Baltic port of Lübeck. The city was the capital of the Hanseatic League, a powerful medieval trade association of cities and merchants.

6 ounces very small to miniature unshelled raw shrimp
1 tablespoon vegetable oil
1 shallot, peeled and finely minced
1 leek, thoroughly cleaned, trimmed, and chopped
1 medium russet potato, peeled and diced
1 medium red potato, peeled and diced
1 carrot, peeled and chopped
1 ($14\frac{1}{2}$-ounce) can chicken broth, plus more as needed
Salt and freshly milled black pepper
Pinch of ground ginger
Pinch of dried tarragon
$\frac{1}{4}$ cup light cream

4 to 6 servings

1. Bring salted water to a boil in a large pot. Add the shrimp and cook for 2 to 3 minutes, or until pink. Shell and devein them and reserve the shells. Simmer the shells with 2 cups water for 15 minutes to make stock.

2. Meanwhile, heat the oil in another large saucepan. Sauté the shallot until translucent. Add the leek and cook for about 3 minutes. Add the potatoes, carrot, and chicken broth.

3. Strain the shrimp stock, add it to the soup and stir. Reduce the heat and cook over medium heat for 20 minutes, or until the potatoes are tender.

4. Puree the soup in a blender for just a few seconds so that some of the vegetables remain in chunks. If the soup is too thick, add more broth.

5 Add the shrimp and reheat the soup thoroughly. Season with salt, pepper, ginger, and tarragon. Stir in the cream and serve at once.

Crab Soup with Vegetables

Hamburger Krebssuppe

Over the centuries, the cuisine of Hamburg established a well-deserved reputation for its sophistication. The wealthy traders of this city-state played a leading role in the Hanseatic League, and they certainly ate well.

This crab soup is a classic made with live crabs, but you can also substitute good-quality canned crabmeat.

---

2 tablespoons unsalted butter
1 medium yellow onion, peeled and finely chopped
1 carrot, peeled and chopped
1 leek, thoroughly cleaned, trimmed, and chopped
1 stalk celery, trimmed and chopped
2 ($14\frac{1}{2}$-ounce) cans chicken broth
$\frac{1}{2}$ cup fresh shelled or frozen green peas
1 tablespoon all-purpose flour
6 spears fresh cooked or canned white asparagus, drained (see box opposite page)
$\frac{1}{2}$ cup heavy cream
$\frac{1}{2}$ (16-ounce) can pasteurized crabmeat, or $\frac{1}{2}$ pound fresh crabmeat
2 tablespoons cognac, or some other good brandy
Salt and freshly milled black pepper

6 servings

1. Heat the butter in a pot and sauté the onion until translucent. Add the carrot, leek, celery, and chicken broth. Bring to a boil, then reduce the heat and simmer for 15 minutes.

2. Strain the soup through a fine sieve and transfer the broth back to the pot. Add the peas and cook 5 to 10 minutes, depending on whether you use fresh or frozen.

3. Mix the flour with a few tablespoons of the broth in a small bowl until the flour is entirely dissolved, then whisk it into the soup. Simmer until the soup thickens, stirring constantly.

4. Cut the asparagus into 1-inch chunks and add to the soup with the cream. Drain the crabmeat, if necessary, and add it to the soup. Stir in the cognac and season with salt and pepper. Reheat the soup thoroughly and serve hot.

How to Cook White Asparagus

Germany is famous for its white asparagus, also called blanched asparagus. Unlike green asparagus, white asparagus always requires peeling, regardless of the thickness of the stalks.

If you are lucky enough to find white asparagus, check whether it is fresh by gently knocking two stalks against each other—they should make a springy sound. Also, the cut ends must be light-colored and moist.

First wash the asparagus. Then, carefully peel each stalk away from the tips without damaging them (the tips are considered the finest part). Make sure to remove the skin all the way around. Trim ½ to 1 inch from the ends. If you are not cooking the asparagus right away, wrap it in a clean damp kitchen towel and store in the vegetable compartment of your refrigerator.

To cook the asparagus, you need a saucepan large enough to lay the asparagus horizontally. Fill it two-thirds with lightly salted water and bring to a boil. Add a pinch of sugar and a dot of butter. Reduce the heat. Put the stalks in the water with all of the tips facing in the same direction. If you cook 1 pound or more, bundle the asparagus with kitchen twine in 1-pound portions.

Simmer the asparagus for 12 to 15 minutes, depending on the thickness. Carefully remove the spears with a slotted spoon and drain on a large plate.

Shrimp Soup with White Asparagus

Krabbensuppe

Although asparagus is mainly grown in southwestern Germany, it is incorporated into fine regional foods all over the country. The original soup is made with the tiny North Sea shrimp.

1 pound very small to miniature unshelled raw shrimp
1 stalk leek, thoroughly cleaned, trimmed, and chopped
1 carrot, peeled and chopped
1 parsnip, peeled and chopped
1 turnip, peeled and sliced
Salt
Pinch of sugar
Pinch of medium-hot curry powder
3 tablespoons unsalted butter
$\frac{1}{3}$ cup all-purpose flour
$\frac{2}{3}$ cup dry white wine, at room temperature
4 spears fresh cooked or canned white asparagus, drained (see page 21)
1 cup heavy cream, at room temperature
Freshly milled black pepper
2 tablespoons finely chopped fresh dill

6 servings

1. Bring salted water to a boil in a large pot. Add the shrimp, reduce the heat, and simmer for 2 to 3 minutes, or until pink. Shell and devein the shrimp, reserving the shells.

2. Cook the shells with 1 quart water and the leek, carrot, parsnip, turnip, salt, sugar, and curry powder for 30 minutes. Strain the broth into a large bowl and set aside. Discard the shells and vegetables.

3. Melt the butter in the pot and stir in the flour. Cook over low heat until it begins to turn beige, stirring constantly. Whisk in the wine and shrimp stock.

4. Cut the asparagus into 1-inch chunks and add to the soup, together with the shelled shrimp and cream. Thoroughly reheat the soup but do not boil. Season with salt and pepper. Stir in the dill and serve hot.

Buttermilk Soup with Poached Pears

Buttermilchsuppe mit Birnen

Dairy products have always played an important role in the North German soup kitchen. In times when meat was a luxury restricted to Sundays, buttermilk soup was often cooked with a chunk of bacon and made more nourishing by adding small flour dumplings, called *Klüten* in the North German dialect.

This is a contemporary light and meat-free version of buttermilk soup. It is served hot or chilled, which is a very refreshing way to start a summer meal.

Pears:
$\frac{1}{2}$ cup sugar
3 ripe but firm pears,
   such as Bosc
1 cinnamon stick

Soup:
3 tablespoons unsalted
   butter
$\frac{1}{4}$ cup all-purpose flour
1 quart lukewarm
   buttermilk
Pinch of salt
Pinch of ground cinnamon

6 to 8 servings

1. For the pears: Bring 2 cups water to a boil with the sugar in a large saucepan. Stir to dissolve the sugar. Peel and core the pears, remove their stems, and cut them in half. Reduce the heat to a simmer and place the pears in the liquid in a single layer. Add the cinnamon stick. Cover and cook for 20 minutes, or until the pears are soft but not falling apart. Remove the cinnamon stick and set the pears aside.

2. For the soup: Melt the butter in a large saucepan. Add the flour and cook for 2 to 3 minutes, stirring constantly with a spatula or wooden spoon, until well blended. Slowly stir in the buttermilk, whisking vigorously. Add the salt and simmer until the soup thickens.

3. Strain the juice from the poached pears—the yield should be about 1½ cups—and gradually stir it into the soup. Simmer the soup for about 5 minutes and then add the cinnamon.

4. Dice the pears and add them to the soup. Chill, if desired. Stir well before serving.

Blueberry Soup with Caramelized Croutons

Blaubeersuppe

This refreshing, velvety soup is one of my summer favorites. In Germany, it is made with *Heidelbeeren* (bilberries or whortleberries), the European cousin of the blueberry. Bilberries are smaller and tarter than the North American blueberries, which are a good substitute for bilberries.

Soup:
2 pints fresh blueberries
$\frac{1}{2}$ cup sugar
1 cinnamon stick
Zest of 1 organic lemon,
    finely grated
2 cups dry red wine
1 tablespoon plus
    1 teaspoon cornstarch

Croutons:
8 thin slices baguette, or
    4 slices firm white bread
1 tablespoon unsalted butter
1 tablespoon sugar

6 to 8 servings

1. For the soup: Clean the blueberries and pick them over for culls. Put them in a large saucepan with 2 cups water, the sugar, cinnamon stick, and lemon zest. Cover and cook over low to medium heat for 15 minutes, stirring occasionally. Press the soup through a fine sieve. Pour it back into the pan and discard the solids. Add the wine and bring the soup back to a simmer.

2. Mix the cornstarch with a few tablespoons of the soup in a small bowl until the cornstarch is completely dissolved, and whisk it into the soup. Simmer until the soup thickens and becomes clear. Remove from the heat. Cool and chill.

3. For the croutons: Cut the bread into $\frac{1}{2}$-inch cubes. Heat the butter in a large skillet and add the bread. Crisp the bread over high heat, turning frequently. Sprinkle the sugar over the bread and caramelize.

4. Stir the soup well, ladle it in individual soup bowls, and top with a few croutons. Serve at once.

Pear and Green Bean Stew with Bacon

Birnen, Bohnen, Speck (Gröne Hein)

This specialty from northern Germany is also known as *Gröne Hein* (Green Henry), most likely named after the green beans in it. The combination of sweet and sour is a characteristic that North German cooking has in common with the cuisines of nearby Scandinavia.

1½ pounds fresh or frozen green beans
10 to 12 thin slices (6 ounces) lean center-cut bacon
1 sprig fresh savory, or ¼ teaspoon dried
8 small firm pears
Pinch of sugar
Salt and freshly milled black pepper
1 tablespoon finely chopped fresh flat-leaf parsley

6 to 8 servings

1. Trim the beans and, depending on their length, cut them in half or thirds.

2. Cut the bacon into small strips and place in a large cold saucepan. Cook over medium heat until the fat has been drawn out. Add 1¼ cups water, the beans, and the savory. Cover and simmer over medium heat for 30 minutes, adding a few more tablespoons of water if the beans start to cook dry.

3. Peel the pears and remove the stems. Put the whole pears in a separate saucepan with the pinch of sugar. Add water to cover and simmer over medium heat for 20 minutes, or until the pears can be easily pierced with a knife. Remove the pears from the pan and drain.

4. Carefully season the beans with salt—they might already be salty enough from the bacon—and pepper and garnish with parsley. Put the beans in a serving dish and place the pears on top. Serve hot.

Kale Stew with Smoked Meat and Sausages

Grünkohleintopf

Kale is a culinary cult item in northern Germany. The season starts with the first night frost and lasts until March, or as long as the temperatures are still below freezing to transform the starch in kale into sugar, which gives it its special taste. Since the mid-nineteenth century, when mass transportation became available, people from the cities have made day trips to the country just to eat kale. Today, these *Kohlfahrten* (kale trips) are part of a thriving tourist industry. Companies, sports clubs, or groups of friends organize social events around kale, which often start with a hike and end with a hearty kale dinner.

Kale stew is always served with a variety of smoked meats and sausages, including the traditional *Pinkel* sausage. This specialty from Bremen, which was named after the part of the cow intestines used to case the sausage, is made with beef and/or pork, onions, oat groats, and bacon. With a bit of luck, you might find it in specialty stores or German-style butcher shops, but you can also use any other smoked boiling sausage, or precooked sausage, such as kielbasa.

Kale stew tastes even better when reheated. It also lends itself to freezing.

$2\frac{1}{2}$ to 3 pounds kale, washed and stems and ribs removed
2 tablespoons vegetable oil
2 medium yellow onions, peeled and chopped
2 tablespoons rolled oats
1 pound smoked pork loin
3 smoked boiling sausages (including 1 Pinkel sausage, if available)
Salt and freshly milled black pepper
Generous pinch of ground nutmeg

6 servings

1. Bring a large pot of salted water to a boil. Plunge the kale into the water and blanch for 1 to 2 minutes. Drain the kale well in a colander and chop it coarsely.

2. Heat the oil in a large saucepan and add the onions. Sauté until translucent. Add the blanched kale and 2 cups water. Stir in the oats and bring to a boil, then reduce the heat and simmer for 30 minutes, adding 1 cup water in $\frac{1}{4}$-cup increments, if necessary. The stew should be very moist but not soupy.

3. Add the pork loin and the Pinkel sausage, and cook over low heat for 30 minutes. Add the smoked sausages and up to $\frac{1}{2}$ cup water, if necessary. Cook for 30 minutes. The smoked sausages should only be added for the last 30 minutes of the cooking time, otherwise they will burst. Season with salt, pepper, and nutmeg. Serve with boiled or caramelized potatoes (see page 37).

Roast Duck with Apple and Rum-Raisin Stuffing

Ente mit Lübecker Füllung

This stuffed duck comes from Lübeck, the historic port city on the Baltic Sea. If you find that duck does not yield enough meat, there is no reason why you cannot use the exquisite stuffing for other poultry, such as Cornish hen or even turkey.

Stuffing:
$\frac{1}{2}$ cup washed and dried raisins
$\frac{1}{4}$ cup golden rum
6 slices firm white bread, cut into small cubes
1 tablespoon vegetable oil
3 large tart cooking apples, cored, peeled, and cubed
Salt
Pinch of ground cardamom
Pinch of ground nutmeg
Pinch of dried sage
3 tablespoons dry white wine

Duck:
1 duck or duckling (4 to 5 pounds)
Salt and freshly milled black pepper
1 tablespoon clarified butter
1 cup dry white wine

4 servings

1. For the stuffing: Steep the raisins in the rum. Place the bread on a baking sheet and leave in the oven set to 350 degrees F until dry and light brown, turning once.

2. Heat the oil in a large nonstick skillet. Sauté the apples until they start to soften. Add the toasted bread, salt, cardamom, nutmeg, and sage. Add the raisins plus the excess rum and the wine. Toss well.

3. Preheat the oven to 400 degrees F.

4. For the duck: Remove the giblets from the body cavity, cut off the neck, if necessary, and discard these parts. Cut out any excess fat from the cavity. Wash the duck under cold water and pat dry with paper towels. Rub the duck inside and out with salt and pepper. Stuff the duck loosely, reserving 1 tablespoon of stuffing for the gravy. Sew or skewer the openings shut.

5. Heat the clarified butter in a large skillet and brown the duck on all sides. Place the duck breast down in a large covered casserole or a roasting pan covered with aluminum foil and roast for 45 minutes.

7. Reduce the heat to 350 degrees and uncover the duck. Prick the skin all over with a fork. Turn the duck on its back and roast for 45 to 75 minutes, depending on whether you like it rare or well done. Baste occasionally with the pan juices.

8. Remove the duck from the pan and keep warm. Absorb the excess fat from the casserole with paper towels and deglaze with the wine. Strain the juice into a small saucepan, bring to a boil, and let simmer for a few minutes to thicken the gravy. Add the reserved 1 tablespoon stuffing and season the gravy with salt and pepper.

9. Carve the duck and arrange the meat on a large serving plate or individual plates with the stuffing. Serve the gravy separately.

Roast Leg of Lamb with Juniper Berry Sauce

Heidschnuckenkeule

For a long time, the Lüneburger Heide, a large heath in Lower Saxony, was associated with shepherds driving their flocks, the typical *Heidschnucken* (North German moorland sheep). This animal got its droll name from the word *schnucken* (to nibble), because it nibbles the shoots of conifers and deciduous trees, preventing the heath from becoming woods. *Heidschnucken* are descended from mouflons (wild sheep from Corsica and Sardinia), which were brought to Germany a thousand years ago.

*2 tablespoons crushed
  juniper berries
1 tablespoon dried thyme
Freshly milled black pepper
1 (5-pound) leg of lamb,
  bone, fell, and most fat
  removed
1½ tablespoons vegetable
  oil
1½ tablespoons clarified
  butter
2 carrots, peeled and chopped
2 medium yellow onions,
  peeled and chopped
1 bay leaf
Salt
1¼ cups dry red wine,
  plus more as needed
⅓ cup sour cream
1 tablespoon all-purpose
  flour*

10 to 12 servings

1. Combine the juniper berries, thyme, and pepper in a small mixing bowl. Rub the lamb with the spices, cover, and refrigerate for 2 hours.

2. Preheat the oven to 400 degrees F.

3. Heat the oil and butter and brown the meat on all sides in a large skillet. Place the meat fat-side up in a roasting pan. Arrange the carrots, onions, bay leaf, and salt around the meat. Pour 1 cup of the wine over it and place in the oven. Roast for 1½ hours, basting frequently with the remaining ¼ cup wine and water if it becomes too dry. Check for doneness with a thermometer: 140 degrees F for rare, 150 to 155 degrees for medium, and 160 degrees for medium-well.

4. Turn off the oven. Remove the meat from the pan, transfer to a large platter and let it sit in the warm oven for 10 minutes with the oven door open.

5. Deglaze the pan with ½ cup hot water, or more, if necessary. Degrease and strain the gravy into a small saucepan. Whisk in the sour cream. Dissolve the flour in 1 to 2 tablespoons water and add to the sauce. Simmer for a few minutes until the sauce thickens. Season with salt and pepper. Slice the meat and place it on a serving platter. Serve the gravy separately.

Sautéed Sole with Rémoulade Sauce

Seezunge mit Remouladensoße

Rémoulade originated in France but this sauce is such an integral part of the German repertoire that I am including it in this book with a clear conscience. Rémoulade is served with fish, seafood, or cold meats and *Bratkartoffeln*, German hash browns.

The sole that you can buy in most stores in North America is different from the European (true) Dover sole, which is pricey and hard to find. A good substitute for sole is flounder.

Rémoulade:
2 hard-boiled eggs
1 very fresh raw egg yolk
Salt
½ cup plus 2 tablespoons vegetable oil
1 tablespoon white wine vinegar
2 teaspoons Dijon mustard
1 tablespoon capers
1 finely chopped medium gherkin (1 tablespoon)
2 tablespoons finely chopped fresh mixed herbs (parsley, chives, dill, and chervil)
Freshly milled black pepper
Pinch of sugar

Fish:
2 pounds sole fillets
Salt
Juice of 1 lemon
¼ cup all-purpose flour
Vegetable oil for sautéing

4 to 6 servings

1. For the rémoulade: Shell the eggs. Separate the yolks from the whites and press the yolks through a fine sieve into a small bowl (set the whites aside for another use or discard). Stir in the raw egg yolk and add salt. Slowly incorporate half of the oil, using a metal whisk or an electric mixer, until you get a thick consistency. Add the vinegar and mustard, then whisk in the remaining oil. Stir in the capers, gherkin, and herbs, and season with salt, pepper, and sugar. Refrigerate until shortly before serving.

2. For the fish: Rinse the fillets under cold running water and pat dry with paper towels. Salt and drizzle with lemon juice. Dredge the fillets in flour.

3. Heat the oil in a large nonstick skillet and cook the fish for 3 to 5 minutes on each side, or until golden in color and cooked through. Gently remove the sole from the skillet—it falls apart very easily—and serve hot with rémoulade.

Haddock Fillets in Mustard Sauce

Schellfischfilets in Senfsoße

The classic accompaniment for this traditional dish is boiled potatoes, but plain white rice is equally good to absorb the delicious creamy mustard sauce.

2 pounds fresh or frozen and thawed haddock fillets
2 tablespoons lemon juice
1 tablespoon unsalted butter
1 shallot, peeled and minced
$\frac{1}{2}$ cup dry white wine
1 bay leaf
1 cup light cream
2 tablespoons Dijon mustard
Salt and freshly milled white pepper

4 to 6 servings

1. Rinse the fish under cold running water, pat dry with paper towels, and drizzle with lemon juice. Set aside.

2. Melt the butter in a large skillet and sauté the shallot over medium heat until translucent. Add the wine and bay leaf and stir well. Place the fish in the skillet and cover. Reduce the heat and simmer for about 10 minutes. Remove the fish from the sauce and set aside.

3. Whisk the cream and mustard into the sauce. Bring to a boil and then immediately reduce the heat . Simmer until the sauce thickens. Season with salt and pepper.

4. Return the fish to the sauce and heat thoroughly over very low heat, bringing the liquid barely to a simmer. Be sure the sauce does not boil or the fish may break apart. Test for doneness with a toothpick or fork; if the fish is flaky when you gently poke it, it's done. Remove the bay leaf and serve immediately.

Plaice on a Bed of Leeks and Bacon

Finkenwerder Scholle

Finkenwerder, which gives this recipe its name, is an island in the Elbe River and is today incorporated into the city of Hamburg.

Plaice is a type of flounder that is widely available in North America. While the very traditional version of *Finkenwerder Scholle* only uses bacon, some recipes add sautéed leeks, which gives it a nice crunchy touch, and more color, too.

3 to 4 thin slices (2 ounces) lean center-cut bacon
2 leeks, thoroughly cleaned, trimmed, and finely chopped
Pinch of ground nutmeg
1 scaled and gutted plaice or flounder (about 2 to 3 pounds)
Juice of 1 lemon
Salt and freshly milled black pepper
Vegetable oil for sautéing
All-purpose flour for dredging

4 to 6 servings

1. Cut the bacon into small strips and place them in a large cold skillet. Cook until crisp. Pour off some of the fat and set it aside. Add the leek to the bacon and cook for 1 to 2 minutes. Do not overcook the leek; it should still be al dente. Season with nutmeg and keep warm.

2. Rinse the fish under cold water and pat it dry with paper towels. Put on a large platter and drizzle with lemon juice. Season with salt and pepper, but go easy on the salt, as the bacon already adds a good amount to the dish.

3. Heat the reserved bacon fat in a large skillet and add a couple of tablespoons vegetable oil.

4. Right before you are ready to sauté the fish, dredge the fish in flour. Cook the fish on both sides, starting with the light-colored side, for 8 to 10 minutes, or until the fish is crisp and lightly browned. If the fish is flaky when you gently poke it with a toothpick, it's done.

5. Arrange the bacon and the leeks in a serving dish and place the fish on top. Serve immediately.

Baked Pears

Birnen im Teig

Schleswig-Holstein, where this dish originated, has close historical and geographical ties to Denmark. As a result of a plebiscite held after World War I, the northern zone became Danish, while the southern area was incorporated into the German Reich.

This is a dish for people who like the typically Scandinavian combination of sweet and savory. The baking dish is lined with thin slices of *Schinkenspeck*, lean pork that is dry-cured and aged and does not require cooking. This German specialty is hard to find in America but you can substitute a good Westphalian ham.

2 pounds firm pears
Small piece of organic
  lemon peel
1 stick plus 1 tablespoon
  unsalted butter, softened
3 eggs
2 cups all-purpose flour
1½ teaspoons baking
  powder
½ cup milk
½ teaspoon plus a pinch
  of salt
½ pound Westphalian
  ham, thinly sliced

6 to 8 servings

1. Peel and core the pears and remove their stems; then, cut them in half. Bring 1 quart water to a boil in a large saucepan. Add the lemon peel. Reduce the heat and poach the pears in batches in a single layer just until tender. Remove them with a slotted spoon, drain, and set aside.

2. Cream the butter with an electric mixer until light. Separate the eggs and add the yolks to the butter. Add the flour, baking powder, milk, and ½ teaspoon salt.

3. Preheat the oven to 400 degrees F and grease a 2-quart gratin dish.

4. Beat the egg whites with a pinch of salt until they stand in stiff peaks and fold them into the batter.

5. Line the bottom and sides of the gratin dish with the ham. Place the pears cut side down in the dish in a single layer and pour the batter over them. Bake for 30 to 35 minutes, or until golden and a knife comes out clean. Serve warm.

Butterhead Lettuce with Tangy Cream Dressing

Kopfsalat mit Sahnesoße

Boston butterhead lettuce is very common throughout Germany. The lemon-cream dressing, however, is a specialty from the northern part of the country where this salad is often served after the main course.

*¼ cup light cream or
plain yogurt
Pinch of salt
Juice of 1 lemon
1 tablespoon sugar
1 large head Boston
butterhead lettuce, or
2 small bibb butterhead
lettuces, washed and
dried*

4 to 6 servings

1. Combine the cream with salt, lemon juice, and sugar and let stand for at least 10 minutes until the dressing thickens.

2. Tear the lettuce into bite-size pieces. Just before serving, toss the lettuce with the dressing until all leaves are nicely coated. Serve at once.

Beet Salad with Horseradish Vinaigrette

Rote-Bete-Salat

Salad recipes are a rarity in the traditional cuisine of northern Germany because greens and vegetables were mainly incorporated into stews, which were the daily regimen of fishermen and farmers. Yet there are several variations of beet salads.

Make this salad two days ahead so it can develop its full flavor. Some recipes also add a grated apple for tanginess.

1 pound small young beets
1 teaspoon caraway seeds
Salt
$\frac{1}{4}$ cup red wine vinegar
$\frac{1}{4}$ cup sugar
2 cloves
$\frac{1}{4}$ cup prepared jarred horseradish
1 thumbnail-size piece of fresh ginger, peeled and finely grated

4 servings

1. Bring a kettle of water to a boil. Cut the tops off the beets, leaving about 1 inch of the stem and the roots on to prevent the beets from bleeding. Place the beets in a saucepan and pour boiling water over them. Add the caraway seeds and salt. Cover and cook over low to medium heat for 30 minutes to 1 hour until tender. Check for doneness with a sharp knife. Drain and cool. Slip off the skins and cut the beets into $\frac{1}{4}$-inch slices.

2. In a small saucepan, mix the vinegar with $\frac{1}{2}$ cup water. Add the sugar and cloves and bring to a boil. Remove from the heat and pour the hot mixture over the warm beets. Toss with the horseradish and ginger. Cover and refrigerate for 2 days before serving.

Caramelized Potatoes

Karamelkartoffeln

When a dish is cooked on both sides of a national border, it is often impossible to tell where it originated. Caramelized potatoes are a specialty of northern Germany as well as Denmark. They are often served with Kale Stew (*see page 26*).

I like to go easy on the sugar, at the expense of less caramelized potatoes, but if you prefer a heavier glaze, add a little more sugar.

1 pound very small new or fingerling potatoes
2 tablespoons unsalted butter, melted
Salt
1 tablespoon sugar, plus more to taste
Pinch of ground nutmeg

4 to 6 servings

1. Scrub the potatoes with a brush and boil them, covered with salted water, until just tender, about 15 minutes, depending on the size.

2. Preheat the oven to 400 degrees F.

3. Mix together the butter, salt, sugar, and nutmeg.

4. Place the potatoes in a greased 2-quart gratin dish in a single layer. Pour the butter mixture over them and toss gently so all of the potatoes are coated. Bake for 50 minutes, or until crisp and lightly browned.

Potato Patties with Dried Fruit Compote

Kartoffelbuletten

Rügen is Germany's largest island, located off the coast of Mecklenburg-West Pomerania and formerly part of the German Democratic Republic. Most traditional dishes from Rügen are simple to prepare but the island's cuisine features a stunning variety. The reason for this is not only the island's many different landscapes: coast, chalk cliffs, forests, moors, heath, farm fields, salt marshes, and hills, with a rich fauna and flora. Foreign invaders also left traces in the cooking pots. Rügen belonged to Sweden before becoming part of Prussia after the Vienna congress in 1815. The Scandinavian influence is still discernible in many dishes, such as these easy-to-make potato patties. They are traditionally eaten with dried fruit compote, but they are a good accompaniment for meat, poultry, and fish dishes as well.

Dried fruit compote:

½ pound mixed dried fruit
¼ cup sugar, plus more to taste

Patties:
2 pounds starchy yellow potatoes (Yukon Gold)
2 tablespoons unsalted butter
2 tablespoons milk
Salt
Pinch of ground nutmeg
1 egg
2 tablespoons all-purpose flour
Vegetable oil for sautéing

10 pieces

1. For the compote: Rinse the dried fruit under cold water and put it in a small saucepan. Add the sugar and just enough water to cover the fruit. Simmer until the fruit is soft, about 30 minutes. Taste for sweetness and add sugar to the hot compote if necessary. Place the compote in a jar and refrigerate. It will keep up to 3 weeks.

2. For the patties: Peel and quarter the potatoes. Bring them to a boil in salted water and cook until tender. Drain and mash the potatoes.

3. Melt the butter and heat the milk together in a small saucepan or in the microwave. Mix the potatoes, butter, milk, salt, and nutmeg in a large bowl. Add the egg and flour and knead to form a soft but solid dough.

4. Heat the oil in a large skillet. Shape the dough into thick 3-inch patties with moist hands and place them in the skillet. Sauté the patties until golden brown on one side; then, carefully turn them with a metal spatula and brown the other side. Serve hot with the cold compote, or with a meat dish.

Potatoes in Béchamel Sauce

Béchamelkartoffeln

As French as it may sound, potatoes in béchamel sauce are typically North German. There are many different variations of them. On the island of Rügen, for example, béchamel potatoes are served with marinated herring. All recipes, though, have one thing in common: the use of bacon.

For a leaner version, replace the heavy cream with half-and-half or milk.

2 pounds red or other low-starch potatoes
4 to 5 thin slices (2 ounces) lean center-cut bacon
$1/4$ cup all-purpose flour
$1/2$ cup beef broth, canned or homemade (see page 200)
1 cup milk, plus more as needed
$1/2$ cup heavy cream
Pinch of ground nutmeg
$1^1/2$ teaspoons white wine vinegar
Salt and freshly milled white pepper

6 to 8 servings

1. Scrub the potatoes with a brush and boil them, covered with water, until just tender, 15 to 20 minutes, depending on the size. Drain and set aside.

2. Cut the bacon into $1/4$-inch strips. Place in a cold skillet and sauté until crisp. Remove the bacon from the skillet and set aside. Pour the bacon fat into a small saucepan and reheat over low heat. Stir in the flour and whisk in the broth, milk, and cream. Simmer for 10 minutes, stirring constantly to avoid lumps. If the sauce is too thick, add more milk, a tablespoon at a time. Add the bacon, nutmeg, and vinegar. Season with salt—carefully, as the sauce may be salty enough from the bacon—and pepper.

3. Peel the potatoes and cut them into $1/2$-inch-thick slices. Toss gently with the sauce in the pot in which you cooked the potatoes. All the potatoes should be generously coated. Reheat but do not boil. Remove from the heat, cover, and let stand for 5 minutes before serving.

Rutabaga Puree

Rübenmus

In World War I, the German population was saved from starvation by a daily rutabaga diet offered by 1,500 public soup kitchens. But the association of rutabagas with wartime and hunger is fading. Today even chefs in fine restaurants deign to put rutabagas on their menus.

Rutabagas, also known as "Swedes" in English, are a root vegetable, a cross between turnips and cabbage. They taste best after they are exposed to light frost, which gives them a sweeter taste. Traditionally rutabagas are served as a hearty stew with various smoked meats. Nowadays they are more often prepared in a lighter dish, as in this recipe. Rutabagas also taste good reheated, so you can prepare this dish ahead of time.

½ rutabaga (about 10 ounces), peeled and diced
1 medium potato, peeled and diced
1 medium carrot, peeled and diced
1 medium tart apple, peeled, cored, and diced
1 medium yellow onion, peeled and chopped
1½ teaspoons vegetable bouillon base
Salt and freshly milled white pepper
Sugar
Lemon juice

4 servings

1. Put the rutabaga, potato, carrot, apple, and onion in a saucepan. Dissolve the bouillon base in 1½ cups warm water and add to the vegetables. Cover and bring to a boil, then reduce the heat and cook for 25 to 30 minutes, until the vegetables are soft.

2. Strain the vegetables and reserve the liquid. Puree the vegetables and return to the pot. If the puree is too stiff, add some of the liquid, 1 tablespoon at a time. Season with salt, pepper, a pinch of sugar, and a dash of lemon juice.

Nutty Meringue

Qualle auf Sand

This is a delicate sand-colored pastry dusted with spelt flour. The name *Qualle auf Sand*, which literally translates as "jellyfish on sand," was inspired by the sandy beaches of the North Sea. Although some restaurants and cafés along the coast and in Hamburg serve this treat, the recipe is more or less a well-kept secret and is not found in many cookbooks. The following recipe is from the Witthüs, a legendary teahouse on the island of Sylt. It closed its doors in 1994, after providing a haven for freezing beach walkers, including my own family, for more than three decades. At the Witthüs, the pastry was topped with whipped cream and a circle of pineapple chunks, but you can let your imagination play: fresh fruit salad, rum-soaked cherries, or chocolate shavings, as long as you stick to the dollops of whipped cream, which is a must.

$\frac{1}{2}$ cup chopped hazelnuts
$\frac{2}{3}$ cup chopped walnuts
5 eggs, separated
1 cup confectioners' sugar
Pinch of salt
1 tablespoon spelt flour

16 pieces

---

1. Grind half of the hazelnuts and half of the walnuts very finely in a food processor.

2. Preheat the oven to 250 degrees F. Line an 11x15-inch jellyroll pan with parchment paper and grease well.

3. Beat the egg yolks with $\frac{1}{2}$ cup of the confectioners' sugar. In a separate bowl, beat the egg whites with a pinch of salt until they stand in stiff peaks, then gradually incorporate the remaining $\frac{1}{2}$ cup confectioners' sugar. Combine the ground nuts and chopped nuts with the egg yolk mixture. Fold in the egg whites. Spread the mixture evenly on the jellyroll pan and dust with the spelt flour, using a sifter for even distribution.

4. Bake the meringue for 2 to 3 hours, or until the inside is completely dry. If the top turns brown but the inside is still soft, reduce the heat to 200 to 225 degrees F.

5. Cool and carefully remove the parchment paper. Cut into 4-inch squares and store the meringues in a tin, with parchment paper between each layer. They keep for several weeks.

Fruity Buttermilk Mousse

Errötendes Mädchen

A refreshing summer favorite with a delicate pink hue and a clearly old-fashioned, romantic name: *Errötendes Mädchen* (blushing maiden). Who came up with this name and when is unknown.

2 egg whites
1 quart buttermilk
2 (3-ounce) packages
raspberry- or cherry-
flavored Jell-O gelatin
$\frac{1}{2}$ cup sugar
2 teaspoons vanilla extract

8 to 10 servings

1. Beat the egg whites until they stand in stiff peaks and set aside.

2. Shake the buttermilk carton very well. Heat 2 cups of the buttermilk in a small saucepan over low heat.

3. Remove the pan from the heat and slowly pour it into a bowl with the Jell-O. Whisk vigorously by hand or with an electric mixer until the Jell-O is completely dissolved. Scrape the bottom of the bowl with a rubber spatula to prevent the Jell-O from sticking to the bottom, and whisk again.

4. Mix the remaining 2 cups cold buttermilk with the sugar and vanilla. Stir into the Jell-O mixture and gently fold in the egg whites. Pour the mousse into 8 individual dessert bowls or 1 large glass serving bowl and chill for several hours until firm.

5. Take the dessert out of the refrigerator 30 minutes before serving so it can develop its full flavor.

Tea Mousse

Friesische Teecreme

Black tea is the regional drink of the northern coastal area of Frisia. The East Frisian tea blend (*Ostfriesenmischung*) is one of the most popular black teas in Germany. It consists mainly of Assam tea from northeast India, and a small portion of another black tea, such as Darjeeling. Frisians drink their tea with cream and rock candy. Given the popularity of tea in the area, it is not surprising that the regional cuisine has produced a dessert like tea mousse.

$1/2$ *cup washed and dried raisins*
$1/4$ *cup golden rum*
1 ($1/4$-ounce) envelope unflavored gelatin
3 egg yolks
$1/2$ *cup sugar*
$1/2$ *cup freshly brewed very strong black tea (Darjeeling or English Breakfast)*
$2/3$ *cup milk*
$1/2$ *cup heavy cream*
Seeds of $1/2$ vanilla bean, or $1 1/2$ teaspoons pure vanilla bean paste

4 to 6 servings

1. Combine the raisins with the rum in a small bowl. Set aside.

2. Soak the gelatin in $1/2$ cup cold water and set aside.

3. Beat the egg yolks until foamy in the top of a double boiler or a metal bowl placed over a pot with gently boiling water. Stir in the sugar.

4. Blend the tea with the milk and cream and pour the mixture into the egg yolks. Add the vanilla and gelatin and stir until the gelatin is entirely dissolved. Remove from the heat and place the bowl in a larger bowl filled with ice water. Drain the raisins and add them to the mixture. Stir until slightly cool. Pour the mousse in a large glass serving bowl or individual dessert bowls and chill for several hours until firm.

Raspberry–Vanilla Trifle with Macaroons

Plettenpudding

When 25-year-old Thomas Mann first submitted the manuscript of his family epic *The Buddenbrocks* to a publisher, he received a devastating answer. The publisher had only made it halfway through the text, found it way too long, and encouraged the young author to reduce it by half, in which case he would be very inclined to consider it for publication. Thomas Mann stubbornly stuck to his original manuscript with its detailed descriptions of the life of an upper-class family in his hometown of Lübeck. He based his oeuvre on his own family archives and, for the culinary part, on recipes that were provided by his mother. If Thomas Mann had not stood his ground, there would be no description of the Buddenbrocks' opulent dinner in the first part of the book, which won him the Nobel Prize for literature in 1929. The dessert served at this dinner was *Plettenpudding*.

$3/4$ pint fresh raspberries, or 1 (12-ounce) bag frozen raspberries
$1/4$ cup plus 2 tablespoons sugar
6 slices pound cake, cut into 1-inch cubes
$1/4$ cup sherry
$1/4$ cup strained red raspberry preserves
1 cup heavy cream
4 egg yolks
1 cup milk
Seeds of 1 vanilla bean, or 1 tablespoon pure vanilla bean paste
$1\frac{1}{2}$ teaspoons unflavored gelatin
10 coarsely crushed macaroons

8 to 10 servings

1. Mix the raspberries with 2 tablespoons of the sugar and simmer until they release their juices but do not fall apart. Strain the raspberries to remove any seeds.

2. Place half of the pound cake on the bottom of a glass serving dish with a flat bottom. Drizzle with half of the sherry and evenly spread with half of the raspberries. Top with the remaining pound cake, drizzle with the remaining sherry, and spread evenly with the preserves. Set aside.

3. Whip the cream in a chilled bowl until it stands in soft peaks. Refrigerate.

4. Beat the egg yolks with the remaining $\frac{1}{4}$ cup sugar until light and pale yellow, using an electric mixer. Bring the milk and vanilla to a boil in a saucepan. Remove from the heat and slowly incorporate the egg yolks while stirring constantly. Continue beating the mixture over very low heat until the custard thickens, but do not boil it.

5. Fill a large bowl with ice water and set aside.

6. Soak the gelatin in $\frac{1}{4}$ cup cold water and stir it into the custard. Remove the pan from the heat immediately and set it in the bowl of ice water. Stir constantly while the custard is cooling. When it starts to set, fold in the whipped cream.

7. Spread the remaining raspberries on the preserves and top with half of the custard. Sprinkle with the crushed macaroons and top with the rest of the custard. Chill for several hours until set.

Vanilla Custard with Wine Mousse Topping

Welfenspeise

This is a popular dessert at weddings and other celebrations. It was named after the powerful medieval dynasty of the Welfen, whose colors are white and yellow.

Custard:
2 cups milk
2 tablespoons sugar
Seeds of $\frac{1}{2}$ vanilla bean,
*   or $1\frac{1}{2}$ teaspoons pure*
*   vanilla bean paste*
1 strip organic lemon peel
Pinch of salt
$\frac{1}{3}$ cup cornstarch
3 egg whites

Topping:
3 egg yolks
$\frac{1}{3}$ cup sugar
1 cup dry white wine
1 tablespoon cornstarch

8 to 10 servings

1. For the custard: Bring $1\frac{1}{2}$ cups of the milk to a boil in a small saucepan with the sugar, vanilla, lemon peel, and salt. Dissolve the cornstarch in the remaining $\frac{1}{2}$ cup milk. Remove the milk mixture from the heat and whisk in the cornstarch mixture. Bring the custard to a boil while whisking constantly. Remove from the heat and continue whisking for a few more minutes to avoid lumps. Set aside.

2. Beat the egg whites until they stand in stiff peaks. Fold them into the hot custard. Remove the lemon peel and pour the custard into a large glass serving dish or individual dessert bowls. The dish/bowls should be only half full to leave space for the topping.

3. For the wine mousse topping: Mix the egg yolks with the sugar in a metal bowl and whisk with an electric mixer to a thick consistency. Add the wine. Pour into the top of a double boiler or place the metal bowl over a pot with gently boiling water. Add cornstarch. Beat the mousse until it thickens and the cornstarch becomes clear. Place the bowl in a larger bowl filled with ice water and beat until slightly cool.

4. Pour the mousse on top of the custard and chill for at least 2 hours before serving.

Chilled Cherry Soup with Egg-White Dumplings

Kirschkaltschale

The top-of-the-crop German cherries owe their existence to the sweat of Dutch settlers, who dug and installed drains in a marsh near the city of Hamburg called *Altes Land* (Old Country) 700 years ago. With 10 million fruit trees, the *Altes Land* is one of the largest fruit growing areas in Germany today and is especially renowned for its cherries.

This recipe from Hamburg should be prepared with fresh cherries. Depending on their sweetness, you might want to adjust the amount of sugar.

Soup:
1 pound sweet cherries, stemmed
1 cup dry red wine
$\frac{1}{2}$ cinnamon stick
$\frac{1}{2}$ cup sugar, plus more to taste
2 tablespoons cornstarch

Dumplings:
2 egg whites
2 tablespoons sugar
Ground cinnamon for garnish

6 servings

1. For the soup: Pit the cherries and combine them with $2\frac{1}{2}$ cups water, the wine, cinnamon stick, and $\frac{1}{2}$ cup sugar in a large saucepan. Bring to a boil, reduce the heat, and simmer for 15 to 20 minutes. Taste for sweetness and add more sugar if necessary. Dissolve the cornstarch in a few tablespoons of the cooking liquid and add it to the soup. Continue simmering until the soup becomes clear again, stirring vigorously to avoid lumps. Remove from the heat, cool, and chill.

2. For the egg-white dumplings: Bring 1 quart water to a boil. Beat the egg whites until they form soft peaks. Add the sugar and continue beating until they stand in stiff peaks. Scoop out little dumplings with a soup spoon. Reduce the heat and lower the dumplings into the barely simmering water. Cover and cook for 5 minutes. Remove the dumplings with a slotted spoon and drain in a colander.

3. Remove the cinnamon stick and serve the soup in individual soup bowls, topped with the dumplings. Sprinkle the dumplings with a pinch of cinnamon.

Applesauce with Pumpernickel Crunch

Verschleiertes Bauernmädchen

This dish is as easy and quick to make as its name is poetic and mysterious (*Verschleiertes Bauernmädchen* means "veiled farm girl"). It originated in the Holsteinische Schweiz (the Switzerland of Holstein), a breathtakingly beautiful area in the eastern part of the state of Schleswig-Holstein. With almost 200 lakes, gentle hills, large forests, and grand castles and manors, it is the perfect setting for a typically German film genre called *Heimatfilm*, a tearjerker with a regional plot. No wonder so many famous movies and TV series have been made in this area.

Applesauce:

2 pounds tart cooking apples, cored, peeled, and cut into chunks

1 cinnamon stick

about 3 cups

1. For the applesauce: Put the apples and cinnamon stick in a saucepan. Add ½ cup water (you can always add a little more water, or boil down excess water, to make a thick but not too dry applesauce). Cover and cook the applesauce over low heat for 15 to 20 minutes, or until the apples are completely tender, stirring occasionally. Pass the apples through a food mill or puree them in a blender. Let the applesauce cool before processing it any further.

Crunch:
4 (2-ounce) slices authentic (imported) pumpernickel
2 tablespoons unsalted butter
2 tablespoons plus 1 teaspoon sugar, plus more to taste
1 cup (9 ounces) red raspberry preserves
$^3/_4$ cup heavy cream
1 teaspoon vanilla extract

6 to 8 servings

2. For the crunch: Preheat the oven to 400 degrees F. Crumble the pumpernickel into $^1/_4$-inch bits and spread them on a greased baking sheet. Leave them in the oven until they are crunchy, tossing them occasionally so all the crumbs dry evenly.

3. Melt the butter in a large skillet over medium heat. Add the crumbs and 2 tablespoons of the sugar and caramelize, stirring constantly. Set aside to cool.

4. Stir the raspberry preserves to a smooth consistency. If necessary, add a few drops of water.

5. Sprinkle a thin layer of crumbs on the bottom of a serving dish, preferably a glass dish so that the different layers are visible. Layer some applesauce, crumbs, and preserves on top. Continue layering in this order until all the ingredients are used up, ending with a layer of crumbs. Chill for at least a couple of hours.

6. Just before serving, whip the cream with the vanilla and remaining 1 teaspoon sugar, or more to taste, in a chilled bowl until soft peaks form. Cover the bread-crumbs evenly with the cream and serve.

Red Berry Pudding with Vanilla Sauce

Rote Grütze mit Vanillesoße

In recent decades, this pudding went from an old-fashioned dessert to a culinary blockbuster. Although recipes vary greatly, almost all call for red currants (*see page 229*). Which other fruits you add—raspberries, cherries, blackberries, strawberries, or blueberries—depends on availability and your personal taste, but there is one rule of thumb: you should include at least one tart fruit. There are also several ways to top *Rote Grütze*: with vanilla sauce, whipped cream, cream, vanilla ice cream, or just milk.

If you use fruits that do not yield much juice, or if you prefer a softer consistency, you might want to reduce the amount of cornstarch. Likewise, the amount of sugar you use depends on the ripeness of the fruit, so taste the fruit before cooking it. The juicier and sweeter the fruit, the better the taste of the pudding.

Pudding:
2 pounds ripe berries (fresh or frozen) and pitted cherries, washed and picked over
Sugar
1/2 cup cornstarch

Vanilla sauce:
3 egg yolks
3 tablespoons sugar
1 tablespoon cornstarch
1 1/2 cups milk
1 vanilla bean, or
    1 tablespoon pure vanilla bean paste

6 to 8 servings

1. For the pudding: Put the blueberries, if using, and cherries in a large saucepan with 2 to 3 tablespoons water. Bring to a boil and cook until they pop or release their juice. Hull the strawberries, if using, and cut very large ones into quarters. Add the more delicate fruit like strawberries and raspberries last and then immediately remove the pan from the heat. Taste for sweetness and add sugar to taste and stir to dissolve.

2. Dissolve the cornstarch in at least 1/4 cup cold water. Stir the cornstarch mixture into the fruit mixture. Return the pot to the heat and cook briefly over low to medium heat, stirring constantly. When the pudding turns clear and thickens, immediately remove the pan from the heat. Continue stirring for another 1 to 2 minutes. Make sure not to undercook the pudding, otherwise it will taste chalky.

3. Pour the hot pudding into a glass serving bowl or individual dessert bowls. To prevent the glass from cracking when you pour the hot pudding into it, put a damp dishtowel underneath the bowl. Refrigerate for several hours until set. Serve the pudding cold, but take it out of the refrigerator 30 minutes before serving, so it can develop its full flavor.

4. For the vanilla sauce: In a small saucepan, whisk the egg yolks with the sugar and cornstarch. Add the milk and vanilla—if using a vanilla bean, slit it lengthwise, scrape out the seeds with a sharp knife, and add the bean and the seeds to the mixture. Cook over low heat until the sauce thickens, whisking constantly. Make sure that the sauce does not boil. Remove the vanilla bean, if using. Refrigerate. Stir the sauce well before serving.

Sand Cookies

Heidesand

The sandy soil of the Lüneburger Heide heath was the inspiration for these cookies, which get their special flavor from browning the butter before adding it to the dough.

2 sticks unsalted butter, softened
1 cup sugar
2 teaspoons vanilla extract
2 tablespoons heavy cream
Pinch of salt
2 cups all-purpose flour
2 teaspoons baking powder

45 cookies

1. Brown the butter in a small saucepan while monitoring it closely. The butter should be browned but not burnt. Cool.

2. Beat the browned butter until foamy and combine it with the sugar, vanilla, cream, and salt, beating to a creamy consistency using an electric mixer.

3. Combine the flour with the baking powder and add to the butter mixture. Knead the dough with your hands and shape it into two 1½-inch diameter rolls. Wrap them separately in plastic wrap and refrigerate for 30 minutes.

4. Preheat the oven to 350 degrees F. Line a baking sheet with parchment paper.

5. Carefully cut the rolls into ¼-inch slices. Place the cookies 2 to 3 inches apart on the baking sheet and bake for 10 minutes, or until light yellow and still soft. Cool on racks. Store in an airtight container.

Cinnamon Rolls

Franzbrötchen

Franzbrötchen (Franz's rolls) are an exclusive specialty of Hamburg, although their reputation as a breakfast treat has spread across Germany. Whether it was a drunken bakery apprentice named Franz who accidentally sat on a baking sheet with dough at night, or whether the cinnamon rolls developed from a buttery baguette-style bread named *Franzbrot* (Franz's bread), the origin of this pastry lies in the dark.

Dough:
2 ($1/4$-ounce) envelopes
  active dry yeast
$1/3$ cup plus 2 to 3 tablespoons lukewarm milk
$2^{1}/_{2}$ cups plus $1/3$ cup
  all-purpose flour
$3/4$ teaspoon salt
4 tablespoons unsalted
  butter, softened
$1/3$ cup sugar
$1/2$ teaspoon ground
  cinnamon

Filling:
1 stick unsalted butter,
  chilled
$3/4$ cup sugar
1 tablespoon ground
  cinnamon

15 pieces

1. For the dough: Combine yeast with the milk in a small bowl and let stand for 10 minutes until frothy.

2. Mix the flour and salt in a large mixing bowl. Gradually add the yeast mixture. Stir in the butter and sugar. Knead into a smooth dough using the kneading attachment of an electric mixer. Cover and let rise for 20 minutes.

3. Work the cinnamon into the dough and roll with a heavy rolling pin into a rectangle, approximately 11 x 27 inches.

4. For the filling: Cut the butter into small chunks and distribute them evenly onto the dough. Sprinkle with the sugar and cinnamon. Roll up the dough from the long side to a flat roll and let rest for 20 minutes.

5. Cut the dough into 2-inch-thick slices with a sharp knife. To give the *franzbrötchen* their typical compressed, dimpled shape, use the handle of a wooden spoon or the blade of a dinner knife to make a deep dent parallel to the cut side in the middle of each piece. Grease a $17^{1}/_{2}$ x 14-inch baking sheet. Place the rolls at least 2 inches apart on the sheet and let them rest for 20 more minutes. Meanwhile preheat the oven to 400 degrees F.

6. Bake rolls for 15 to 20 minutes, or until well risen and golden. Serve fresh from the oven.

Butter Sheet Cake

Butterkuchen

Large sheets of freshly baked butter cake are an integral part of every large family gathering in northern Germany. Because it is also widely served at funeral receptions, some people sarcastically nickname it *Beerdigungskuchen* (burial cake), but that should be no reason for you to shy away from this simple and scrumptious cake.

This cake is best when eaten within a few hours of baking. I recommend that you freeze any leftovers in an airtight container and reheat them in an oven preheated to 350 degrees F.

Dough:
2 (¼-ounce) envelopes active dry yeast
1 cup lukewarm milk
3½ cups all-purpose flour
1 teaspoon salt
3 tablespoons unsalted butter, softened
1 egg, at room temperature
¼ cup sugar

1. For the dough: Combine the yeast with ½ cup of the milk in a small bowl and let stand for 10 minutes until frothy.

2. Mix the flour and salt. Mix the butter with the remaining ½ cup milk in another large bowl. Add the yeast mixture, then gradually add the flour mixture.

3. Lightly beat the egg and add to the dough with the sugar. Work into a smooth dough in a food processor with a dough blade or with the kneading attachment of an electric mixer. The dough has the right consistency if it does not stick to the bowl any longer. Cover and let rise for 1 hour.

4. Grease a 17½ x 14-inch baking sheet. Dust the work surface and a rolling pin with flour. Knead the dough gently with floured hands until it is smooth and no longer sticky. Roll the dough with a heavy rolling pin to a size large enough to fit the baking sheet plus ¼ to ½ inch on each side for the edges. Spread the dough on the baking sheet. Push the edges up the sides of the pan to make a rim. Prick the dough with a fork in several places. Cover it with a clean dishtowel and let stand for 30 minutes.

5. Preheat the oven to 350 degrees F.

Topping:

$1\frac{1}{4}$ sticks unsalted butter, softened

$\frac{1}{2}$ cup sugar

1 teaspoon ground cinnamon

1 cup sliced blanched almonds

12 to 16 servings

6. For the topping: Mix the butter, sugar, and cinnamon with an electric mixer. Make a dent in the dough with your index finger every inch or so; these are the typical *Butterlöcher* (butter holes) that give the cake its buttery flavor. Spread the butter mixture evenly on the dough and sprinkle it with almonds.

7. Bake for 20 minutes, or until a toothpick comes out clean and the cake has a nice golden top. Serve very fresh.

Windmill Cake

Friesentorte

There are several variations of this scrumptious and festive cake from Frisia. What they all have in common is the plum butter, whipped cream filling, and the "windmill" on top. I doubt that the sleek high-tech wind turbines that line the coast of Frisia today would have inspired a cake like this!

Unless you can find genuine imported German plum butter (*Pflaumenmus*), this cake requires making your own from Italian or Damson plums that you can identify by their yellow to orange flesh. Plum butter takes several hours to make but is very little work except for the stirring.

Plum butter:
2 pounds Italian or Damson plums, washed, halved, and pitted
2 cups sugar
¼ teaspoon ground cloves
1 teaspoon ground cinnamon

Crust:
4 tablespoons cold unsalted butter
1 cup all-purpose flour
¼ cup sugar
1 egg yolk
⅛ teaspoon ground cloves
⅛ teaspoon ground cinnamon
Pinch of salt
1 package puff pastry (2 sheets), thawed according to package directions

1. For the plum butter: Preheat the oven to 300 degrees F. Set an oven rack in lower third of the oven. Put the plums in an ovenproof casserole dish with a lid (a cast-iron Dutch oven is ideal). Cook over medium heat, stirring occasionally, until the plums are soft. Add ½ cup of the sugar and the spices, and stir to dissolve.

2. Cover with a lid and transfer the casserole to the oven. Cook for 30 minutes and then stir in another ½ cup of sugar. Repeat this step twice more, stirring well after each addition of sugar, and scraping over the bottom and down the sides of the casserole to prevent the plum butter from scorching.

3. Continue cooking until the mixture is very thick and a spoon leaves a trace in the plum butter, about 4 hours total. Pour into a sterilized jar with a screw-top lid. Cool and store the plum butter in the refrigerator if not using right away. Bring to room temperature 1 hour before using so it is spreadable.

4. For the bottom crust: Cut the butter into small chunks and quickly knead with the flour, sugar, egg yolk, cloves, cinnamon, and salt until a moist but not sticky dough forms. If the dough is sticky, add more flour, a teaspoon at a time, until it does not stick to your hands any more. If it is too dry, add a few drops of ice-cold water. Form dough into a ball and wrap in plastic wrap and refrigerate for 1 hour.

Filling:

1 scant tablespoon gelatin

2 cups heavy cream

1 teaspoon vanilla extract

¼ cup sugar

¾ cup (8 ounces) coarsely chopped unpeeled almonds

12 to 16 servings

5. Preheat the oven to 400 degrees F. Line a baking sheet with parchment paper. Unfold the puff pastry sheets on a lightly floured surface and cut out two 9-inch circles. Pierce each circle several times with a fork. Cut the scraps into as many triangles of equal size as possible, and place them and the circles on the baking sheet. Bake in the preheated oven for 15 minutes, until golden brown. Transfer to a rack to cool.

6. Increase the oven temperature to 425 degrees F. Grease the bottom and sides of a 9-inch springform pan. Roll the dough for the bottom crust into an 11-inch circle. Place in the pan and 1-inch up the sides. Bake in the preheated oven for 15 minutes, until golden brown. Transfer crust to a rack to cool.

7. For the filling: Soak the gelatin in ½ cup cold water. Beat the cream with the vanilla extract, gradually adding the sugar until it stands in stiff peaks. Toast the almonds in an ungreased skillet and set aside.

8. Bring some water to a boil in a small saucepan, then reduce to a simmer. Put the soaked gelatin in a large ladle and dip it into the simmering water, making sure no water spills into the ladle, and keep there until the gelatin is fully dissolved. Stir a few tablespoons of the whipped cream into the gelatin, then quickly fold this mix into the whipped cream.

9. Return the bottom crust to the springform pan and attach the rim. Grease the sides of the pan to prevent the filling from sticking. Spread half the plum butter over the bottom crust; top with one-third of the whipped cream mixture and one-third of the almonds. Place a puff pastry disk on top and spread with the remaining plum butter. Top with another one-third of the whipped cream mixture and another one-third of the almonds. Place the second puff pastry disk on top and spread with the remaining whipped cream mixture. Place the puff pastry triangles at equal distance in a decorative circle, slanting them slightly. Sprinkle with the remaining almonds. Refrigerate for 3 to 4 hours, until the filling is fully set.

Brown Spice Cookies

Braune Kuchen

These classic Christmas cookies from Hamburg traditionally came in pairs: Brown Spice Cookies (*Braune Kuchen*) made with molasses, and White Spice Cookies (*Weiße Kuchen, see opposite page*). For best taste, let the cookies age for a couple of weeks in tin cans.

$1/2$ cup plus 2 tablespoons dark unsulphured molasses
5 tablespoons unsalted butter
$1/3$ cup sugar
2 tablespoons finely chopped candied orange peel, plus more for garnish
2 tablespoons finely chopped candied citron or candied lemon peel
$1/4$ cup chopped blanched almonds
1 teaspoon ground cinnamon
1 teaspoon ground cardamom
$1/2$ teaspoon ground cloves
$2 1/2$ cups all-purpose flour
$1 1/2$ teaspoons baking powder
Blanched almond halves for garnish

60 cookies

1. Heat the molasses, butter, and sugar in a small saucepan over very low heat. Remove from the heat and stir until completely cool. Add the orange peel, citron, almonds, cinnamon, cardamom, and cloves. Mix the flour with the baking powder and stir it into the mixture. Knead the dough with your hands until it reaches a smooth consistency.

2. Preheat the oven to 375 degrees F. Line at least two baking sheets with parchment paper.

3. Roll the dough between layers of plastic wrap to about $1/4$ inch thick or a little thicker. Cut out the cookies with cookie cutters and place them on the baking sheets 1 to $1 1/2$ inches apart. Use up all the dough by kneading and rerolling the scraps. Garnish each cookie with an almond half or orange peel.

4. Bake each batch for 8 minutes, or until golden brown. Transfer the cookies to racks to cool. Store in airtight containers.

White Spice Cookies

Weiße Kuchen

Unlike Brown Spice Cookies (*see opposite page*), this white variation has all but disappeared, and recipes for it are scarce. This is a pity because White Spice Cookies are indeed lighter (without butter) and wonderfully crisp—perfect for dunking.

3 eggs
1½ cups sugar
2 teaspoons finely grated organic lemon zest
⅓ cup packed finely chopped candied citron or candied lemon peel, plus more for garnish
½ teaspoon ground cinnamon
¼ teaspoon ground cloves
1½ teaspoons baking soda
2½ cups all-purpose flour

80 cookies

1. Beat the eggs with the sugar until pale and creamy. Add the lemon zest, citron, spices, baking soda, and flour and mix well. The dough will be very stiff.

2. Transfer the dough to a container with a tight-fitting lid. Let sit in the refrigerator overnight.

3. Preheat the oven to 300 degrees F. Grease at least two baking sheets.

4. Roll the dough ⅛-inch thick on a well-floured work surface. Using a small plastic storage container or any other small rectangular mold about 2 x 2 inches, cut out the cookies and place them on the prepared baking sheets about 1 to 1½ inches apart. Use up all the dough by kneading and rerolling the scraps. Garnish each cookie with a piece of candied citron in the center.

5. Bake in the preheated oven for 20 minutes, until the cookies are pale yellow. Let cool for 3 minutes, then, transfer to racks to cool. Store in airtight containers.

Fruit Marinated in Rum

Rumtopf

Rumtopf is a great old-fashioned way to capture the flavor of all the fruit harvested during the summer. And where else could this recipe have originated than in Schleswig-Holstein, also known as "rum country."

The marinated fruit can be served with vanilla ice cream or Bavarian cream (*see page 230*), or simply topped with whipped cream. How you compose your *Rumtopf* depends on your personal taste, but here are the basics:

1. A *Rumtopf* is created in several steps over time, starting with the earliest summer fruit, strawberries, and then adding whatever the orchard yields. However, do not use apples, blueberries, and blackberries, as they do not mix well.

2. Use only high-quality, ripe, unblemished fruit, and quality rum with at least 40 percent alcohol.

3. Before adding a new layer, gently stir the mixture with a clean spoon.

4. Each layer takes about 6 weeks to marinate.

5. The fruit must always be immersed in rum, otherwise it might mold. To prevent this, place a small plate on top of the mixture to push the fruit into the rum.

6. Keep the *Rumtopf* in a cool and dark place.

7. After adding the last layer, the fruit has to marinate for at least 2 more months. That means that if you add the last fruit in the early fall, your *Rumtopf* will be ready for Thanksgiving or Christmas.

8. And the most important: be patient.

Special equipment needed: a tall glazed ceramic container with a lid, holding at least 1 gallon.

Getting started:

1 pound strawberries
1¼ cups sugar
3 cups rum

1. Wash, hull, and dry the strawberries. Gently toss them with the sugar in a large bowl and let stand for 1 hour.

2. Place the strawberries in the glazed ceramic container and pour the rum over them. The fruit should be covered with rum by about 1 inch. Cover with the lid and check occasionally to see whether all of the strawberries are immersed in rum. If not, place a plate on top of the fruit to hold it down in the rum. If the plate does not help, add more rum.

The following is a guideline for the amounts of fruit, sugar, and rum: For each pound of fruit, use 1¼ cups sugar and enough rum to cover the fruit by 1 inch. But you may modify quantities of fruit, sugar, and rum to personal taste. A few weeks after adding the last fruit and no later than 1 month afterwards, add an additional 1½ cups rum. Because of its high alcohol content, *Rumtopf* keeps for years.

	Preparation
Cherries	Remove stems.
Apricots	Remove skins by blanching. Cut in half and remove pits.
Raspberries	Pick over very carefully.
Peaches, nectarines	Remove skins by blanching. Cut in half and remove pits.
Plums	Remove skins by blanching. Cut in half and remove pits.
Pears	Peel, core, and remove stems. Quarter.

Real Marzipan

Lübecker Marzipan

That marzipan was invented in the city of Lübeck is a widespread and well-known legend—pure legend. The truth is that marzipan was brought to Europe from the Middle East. But to give due credit to Lübeck, its marzipan does have a long tradition. A decree in 1530 exclusively allowed the city's pharmacists to produce marzipan, which they used to coat bitter pills in order to improve their taste. Only in the early nineteenth century did confectioners take over the marzipan business. The real breakthrough came at the 1873 World's Fair in Vienna, when the fine marzipan from the Lübeck-based Niederegger Company received an award.

Blanching almonds takes a little bit of time but I think the fresher taste is worth the effort. Simply pour boiling water over the shelled almonds and let them stand for 1 minute; the hulls will be easy to squirt out of the skins. Dry the almonds well with paper towels before processing them.

2 cups blanched almonds
2⅓ cups confectioners'
sugar
1 tablespoon rose water

60 to 80 pieces

1. Grind the almonds in the food processor to a very fine powder. Add the confectioners' sugar and rose water and keep grinding until a thick, smooth paste forms. Add drops of water to get the desired consistency but do not overdo it, otherwise your marzipan will become difficult to shape. Scrape down the sides of the food processor bowl frequently to ensure that all the paste is smooth.

2. Shape into a compact ball if you intend to use the marzipan for another recipe, or roll the paste about ½-inch thick with a heavy rolling pin. If the marzipan is too sticky and moist, dust the work surface with confectioners' sugar. Cut the marzipan into 1-inch squares.

3. Store in an airtight container, inserting aluminum foil between the individual layers. Homemade marzipan keeps for 1 to 2 weeks; after that, it becomes a bit dry but still tastes good.

Apple Dumplings

Apfelklöße

Germans love apples; they are the most popular fruit in the country. The apple of choice for many German recipes is the tart and juicy Boskoop, or Belle de Boskoop, which originated in the Netherlands in the mid-19th century.

In traditional German cuisine these apple dumplings were served as a light lunch, but today they more frequently appear as dessert.

2 eggs
¼ teaspoon salt
2 teaspoons sugar
⅓ cup plus 1 tablespoon milk
⅛ teaspoon ground nutmeg
1 tablespoon unsalted butter, melted
2 cups all-purpose flour
1 tart apple, peeled, cored and finely chopped (about 2 cups)

Topping:
Sugar
Ground cinnamon
Unsalted butter

4 servings

1. Beat the eggs with the salt, sugar, milk, nutmeg, and melted butter. Gradually add the flour and stir well until the dough is smooth and free of lumps. Fold the chopped apple into the dough until evenly distributed.

2. Bring salted water to a boil in a pot that is large enough to hold the dumplings without touching each other. Reduce the heat.

3. Using an ice-cream scoop, shape 12 dumplings, dipping the scoop into hot water after shaping each one. (Alternatively, you can also shape the dumplings with moistened hands, but they will be less compact and lighter if you use a scoop.)

4. Gently lower the dumplings into the hot water and simmer for 15 minutes. Makes sure the water does not boil or the dumplings will fall apart. Remove the dumplings with a slotted spoon and drain in a colander.

5. For the topping: Mix sugar with a few pinches of cinnamon. Lightly brown some butter in a small saucepan and drizzle it over the dumplings. Sprinkle with cinnamon sugar and serve immediately.

Coffee with Rum and Whipped Cream

Pharisäer

The correct ratio between coffee and rum in this drink is a very serious matter, and to avoid any cheating, a German court determined a few years ago that this drink has to contain 4 centiliters (about $1\frac{1}{3}$ fluid ounces) to be lawfully labeled *Pharisäer* (Pharisee). In German, the word "Pharisee" is an old-fashioned synonym for a hypocritical person. Here's how the drink got its name: In 1873, a farmer's family celebrated the christening of their seventh child. Among the guests was the pastor, a fierce teetotaler. Rum is to the people of the North Sea what vodka is to the Russians. The host found a way to sneak some rum into the coffee and topped each cup lavishly with whipped cream to disguise the smell of the alcohol. Everybody had a good time until the pastor was served a coffee with rum by mistake, and he yelled "What Pharisees you are!"

$\frac{1}{2}$ cup heavy cream
2 cups freshly brewed
  strong hot coffee
$\frac{2}{3}$ cup golden rum
Sugar

4 to 6 servings

1. Whip the cream until soft peaks form.

2. Divide the coffee and rum into 4 cups and add sugar to taste. Top with whipped cream and serve immediately. Do not stir—*Pharisäer* is sipped from underneath the whipped cream topping.

Black Tea Punch with Orange and Cognac

Seelenwärmer

A stiff drink for chilly days, on the coast or elsewhere—that's why it is called *Seelenwärmer* (soul warmer).

Zest and juice of 1 organic orange
Juice of $1\frac{1}{2}$ organic lemons
$\frac{1}{4}$ cup cognac or any other fine brandy
$1\frac{1}{2}$ cups freshly brewed black tea (Darjeeling or English Breakfast)
$\frac{1}{4}$ cup honey, plus more to taste
$\frac{1}{2}$ cup golden rum

4 to 6 servings

1. Mix the orange zest and juice with the lemon juice and cognac. Let stand for 2 to 3 hours.

2. Strain the juice and mix with the tea, honey, and rum. Reheat in a saucepan but do not boil. Serve in individual punch glasses.

Mulled Wine with Rum

Sylter Welle

Of all the German islands, the narrow island of Sylt in the North Sea has always been the most chic, not unlike the Hamptons on Long Island. But away from the places where the rich and beautiful wine, dine, shop, and sunbathe—often on nudist beaches, for which the island is as famous as for its thatched houses—unspoiled nature and genuine local traditions can still be found. The island's toughest enemy, however, is erosion, and without protective measures, Sylt is likely to disappear over the next millennium. Everything is being done to save the island so that future generations will, among other things, be able to savor *Sylter Welle* where it originated.

$1/2$ cup sugar, plus more to taste
$2/3$ cup boiling water
$2/3$ cup dry red wine
$2/3$ cup golden rum
4 whole cloves
Ground nutmeg
4 organic lemon slices

4 to 6 servings

1. Rinse 4 punch glasses with hot water. Put 2 teaspoons sugar in each glass and add 2 to 3 tablespoons boiling water. Stir until the sugar is completely dissolved.

2. Heat the red wine with the rum and cloves, but do not boil. Divide between the 4 punch glasses. Sprinkle with a pinch of nutmeg and garnish with a slice of lemon. Serve immediately.

Egg Grog

Eiergrog

Flensburg, Germany's northernmost city located near the Danish border, became the country's rum capital for more than one reason. Since the mid-fifteenth century, the port city belonged to the kingdom of Denmark. Sailing under the Danish flag allowed ships from Flensburg to safely transport their merchandise, including rum from the Danish West Indies, even during times of war. It did not take the smart merchants of Flensburg long to discover that the excellent quality of the city water helped to refine the raw rum that ships brought in from overseas. This was the start of rum processing in Flensburg, which is a major industrial sector until the present day.

4 egg yolks
¼ cup sugar
1 cup golden rum
Hot water

4 servings

1. Beat the egg yolks with the sugar in a small bowl until foamy.

2. Heat the rum in the top of a double boiler or in a metal bowl placed over a pot of gently boiling water. Slowly pour in the egg yolks and continue beating until the entire mixture is thoroughly heated.

3. Pour the grog into 4 mugs or grog glasses (with a handle) and add hot water to taste. Serve right away.

Eastern Roots

Germany's eastern region is mainly comprised of the former German Democratic Republic, which ceased to exist when Germany was reunified in 1990. This collection includes recipes from Berlin, the states of Brandenburg, Saxony, Saxony-Anhalt, and Thuringia. Although East Prussia (which was divided between the Soviet Union and Poland after World War II) and Silesia (now Poland) no longer belong to Germany, I have included those areas, because dishes like *Königsberger Klopse* (meatballs in creamy caper sauce) are an integral part of the traditional German menu.

The cuisine of the East is very diverse. It includes meats and sausages, game, poultry, freshwater fish from the many rivers and lakes, and locally grown vegetables. Thuringia has a panoply of dumplings every bit as impressive as Bavaria's proud parade of dumplings. Saxonians are the hands-down pastry champions. With the exception of a few classic dishes from the urban cuisine, such as *Leipziger Allerlei* (mixed spring vegetables with morels) or chicken fricassee from Berlin, the majority of East German specialties are hearty and filling.

During the forty plus years of the socialist regime, the menus in East Germany were unappealing and loaded with socialist food jargon. Side dishes, for example, carried a prefix that bluntly dictated their purpose: to fill you up. Potatoes, rice, and vegetables were listed on menus as *Sättigungsbeilage* (filling side dish), rather than the plainer, common word, *Beilage* (side dish). Thankfully, there were exceptions. Several appealing foods from eastern producers have made the transition into the capitalist economy of a united Germany.

After the wall between East and West Germany fell in 1989, many easterners flooded supermarkets in the West. The wide-eyed easterners marveled at the variety and fully stocked shelves. Once the thrill wore off and appetites were satiated, many easterners developed a craving for the foods from the socialist era. This longing is known in German as *Ostalgie*, a pun on *Ost* (the East) and *Nostalgie* (nostalgia).

Sour Cream Spread with Chives

Schmand und Glumse

East Prussia was, as the name indicates, the easternmost part of the kingdom of Prussia. After World War II, it was divided between Poland and Russia. In East Prussia, winters were long and cold, and the food was hearty and solid. *Schmand*, a thick cream with at least 20 percent fat, was an indispensable ingredient in many dishes and so popular that it even found its way into nostalgic poems about this land lost forever. Sour cream is a substitute for *Schmand*. This dip is served as a bread spread or with potatoes cooked in their skins.

1 medium yellow onion, peeled and coarsely chopped
1 cup Greek yogurt
¼ cup sour cream
1 tablespoon olive oil
1 hardboiled egg, finely chopped
1 small bunch chives, trimmed and snipped
Lemon juice
Salt and freshly milled black pepper
Pinch of sugar

4 servings

1. Bring water to a boil in a small saucepan. Blanch the onion for 1 minute. Drain well and cool, then finely chop.

2. In a small bowl, stir the Greek yogurt with the sour cream and olive oil until smooth. Add the blanched onion, egg, and chives, and season with a dash of lemon juice, salt, pepper, and sugar. Refrigerate until serving.

Open-Faced Sandwich with Smoked Ham and Egg

Strammer Max

Of all German dishes, I think *Strammer Max* would be the most prone to be rated "R" for its suggestive name. As the *Dictionary of the Upper Saxonian Dialects*, published in the 1990s by the Saxonian Academy of Sciences in Leipzig, tells us, *Strammer Max* means two things: the erect male organ, aka *Max*, and the popular snack. The snack was so named because it is believed to boost sexual performance.

1 tablespoon unsalted butter, at room temperature
1 large slice fresh, country-style bread
1 thick slice (3 ounces) smoked ham
1 egg
Salt and freshly milled black pepper
½ large tomato, sliced
1 gherkin
1 teaspoon snipped chives

1 serving

Spread ½ tablespoon of the butter on the bread and place the ham on it. Heat the remaining ½ tablespoon butter in a nonstick skillet and cook the egg sunny side up. Slide the hot egg onto the sandwich. Season with salt and pepper and garnish with the tomato slices, gherkin, and chives. Serve immediately.

Bratwurst with Curry Ketchup

Currywurst

Gourmets please forgive me, but the collection of recipes in this book would not be complete without *Currywurst*, one of Germany's top fast foods. Here is the story of a big success borne out of boredom on a rainy day in Berlin in September 1949.

Herta Heuwel was standing in her snack bar at Stuttgarter Platz. She only had a few customers, so she started experimenting with tomato ketchup and spices. She poured the mixture over a sliced sautéed sausage—the *Currywurst* was invented. In 1959, she patented her invention so the facts about the origin of this popular fast food appear clear.

Not quite, though. Almost half a century and billions of sausages later, the cities of Berlin and Hamburg both claimed that the fast food had been invented in their realm. Two authors, one from Berlin and the other from Hamburg, each published a book to support their cause. Finally, 83-year-old Frau Heuwel came forward and reminded the world of her patent, deciding the argument in favor of Berlin.

However, the question remained unanswered as to which of the two cities can call itself the *Currywurst* capital. Boasting 72 million sausages per year, Hamburg, a city with 1.7 million inhabitants, led the *Currywurst* consumption, compared to Berlin with "only" 70 million sausages.

Having a *Currywurst* at one of the numerous snack bars in Berlin is a must for visitors to the capital. Several U.S. presidents as well as many foreign celebrities have been seen snacking on the hot and spicy legend.

Currywurst is eaten with French fries or on a roll. If you want to stay true to the real thing, serve it on disposable plates.

Curry ketchup:
1 tablespoon vegetable oil
1 small yellow onion,
    peeled and finely
    chopped
1 (14½-ounce) can whole
    peeled tomatoes, drained
1 tablespoon brown sugar
½ cup cider vinegar
Pinch of powdered mustard
Pinch of ground allspice
Pinch of ground cloves
Pinch of ground mace
Pinch of ground cinnamon
½ bay leaf
Salt and freshly milled
    black pepper

Sausage:
1 tablespoon vegetable oil
4 large fresh sausages,
    preferably bratwurst
Mild to medium curry
    powder

4 servings

1. For the curry ketchup: Heat the oil in a small saucepan and sauté the onion until translucent. Add the tomatoes, sugar, vinegar, mustard, allspice, cloves, mace, cinnamon, and bay leaf. Simmer, uncovered, for 45 minutes, or until a thick paste forms. Remove the bay leaf and puree the ketchup. Season with salt and pepper and cool. The curry ketchup can be kept refrigerated for 3 to 4 weeks.

2. For the sausage: Heat the oil in a large skillet. Sauté the sausages until cooked through and browned, turning them frequently. Top each sausage with the curry ketchup and sprinkle with a pinch of curry powder. Serve at once.

Pork Schmalz Spread with Apple and Fried Onion

Schmalz mit Äpfeln und Zwiebeln

Well-seasoned with marjoram and/or apples and onions, *Schmalz* (rendered lard) is a delicious spread. Country-style restaurants sometimes serve it with freshly baked bread as a hearty greeting from the chef. There are many different versions of *Schmalz* all over Germany. Here is a rather lean version, where the apples and onions are nicely balanced with the lard. Instead of buying industrial lard in a supermarket, try to get it from your local butcher.

Serve the spread with a saltshaker on the table, as it should be salted to individual taste. The spread keeps for up to 1 month in the refrigerator.

*1 cup (6 ounces)
unflavored rendered lard,
at room temperature
1 medium yellow onion,
peeled and sliced into
thin rings
1 large tart cooking apple,
cored and peeled
Salt
$^1\!/_2$ teaspoon marjoram*

16 servings

1. Heat 2 tablespoons of the lard in a large skillet over medium heat. Add the onion rings and fry until crisp. Grate the apple and add to the onion. Reduce the heat and cook until the apple is soft but not yet falling apart. Season with salt and marjoram and cool.

2. Put the remaining lard in a bowl and mix well with the apple and onion. Put the spread into an airtight container and refrigerate.

Onion Quiche

Zwiebel-Speck-Kuchen

Every October, the picturesque city of Weimar hosts the onion market, a tradition that goes back as far as 1653. The market's symbol is an onion garland, and every year a competition is held for the longest garland.

Of course you don't have to wait for the month of October to savor this pie with a glass of chilled white wine. In the unlikely event of leftovers, reheat the quiche in a hot oven, not in the microwave, or it will become soggy.

Dough:
1 ($\frac{1}{4}$-ounce) envelope active dry yeast
$\frac{2}{3}$ cup lukewarm milk
$2\frac{1}{4}$ cups all-purpose flour
1 teaspoon salt
Pinch of sugar
3 tablespoons unsalted butter, melted

Topping:
10 thin slices (5 ounces) lean center-cut bacon
4 large yellow onions, peeled and thinly sliced
3 eggs
1 cup sour cream
Salt and freshly milled black pepper
$\frac{1}{2}$ teaspoon ground caraway

12 servings

1. For the dough: Combine the yeast with the milk in a small bowl and let stand for 10 minutes, until frothy.

2. Mix the flour with the salt and sugar. In a large bowl mix the melted butter and the yeast mixture. Gradually add the flour mixture. Knead into a smooth dough using the kneading attachment of an electric mixer. Cover and let stand for 1 hour.

3. For the topping: Cut the bacon into small strips and place them in a large cold skillet. Sauté slowly until the fat has been drawn out. Pour off the fat and reserve it in a small bowl. When the bacon is crisp, remove it from the skillet. Pour the fat back into the skillet and sauté the onions in the bacon fat until translucent. Set aside to cool.

4. Beat the eggs in a mixing bowl and whisk in the sour cream. Add the salt, pepper, caraway, bacon, and onions.

5. Preheat the oven to 400 degrees F. Grease an 11x15-inch jellyroll pan. Knead the dough briefly on a floured surface. Roll the dough to fit the prepared pan plus 1 to 2 inches on all sides. Evenly spread the dough onto the pan, gently pressing it up the sides. Trim the excess and prick in several places with a fork. Spread the topping evenly over the dough. Bake for 30 to 35 minutes. Serve hot with white wine.

Browned Potatoes with Ham and Eggs

Bauernfrühstück

Bauernfrühstück means "a farmer's breakfast." It makes a solid brunch or a light dinner.

$1\frac{1}{2}$ *pounds red or other low-starch potatoes*
3 tablespoons unsalted butter or vegetable oil
1 medium yellow onion, peeled and finely chopped
1 cup (4 to 5 ounces) diced smoked ham
3 eggs
3 tablespoons milk
Salt and freshly milled black pepper
1 tablespoon snipped chives

4 servings

1. Scrub the potatoes with a brush and boil them in their skins until tender. Cool, peel, and cut into $\frac{1}{2}$-inch slices.

2. Heat the butter in a large nonstick skillet and brown the potatoes on all sides. Add the onion and cook until soft. Add the diced ham.

3. Beat the eggs and blend them with the milk. Season with salt and pepper and pour the mixture into the pan. Cover and cook for 2 to 3 minutes, or until the liquid is set. Do not overcook—it should still be moist. Sprinkle with chives and serve.

Quick Rye Rolls

Schusterjungen

These rustic rye rolls are a specialty from Berlin that originated in Silesia. They were nicknamed *Schusterjungen* (cobbler's apprentices) because they lack the typical center groove of regular rolls, making them flawed. *Schusterjungen* are sometimes equated with *Salzkuchen*, a different type of roll from Berlin that was made with coarse white flour, which made them very cheap.

I found *Schusterjungen* recipes with and without yeast, and liked this quick version. They taste best eaten the same day they are baked.

2½ cups rye flour
2 cups bread flour
1 scant tablespoon baking
  powder
1 teaspoon salt
1 teaspoon caraway seeds,
  plus more for sprinkling
2½ cups beer, at room
  temperature
Coarse (kosher) salt

12 to 15 rolls

---

1. Preheat the oven to 400 degrees F. Line a baking sheet with parchment paper.

2. Combine the flours with the baking powder, salt, and caraway seeds. Gradually add the beer, kneading into a smooth dough with your hands, or with the kneading attachment of an electric mixer.

3. Put some caraway seeds on a small plate, and some kosher salt on another plate. With well-floured hands, shape the dough into 2-inch round rolls. Dip them first in the caraway seeds, then in the salt.

4. Place the rolls 2 inches apart on the prepared baking sheet and bake for 30 minutes, or until brown. Place on a rack to cool.

East Prussian Fish Chowder

Ostpreußische Fischsuppe

Ideally the fish base for this easy and quick chowder is made from scratch but if you must, substitute with ready-made, good-quality fish stock.

3 pounds mixed bones and heads of white-fleshed fish, gills removed and rinsed well
1 carrot, peeled and diced
1 stalk celery, trimmed and chopped
1 medium yellow onion, peeled and finely chopped
1 leek, thoroughly cleaned, trimmed, and chopped
1 small bunch flat-leaf parsley, chopped
1 bay leaf
5 allspice berries
2 black peppercorns, crushed
1 pound cod or haddock fillet, skin removed
3 tablespoons unsalted butter
3 tablespoons all-purpose flour
1 cup dry white wine
Salt
3 tablespoons heavy cream
2 tablespoons sour cream
Pinch of sugar
5 ounces cooked shrimp, coarsely chopped
Freshly milled black pepper
Pinch of sugar
Finely chopped fresh dill

6 servings

1. Put the fish bones and heads in a soup pot with the carrot, celery, onion, leek, parsley, bay leaf, allspice, and peppercorns. Add 6 cups cold water and bring to a boil. Remove the scum that forms on top and cook, covered, for 15 minutes. Strain through a fine sieve and discard solids. Set broth aside. Rinse the pot.

2. Cut the fish fillet into bite-size pieces. Melt the butter in the soup pot. Stir in the flour and cook over low heat until it begins to turn beige, stirring constantly. Stir in the wine and continue stirring until the mixture is thickened and free of lumps.

3. Measure 5 cups of the fish stock and add it to the pot with 1 teaspoon salt. Add the fish fillet and cook over low heat for 5 minutes, until the fish is no longer translucent.

4. Stir in the heavy cream and sour cream until well incorporated. Add the shrimp. Season with salt, pepper, and sugar. Stir in some dill and serve hot.

Sauerkraut Soup

Sauerkrautsuppe

Contrary to popular belief, sauerkraut has never been a German national dish, according to German journalist Hans Hermann von Wimpffen, who has researched and written on the topic extensively. Sauerkraut with sausage and bacon is actually the signature dish of Alsace, where sauerkraut was first produced.

I should note that this recipe is not to satisfy those who think a German cookbook must contain at least one recipe with sauerkraut *(for sauerkraut as a side dish, see page 167)*. Rather I am including this recipe from Thuringia because it is a tasty soup perfect for cold days.

1 (14½-ounce) can sauer-
kraut or fresh sauerkraut
2 tablespoons vegetable oil
1 medium yellow onion,
peeled and chopped
1 quart beef broth, canned
or homemade (see page
200)
1 bay leaf
2 juniper berries
½ teaspoon caraway seeds
1 medium potato, peeled
and grated
3 tablespoons sour cream
Salt and freshly milled
black pepper
1 teaspoon dark brown sugar

4 servings

1. Place the sauerkraut in a colander. Drain, rinse with cold water, and drain again.

2. Heat the oil in a pot and cook the onion over medium heat until translucent. Add the sauerkraut, broth, bay leaf, juniper berries, and caraway seeds. Cover and simmer for 10 minutes.

3. Add the grated potato and cook, covered, for 20 more minutes.

4. Stir in the sour cream, and season with salt, pepper, and sugar. Remove the bay leaf and serve hot.

Mixed Vegetable Soup with Frankfurter Sausages

Thüringer Schnippelsuppe

This hearty soup from Thuringia is almost a full meal. It can be supplemented by other vegetables of the season. If you do not eat it all at once, don't worry—*Thüringer Schnippelsuppe* tastes even better reheated the next day.

1 pound red or other low-starch potatoes, peeled
1 turnip, peeled
2 carrots, peeled
1 leek, thoroughly cleaned and trimmed, white parts only
6 brussels sprouts
3 (14½-ounce) cans beef broth, or 1½ quart homemade beef broth (see page 200)
¼ teaspoon black peppercorns
1 bay leaf
1 cup fresh shelled or frozen green peas
6 thin slices (3 ounces) lean center-cut bacon
2 medium yellow onions, peeled and chopped
1 cup coarsely chopped fresh flat-leaf parsley
2 frankfurters (about ½ pound), cut into ½-inch slices
Salt and freshly milled black pepper
2 teaspoons white wine vinegar

6 to 8 servings

1. Cut the potatoes, turnip, carrots, and leek into 1-inch cubes or slices. Trim and halve the brussels sprouts.

2. Put the broth in a stockpot. Add the potatoes, turnip, carrots, leek, brussels sprouts, peppercorns, and the bay leaf. Bring to a boil, reduce the heat, and cover. Cook over low heat for 40 minutes, or until the vegetables are tender. Add the peas 5 to 10 minutes before the end of the cooking time.

3. While the soup is cooking, cut the bacon into small strips. Place them in a large cold skillet and sauté them. Add the onions and cook until the bacon is crisp and the onions are soft. Add the bacon, onions, and parsley to the finished soup.

4. Add the frankfurters and heat thoroughly in the soup. Season with salt and pepper and add the vinegar. Remove the bay leaf and serve hot.

Red Wine Soup

Rotweinsuppe

Wine soup is a dish with a long tradition that is now being rediscovered by German chefs and home cooks. It is a great way to start a dinner on a chilly fall or winter night, assuming that your guests are either staying overnight or walking home.

Wine soup in the West, such as *Pfälzer Weinsuppe* (Palatinate Wine Soup), is usually made with white wine and meat broth, while the sweet eastern versions use red wine and bear a clear resemblance to wine soup in eastern Europe. In a book about Polish cuisine, I learned that wine soup was usually served for breakfast, not for dinner.

This recipe was inspired by a 1910 wine soup recipe from the Siebenbürger Sachsen, a German minority in Transylvania, Romania—yes, the land of Count Dracula—and recipes from eastern Germany.

1 organic orange
1 organic lemon
$1/4$ cup raisins
2 cups dry red wine
2 tablespoons plus
  2 teaspoons tapioca
  pearls
$1/3$ cup sugar
$1/2$ cinnamon stick
1 whole clove
Pinch of ground nutmeg
$1/2$ cup heavy cream

4 to 6 servings

1. Remove the peel of the orange and lemon with a citrus stripper or a vegetable peeler in as few pieces as possible to make them easier to remove from the soup afterward. Juice the orange and lemon.

2. Rinse the raisins under cold water. Place $1\frac{2}{3}$ cups water, the orange and lemon zest and juice, raisins, wine, tapioca, sugar, cinnamon stick, clove, and nutmeg in a large saucepan and bring to a simmer. Cook for 15 minutes, stirring occasionally.

3. Remove the citrus strips, clove, and cinnamon stick with a slotted spoon. (You might find it easier to strain the soup to remove the spices and the zest, and then put the soup and tapioca back together.)

4. Whisk the cream into the soup and reheat it briefly but do not boil. Serve hot.

Swiss Cheese Salad with Pears and Apples

Brandenburger Käsesalat

Golden pears from the Havelland, the lowland around the Havel River, west of Berlin, inspired nineteenth-century writer Theodor Fontane to write one of the most beautiful and most famous German food poems.

The poem is about a nobleman, Herr von Ribbeck, who had a pear tree on his property. Every fall, he filled his pockets with pears and generously gave them to the village children he met on his daily walk. In his will, he ordered that a pear be buried with him. After the old man's death, his son, known for his stinginess, never gave any pears away. But that did not matter, because a gorgeous pear tree grew on the grave, providing the village children with delicious pears for years to come.

---

1 medium Golden or Red Delicious apple, cored and peeled
1 slightly under-ripe medium Bosc or Bartlett pear, cored and peeled
Juice of 1 lemon
3 tablespoons plain yogurt
1 teaspoon honey mustard
1/4 teaspoon honey
Salt and freshly milled black pepper
1/4 cup walnut pieces
7 ounces Swiss cheese, cut into 1/2-inch cubes

4 servings

---

1. Cut the apple and pear into 1-inch cubes. Put them in a bowl, sprinkle with lemon juice to prevent them from turning brown, and set aside.

2. Whisk together the yogurt, mustard, and honey. Season with salt and pepper.

3. Lightly toast the walnuts in an ungreased pan. Cool.

4. Toss the walnuts with the apple and pear mixture, the cheese and spoonfuls of the dressing. Let stand at room temperature for about 1 hour before serving. Serve with fresh wholesome bread or a baguette.

Eggs in Mustard Sauce

Eier in Mostrichsoße

During the industrial age, Berlin, like other large cities, was a place where many people had to struggle to make ends meet. The lives of the urban poor in the late nineteenth and early twentieth centuries was depicted in detail by lithographer and photographer Heinrich Zille, one of the city's most beloved artists. Through his caricatures with captions in a strong Berlin dialect, he made the life of Berlin's small people known far beyond Berlin. *Zille sein Miljöh* (Zille's social surroundings) became a real trademark.

The names of a number of typical dishes from Berlin reflect that modest lifestyle. For example, a white sauce with bits of bacon or a small amount of ground beef was nicknamed *Beamtenstippe* (clerk's dip). Eggs were another cheap and quick way of feeding a family. Many pubs in Berlin still sell *Soleier* (boiled eggs in brine), which are displayed in large glass jars on the counter.

This is a popular egg dish from Berlin. It is traditionally served with boiled potatoes and mixed salad greens.

---

8 eggs
2 tablespoons unsalted butter
2 tablespoons all-purpose flour
½ (14½-ounce) can lukewarm beef broth, or 1 cup homemade beef broth (see page 200)
1 cup lukewarm milk
2 tablespoons Dijon mustard
1 tablespoon white wine vinegar
¼ teaspoon sugar
Salt and freshly milled white pepper

4 to 6 servings

1. Put the eggs in a large saucepan and cover with cold water. Bring the water to a boil and reduce the heat. Let the eggs simmer for 8 minutes, or a little longer if you prefer them hard. Plunge them into cold water immediately and then peel them.

2. Melt the butter over low heat. Blend in the flour and cook until the mixture begins to turn beige, stirring constantly with a wooden spoon. Slowly add the broth and milk and simmer for 10 minutes while stirring constantly to avoid lumps. Add the mustard, vinegar, and sugar, and season with salt and pepper.

3. Cut the eggs in half and place them in a serving dish. Pour the very hot sauce over them and serve right away.

Crisped Meat Patties

Berliner Buletten

When a language has many different words for one thing, it usually indicates its importance. Meat patties, often sold by butchers as a popular meal on the run, are called *Fleischpflanzerl* in Bavaria, *Buletten* in Berlin, and *Frikadellen* in other parts of the country. Of course Berliners claim that their meat patties, eaten with *Mostrich* (mustard) and *Knüppel* (oblong rolls) are the real stuff and far superior to the competition from the rest of the nation. See for yourself. Should you prefer to use 100 percent beef instead of a 50:50 mixture of pork and beef, Berliners will forgive you.

$1\frac{1}{2}$ *(4- to 5-inch) dry bread rolls*
$\frac{1}{2}$ *tablespoon unsalted butter*
1 medium yellow onion, peeled and finely chopped
1 clove garlic, crushed
10 ounces lean ground beef
10 ounces ground pork
1 egg
1 tablespoon finely chopped fresh flat-leaf parsley
Pinch of ground caraway
Salt and freshly milled black pepper
2 tablespoons vegetable oil

12 pieces

1. If the rolls are still soft, slice them, place them on a baking sheet, and put them in the oven at 350 degrees F until they are dry. Soak the rolls in a small bowl of hot water.

2. Melt the butter in a skillet and sauté the onion and garlic until translucent. Set aside.

3. Put the rolls in a large sieve and squeeze out the excess liquid over the sink. Combine them with the meat, onion, garlic, egg, parsley, caraway, salt, and pepper in a large bowl. Don't be shy about using your hands to mix it well.

4. Form the meat into 2- to 3-inch balls with your hands lightly moistened with water if necessary. Lightly press on the balls to shape them into patties. Heat the oil in a large nonstick skillet over high heat. Add the patties and cook on one side until nicely browned. Turn and brown on the other side. Reduce the heat to medium and cook until no pink remains. Do not cover, or the meat patties will become soggy.

Bratwurst in Beer Sauce

Bratwurst in Biersoße (Stolzer Heinrich)

This East German specialty is also called *Stolzer Heinrich*, which means "proud Henry." The beer sauce is often thickened with spiced Christmas cookies. I use the readily available gingersnaps, which work just as well. This dish is traditionally served with mashed potatoes.

6 bratwurst
2 tablespoons vegetable oil
1/2 (12-ounce) bottle dark beer, plus more to taste
6 gingersnaps, crushed
Salt and freshly milled black pepper
Pinch of sugar

4 servings

1. Put the bratwurst in a large skillet and barely cover with water. Gently simmer for 10 minutes to prevent them from bursting while cooking. Remove them from the water and drain.

2. Heat the oil in the same skillet and sauté the bratwurst over medium heat until lightly browned on all sides. Take them out of the skillet and keep warm.

3. Deglaze the pan with the beer. Add the gingersnaps and simmer over low heat until the gingersnaps are completely dissolved, stirring the sauce occasionally. If you like the sauce a little thinner, add more beer. Season with salt, pepper, and sugar. Pour the sauce over the bratwurst and serve.

Beef Roll-ups with Bacon and Gherkins

Rinderrouladen

Rouladen (from the French *rouler*, "to roll up"), a word coined by French immigrants in Berlin, is one of those dishes that younger generations find too time-consuming to prepare themselves, but devour with delight when mothers or grandmothers make it. Recipes vary from family to family, restaurant to restaurant, and region to region. The traditional accompaniment is boiled potatoes, but any other form of potatoes that soak up the delicious gravy works as well.

Finding the right meat for roll-ups might be a little tricky but it's worth the search. Try to find a butcher who is willing to cut you a few very thin slices off a large roast without requiring that you buy the entire piece. If you want to cut the meat yourself, wrap it tightly in plastic wrap and freeze it for about 30 minutes. When the meat is slightly frozen, it is easier to cut to the desired thinness.

8 thin slices (4 ounces)
  lean center-cut bacon
2 medium yellow onions,
  peeled
$^1/_4$ cup very finely chopped
  gherkins
4 very thin (about $^1/_4$-inch)
  large slices lean bottom
  round roast
Freshly milled black pepper
2 teaspoons Dijon mustard
2 tablespoons vegetable oil
1 (14$^1/_2$-ounce) can beef
  broth, or 2 cups home-
  made beef broth (see
  page 200)
1 tablespoon sour cream or
  crème fraîche (see box
  opposite page)
Salt

4 servings

1. Cut the bacon into small strips and place them in a cold skillet. Cook over medium heat until crisp. Very finely chop 1 of the onions. Discard some of the bacon fat and sauté the onion with the bacon until translucent. Remove from heat and add the gherkins.

2. Spread the meat slices on a large cutting board or a clean work surface. Rub each piece with pepper and brush with $^1/_2$ teaspoon mustard. Divide the filling into 4 equal portions and spread them on the meat, leaving $^1/_2$ inch on each long side to keep the filling inside the roll-up. Roll up the meat tightly, starting from the narrow side, and tie securely with twine.

3. Heat the vegetable oil in a saucepan large enough to hold all roll-ups in a single layer. Brown the roll-ups on all sides. Quarter the remaining onion and add it to the meat along with the broth. Cover and simmer for $1\frac{1}{2}$ hours, or until the meat is tender. Turn the roll-ups every so often and check that there is always at least 1 inch of liquid at the bottom of the pan. Add a little hot water if necessary.

4. Remove the twine from the roll-ups. Keep them warm while you puree the gravy. Pour the pureed gravy back into the pan and increase the heat to reduce the gravy. When it thickens, remove the pan from the heat. Add sour cream, salt, and pepper. Serve the roll-ups and the gravy separately.

Make Your Own Crème Fraîche

Nowadays crème fraîche is available in specialty food stores. But if you cannot find it or want to be more economical (unlike Germany, where it is a standard dairy product, crème fraîche is quite pricey in the United States) you can very easily make your own, which will keep for 4 to 5 days in the refrigerator.

1 cup heavy cream
2 tablespoons buttermilk

Or for a lighter (and equally good) version, use:

$\frac{1}{2}$ cup heavy cream
$\frac{1}{2}$ cup sour cream

Makes 1 cup

Mix the heavy cream and buttermilk (or sour cream) well in a glass jar or plastic container. Cover and let stand at room temperature for 8 to 12 hours, until the crème fraîche has thickened. Refrigerate.

Meat Loaf with Gravy

Falscher Hase

The slightly snotty quick-wittedness of Berliners, also known as *Berliner Schnauze* (Berliner snout) is legendary among other Germans. Berliners have also come up with quirky names for some local dishes. *Falscher Hase* (fake hare), a well-seasoned meat loaf, is one of them. It is usually served with red cabbage and/or mashed potatoes.

2 (4- to 5-inch) dry rolls
6 thin slices (3 ounces) lean center-cut bacon
2 medium yellow onions, peeled
10 ounces lean ground beef
10 ounces ground pork
2 eggs
3 tablespoons finely chopped fresh flat-leaf parsley
1 teaspoon Dijon mustard
1/4 teaspoon paprika
1/4 teaspoon ground caraway
Pinch of dried oregano
Pinch of ground nutmeg
Pinch of cayenne pepper
Pinch of ground marjoram
Pinch of dried thyme
Pinch of ground coriander
Salt and freshly milled black pepper
1 tablespoon vegetable oil
1 tablespoon unsalted butter
1 medium tomato, quartered
1 cup canned or homemade beef broth (see page 200)
Continued

1. If the rolls are still soft, slice them, place them on a baking sheet, and put them in the oven at 350 degrees F until they are dry. Soak the rolls in a small bowl of hot water.

2. Cut the bacon into small strips. Place them in a large cold skillet and sauté. Chop 1 of the onions and add it to the bacon. Cook until all the bacon fat has been drawn out and the onion is translucent; set aside.

3. Preheat the oven to 400 degree F.

4. Place the rolls in a large sieve and squeeze out the excess liquid. Combine the rolls with the meat, onion and bacon mixture, eggs, parsley, mustard, paprika, caraway, oregano, nutmeg, cayenne pepper, marjoram, thyme, coriander, salt, and black pepper. Combine very well, using your hands if necessary. Shape into a loaf that will fit in an ovenproof casserole with a lid, allowing about 1-inch space all around the loaf (the casserole should not be much larger than the loaf).

5. Heat the oil and the butter in the same skillet you used before and brown the loaf on both sides, turning it carefully. Place the loaf in the ovenproof casserole. Quarter the remaining 1 onion and place around the meat loaf along with the tomato quarters. Pour 1/4 cup broth over it.

$1/4$ cup sour cream
1 teaspoon all-purpose flour

6 servings

6. Cover and bake for 20 minutes. Uncover and bake for 40 minutes, or until the top is brown and crisp, gradually adding another $1/2$ cup of the broth. Remove the meat loaf from the casserole and keep warm.

7. Deglaze the casserole with the remaining broth and pour into a small saucepan and bring to a boil. Remove from the heat and strain. Mix the sour cream with the flour and whisk into the gravy. Simmer for a few minutes until the gravy thickens. Season with salt and pepper.

8. Cut the meat loaf into $1/2$-inch-thick slices and serve the gravy separately.

Breaded Ham Slices

Kloppschinken

Kloppschinken ("pounded ham") was a special treat for Sundays and holidays in the Uckermark, a region between Berlin and the Baltic Sea. Traditionally the dish is prepared with either boiled ham or smoked ham and often served with applesauce.

2 cups milk
¼ teaspoon ground nutmeg
4 thick slices (1 pound) boiled and lightly smoked ham
1 egg
⅔ cup dry breadcrumbs
¼ cup vegetable oil

4 servings

1. Pour the milk into a large shallow dish and stir in the nutmeg. Add the ham and marinate for 2 to 3 hours at room temperature.

2. Remove the ham from the marinade and pat dry with paper towels. Discard the marinade. Pound each slice of ham a few times. Lightly beat the egg in a shallow baking dish. Spread the breadcrumbs on a platter right next to it. Dip the ham slices, one at a time, first in the egg, then in the breadcrumbs. Make sure both sides are well coated.

3. Heat the oil in a large nonstick skillet and sauté the ham slices on each side until golden, carefully flipping them over once. Serve hot.

Schnitzel Pancake

Hoppel-Poppel

*H*oppel-Poppel is a popular dish from Berlin, whose name is as cute as it is obscure. It is a good fit for a homey brunch. Since the potatoes are best when they are not freshly cooked, I recommend that you make them the night before.

$1\frac{1}{2}$ *pounds red or other low-starch potatoes, peeled and sliced*
$\frac{3}{4}$ *pound lean pork loin*
$\frac{1}{4}$ *cup vegetable oil*
1 large yellow onion, peeled and finely chopped
Salt and freshly milled black pepper
$\frac{1}{4}$ *teaspoon caraway seeds*
$\frac{1}{4}$ *teaspoon ground marjoram*
4 eggs
2 tablespoons snipped chives
Pinch of ground nutmeg
1 tomato for garnish
2 to 3 gherkins for garnish

6 servings

1. Scrub the potatoes with a brush and boil them in their skins until tender. Cool, peel, and cut into $\frac{1}{2}$-inch slices.

2. Cut the meat into very small strips. Heat 2 tablespoons of the oil in a large nonstick skillet and sauté the onions until translucent. Add the meat and cook until nicely browned and cooked through. Season with salt and pepper. Remove from the skillet and keep warm.

3. Heat the remaining 2 tablespoons oil in the skillet and brown the potatoes on both sides. Season with salt, pepper, caraway seeds, and marjoram. Toss carefully with the meat in a large bowl.

4. Lightly beat the eggs and stir in the chives. Season with nutmeg, salt, and pepper. Place the meat and the potatoes in the skillet, flatten them gently with a wooden spoon or spatula, and pour the eggs over them. Cover and cook over low to medium heat until the eggs have set.

5. Wash, seed, and slice the tomato. Slide the pancake from the skillet onto a large round serving platter and garnish with tomato and gherkins. Serve at once.

Smoked Pork Chops

Kasseler Rippenspeer

Kasseler, a cured and smoked meat specialty, was not named after the city of Kassel in west central Germany, as many people believe. It was named after its inventor, the butcher Cassel, on the eve of the twentieth century in Berlin. The authentic accompaniment is mashed potatoes and sauerkraut.

1 carrot, peeled and chopped
1 large yellow onion, peeled and sliced
1 bay leaf
$1/4$ teaspoon crushed allspice
$1/4$ teaspoon crushed black peppercorns
2 whole cloves
2 pounds lightly smoked thick pork chops
1 cup dry red wine
1 tablespoon all-purpose flour
$1/2$ cup sour cream
Salt (optional)
Freshly milled black pepper

4 servings

1. Preheat the oven to 400 degrees F.

2. Toss the carrot, onion, bay leaf, allspice, peppercorns, and cloves and arrange them in a large roasting pan. Rinse the chops under cold, running water and pat dry with paper towels. Place them on top of the vegetables and pour 1 cup hot water over them. Roast the pork chops for 30 minutes. Turn them and add 1 more cup hot water. Roast them for 30 more minutes, basting frequently.

3. Remove the chops and vegetables from the pan and deglaze with the wine. Strain the gravy into a small saucepan. Mix the flour with the sour cream and whisk into the gravy. Cook over very low heat until the sauce thickens, stirring frequently to avoid lumps. Season carefully with salt—the pork chops usually provide enough saltiness—and pepper. Serve hot with the chops.

Pork Loin with Onion Sauce

Sächsisches Zwiebelfleisch

This is Saxonian comfort food: tender meat in a gravy that gets its special taste and thick consistency from bread crumbs. There was hardly a menu in the former German Democratic Republic (*DDR* in German) that did not include *Sächsisches Zwiebelfleisch*.

*1 stalk celery, trimmed
and chopped
1 carrot, peeled and chopped
1 turnip, peeled and chopped
1 parsnip, peeled and
chopped
3 medium yellow onions,
peeled and sliced
1 bay leaf
½ teaspoon allspice
¼ teaspoon black
peppercorns
1 teaspoon caraway seeds
2 whole cloves
1 teaspoon mustard seeds
1 teaspoon sugar
2 tablespoons white wine
vinegar
¼ teaspoon finely grated
organic lemon zest
2 pounds boneless pork
loin roast
2 tablespoons vegetable oil
2 tablespoons dry
breadcrumbs
Salt and freshly milled
black pepper*

4 to 6 servings

1. Put the celery, carrot, turnip, parsnip, 1 of the onions, the bay leaf, allspice, peppercorns, caraway seeds, cloves, mustard seeds, sugar, vinegar, and lemon zest in a saucepan with 1 quart water. Bring to a boil.

2. Rinse the meat under cold water and add it to the vegetables. The meat should be just covered with water. Reduce the heat and simmer, covered, for 1½ to 2 hours, or until the meat is tender. Strain the broth and set aside.

3. Heat the oil and sauté the remaining 2 onions until golden. Add the strained broth and simmer for 15 minutes. Stir in the breadcrumbs to thicken the sauce. Season with salt and pepper.

4. Slice the meat and reheat it thoroughly in the sauce. Serve hot with potato dumplings (*see page 225*).

Cabbage Casserole

Magdeburger Bördetopf

For a long time I ignored this recipe because it was the signature dish of the former German Democratic Republic, and like so many other "socialist" dishes from the GDR, I thought it could not possibly be tasty. I was dead wrong! It is cabbage at its best, and I am usually not too keen on cabbage.

½ pound lean boneless pork shoulder or neck, cut into ½-inch cubes
½ pound boneless lamb shoulder, cut into ½-inch cubes
1 teaspoon salt, or more to taste
1 teaspoon freshly milled black pepper, or more to taste
Pinch of cayenne pepper
3 cloves garlic, crushed
1 teaspoon coarsely ground caraway seeds
3 to 4 medium russet potatoes (1¼ pounds)
4 medium onions
1 small head white cabbage (about 1 pound)
1 tablespoon vegetable oil
1 tablespoon unsalted butter
1 teaspoon crumbled dried thyme
¾ cup sour cream
2 cups beef broth

4 servings

1. Rub the meat with 1 teaspoon salt, 1 teaspoon pepper, cayenne, garlic, and caraway seeds. Put in a container with a lid and marinate at least 6 hours or overnight in the refrigerator.

2. Peel and thinly slice the potatoes and onions. Wash and trim the cabbage. Quarter it and remove the center core with a sharp knife. Cut each quarter into thin strips. Wash the cabbage in plenty of cold water and drain.

3. Preheat the oven to 450 degrees F. Heat the oil in an ovenproof casserole with a tight-fitting lid, preferably a Dutch oven. Add half of the marinated meat and cook until browned on all sides, then transfer to a bowl. Repeat this with the remaining meat.

4. Melt the butter in the casserole and then remove from the stove. Spread a layer of onions in the casserole, then a layer of potatoes. Season with salt, pepper, and thyme. Add a layer of meat and a layer of cabbage. Repeat this until all the ingredients are used up, seasoning each layer with salt, pepper, and thyme.

5. Whisk the sour cream into the broth until well combined and pour into the casserole. Gently push the layers down with your hands; the liquid should reach up to the top layer. Cover and cook in the preheated oven for 1½ hours. Leave the layers undisturbed and lift the lid only when serving the casserole right at the table.

Meatballs in Creamy Caper Sauce

Königsberger Klopse

These meatballs are a culinary reminiscence from Königsberg, once the cultural and economic center of East Prussia. Since the end of World War II, Königsberg has been part of Russia and was renamed Kaliningrad. The dish, however, has kept its name and its popularity as a staple of traditional German cuisine.

1 (4- to 5-inch) dry bread roll, or 3 thick slices of dry white bread
1 cup hot milk
1 pound ground veal
1 egg
2 shallots, peeled and finely minced
2 teaspoons Dijon mustard
1 teaspoon finely grated organic lemon zest
Salt and freshly milled black pepper
1 ($14\frac{1}{2}$-ounce) can beef broth, or 2 cups home-made (see page 200)
$\frac{1}{4}$ teaspoon black peppercorns
$\frac{1}{2}$ bay leaf
3 tablespoons unsalted butter
3 tablespoons all-purpose flour
1 egg yolk
1 cup light cream
2 tablespoons drained capers
1 tablespoon lemon juice
Pinch of sugar

4 servings

1. If the rolls are still soft, slice them, place on a baking sheet, and put in the oven at 350 degrees F until dry. Pour the milk over the rolls and let stand until all the liquid has been absorbed.

2. Squeeze the excess liquid from the bread. Combine the bread, veal, egg, shallots, mustard, lemon zest, salt, and pepper. Blend well with your hands. Shape into walnut-size meatballs.

3. In a large saucepan, bring the broth to a simmer with the peppercorns and bay leaf. Gently lower the meatballs into the broth in a single layer and cover. Cook over low heat for 20 minutes, or until done, turning the meatballs over just once during the cooking process. Remove the meatballs with a slotted spoon and keep warm.

4. Strain the broth into a separate bowl. Melt the butter in the saucepan and add the flour. Cook until the mixture begins to turn beige, stirring constantly. Gradually whisk in the strained broth.

5. Mix the egg yolk with the cream in a small bowl and stir into the sauce. Add the capers, lemon juice, and sugar, and season with salt and pepper. Add the meatballs to the sauce and carefully reheat over very low heat. Serve immediately with plain rice.

Cabbage Roll-ups with Meat Filling

Thüringische Kohlrouladen

This is an East German dish, however, the cabbage capital of Germany is Dithmarschen in the North. With more than 80 million cabbages per year, Dithmarschen is the largest cabbage cultivation area in Europe. The discovery that the soil and climate in Dithmarschen was optimal for cabbage cultivation was only made by chance in the late 1900s. A canning factory placed an ad in a local newspaper looking for vegetables. A backyard gardener hit upon the idea of planting cabbage and selling it to the factory to fill their cans. The idea clicked and many followed in his footsteps.

---

1 head (3 to 4 pounds) savoy cabbage
1 (4- to 5-inch) dry bread roll, or 3 slices dry white bread
6 thin slices (3 ounces) lean center-cut bacon
1 medium yellow onion, peeled and finely chopped
1 pound ground meat ($\frac{1}{2}$ beef and $\frac{1}{2}$ pork, or beef only)
1 egg
1 tablespoon finely chopped fresh flat-leaf parsley
1 teaspoon Dijon mustard
$\frac{1}{2}$ teaspoon ground caraway
Salt and freshly milled black pepper

Continued

---

1. Bring water to a boil in a large pot. Turn the cabbage bottom up and cut a deep cone-shaped hole into the center to remove the core. Blanch the whole head for 5 minutes, or until the outer leaves can be removed easily. Peel off as many leaves as possible and return the cabbage to the boiling water. Drain the leaves in a colander and repeat the procedure until you have at least 20 large leaves.

2. If the roll is still soft, slice it, place it on a baking sheet and put it in the oven at 350 degrees F until dry. Soak the roll in a small bowl of hot water.

3. Cut the bacon into small strips. Place them in a cold skillet and cook over medium heat until the fat has been drawn out. Discard the fat, leaving only a thin layer in the pan. Sauté the onion in the fat until translucent.

4. Squeeze the excess liquid from the bread. Combine the bread, bacon, onion, meat, egg, parsley, mustard, and caraway in a large mixing bowl. Season well with salt and pepper.

3 tablespoons vegetable oil
1 can (14½-ounce) beef broth, or 2 cups home-made (see page 200)
1 tablespoon all-purpose flour
Pinch of ground nutmeg
Pinch of ground thyme

8 servings

5. Spread the cabbage leaves flat on a clean work surface. Make little incisions in the tough white veins; this makes the leaves smoother and easier to roll. For each roll-up, arrange 2 to 3 leaves in the shape of a fan. Divide the stuffing into 8 portions and put 1 portion in the middle of each fan. Roll up the leaves tightly and neatly while tucking in the sides. Tie each roll-up together with twine or secure with small skewers.

6. Heat the oil in a large saucepan and brown the roll-ups on all sides. Place them in the pan seam-side down and as closely together as possible to prevent them from unrolling. They should fit snugly into the pan. Pour the broth over them, just covering the roll-ups. Cover and simmer for 45 minutes.

7. Remove the roll-ups from the saucepan. Mix the flour with 2 tablespoons cold water and whisk it into the cooking liquid. Let the sauce thicken over low heat. Add the nutmeg and thyme and season with salt and pepper. Remove the twine or skewers from the roll-ups. Transfer them to the saucepan and reheat thoroughly in the sauce.

Chicken Fricassee with Mushrooms and White Asparagus

Berliner Hühnerfrikassee

Chicken Fricassee originated in Berlin and today is a popular dish all over Germany. At the end of the seventeenth century, 20,000 Huguenots (French Protestants) came to Berlin and Brandenburg, escaping severe limitation of their religious freedom under King Louis XIV. At the time, Berlin had only half a million inhabitants, so the influence of the French immigrants was quite noticeable. The Huguenots stimulated the economy, science, arts, education, and gastronomy. Many of Berlin's timeless classics have French-inspired names that go back to the Huguenots. *Hühnerfrikassee* (from French "fricassée") is one of the many culinary reminiscences of the Huguenots.

Chicken:
1 whole roasting chicken (4 pounds)
1 carrot, peeled and chopped
1 leek, thoroughly cleaned, trimmed, and chopped
1 turnip, peeled and sliced
1 parsnip, peeled and sliced
1 sprig rosemary
2 bay leaves
3 stems fresh flat-leaf parsley
½ teaspoon black peppercorns
Salt

1. For the chicken: Remove the giblets. Rinse the chicken under cold running water. Put 2 quarts water in a stockpot with the chicken, carrot, leek, turnip, parsnip, rosemary, bay leaves, parsley, peppercorns, and salt. Bring to a boil, skim the foam off the top, and reduce the heat. Cover and simmer for about 1 hour, or until the chicken is tender.

2. Remove the chicken and vegetables from the pot and strain the broth through a fine sieve. Measure 2½ cups for the sauce and set aside. If you do not have an immediate use for the remaining chicken broth, you can refrigerate it for several days or freeze it. Remove the skin from the chicken, strip the meat from the bones, and cut into bite-size chunks. Discard the bones and skin.

Sauce:

3 tablespoons unsalted butter

2 tablespoons all-purpose flour

8 medium white mushrooms, cleaned, trimmed, and sliced

9 spears cooked fresh or canned white asparagus, drained (see page 21)

$1/4$ cup dry white wine

1 tablespoon lemon juice

1 teaspoon sugar

1 egg yolk

$1/4$ cup heavy cream

Dash of Worcestershire sauce

Salt and freshly milled white pepper

6 servings

3. For the sauce: Melt 2 tablespoons of the butter in a saucepan. Stir in the flour and cook until beige, stirring constantly with a wooden spoon. Gradually add the reserved hot broth and whisk to avoid lumps. Simmer for 5 minutes.

4. Melt the remaining 1 tablespoon butter in another saucepan. Sauté the mushrooms until they begin to soften.

5. Cut the asparagus into 1-inch chunks and add them to the sauce with the mushrooms and chicken. Stir in the wine, lemon juice, and sugar, and simmer for 3 minutes. Combine the egg yolk with the cream and add it to the sauce. Make sure the sauce does not boil. Add the Worcestershire sauce and season with salt and pepper. Serve hot with plain white rice.

Veal Liver with Apples and Onions

Kalbsleber Berliner Art

A classic recipe from Berlin, traditionally served with mashed potatoes.

3 tablespoons vegetable oil
2 large yellow onions, peeled and thinly sliced
2 tablespoons unsalted butter
2 large tart cooking apples, cored, peeled, and thinly sliced
4 slices (1 pound) fresh calves' liver
1 tablespoon all-purpose flour
Salt and freshly milled black pepper

4 servings

1. Heat 2 tablespoons of the oil in a large nonstick skillet and sauté the onions until golden brown. Remove the onions and drain them on paper towels. Keep warm. Do not rinse the skillet; you will need this oil later to cook the liver.

2. In another nonstick skillet, melt the butter and sauté the apples until just soft, stirring them carefully. Keep warm.

3. Rinse the liver slices under cold running water and pat them dry with paper towels. Place the liver on a large cutting board or platter and sprinkle lightly with flour. Heat the remaining 1 tablespoon oil in the skillet in which you sautéed the onions. Brown the liver on both sides for 4 to 6 minutes, or until cooked. Season with salt and pepper. Arrange the liver on a warmed serving platter and top with the onions and apples.

Potato Crescents

Kartoffelhörnchen

The cuisine of Thuringia features potato dishes galore. Of all recipes, Thuringian dumplings are the most widely known, but these potato crescents are every bit as scrumptious as their famous relatives.

2 pounds starchy yellow potatoes (Yukon Gold)
4 tablespoons unsalted butter
6 egg yolks
Pinch of ground nutmeg
$^1/_2$ cup cornstarch
Salt

About 15 pieces

1. Peel and quarter the potatoes. Bring them to a boil in salted water and cook until tender. Drain.

2. Preheat the oven to 350 degrees F. Generously grease a 17½ x 14–inch baking sheet.

3. Mash the potatoes. Melt the butter in a small saucepan. In a large bowl, combine potatoes, butter, 5 of the egg yolks, nutmeg, cornstarch, and salt. Mix thoroughly with a wooden spoon.

4. Shape the potato mixture into 3-inch crescents with your hands moistened with water. Place the crescents on the baking sheet and make a few little incisions in each crescent with a sharp knife. Beat the remaining egg yolk and brush the crescents with it.

5. Bake for 35 minutes, or until golden brown and puffy. Serve immediately.

Potatoes with Quark and Flaxseed Oil

Pellkartoffeln mit Leinöl

Potatoes boiled in their skins served with creamy quark (*see page 174*) and chives are a popular and cheap dish found all over Germany. The addition of flaxseed oil is an East German peculiarity. If you cannot find quark, use Greek yogurt instead.

Cold-pressed flaxseed oil is often praised for its health benefits. It is rich in alpha-linolenic acid, an essential fatty acid believed to help prevent heart disease, inflammatory bowel disease, arthritis, and a variety of other health conditions. You should have no problem finding flaxseed oil in health food stores.

2 pounds very small new potatoes
1 teaspoon caraway seeds
1 (16-ounce) container quark or Greek yogurt
$1/4$ cup snipped chives
Salt and freshly milled black pepper
$1/4$ teaspoon ground caraway
2 teaspoons flaxseed oil, plus more to taste
2 to 3 tablespoons milk (optional)

4 to 6 servings

1. Scrub the potatoes with a brush and bring them to a boil in enough salted water to just cover them. Add the caraway seeds and cook until the potatoes are tender. Drain.

2. Combine the quark or yogurt with the chives. Add salt, pepper, and ground caraway, and stir in the flaxseed oil. Add a small amount of milk and stir until smooth. Serve the hot potatoes and the dip separately. (Instead of incorporating the chives and flaxseed oil into the quark/yogurt, they can also be served on the side and added to taste.)

Creamed Potatoes with Dill

Schmandkartoffeln mit Dill

Made with sour cream, this is a great accompaniment for leftover roast meats, cold cured meats, or grilled fish.

*2 pounds red or other
    low-starch potatoes
2 tablespoons vegetable oil
    or butter
1 medium yellow onion,
    peeled and finely
    chopped
1 cup sour cream
1/4 cup very finely chopped
    fresh dill
Salt and freshly milled
    black pepper*

4 to 6 servings

1. Scrub the potatoes with a brush. Boil them in salted water until just tender. Rinse the potatoes under cold water to cool. Remove the skins and cut them into 1/2-inch slices.

2. Heat the oil in a large skillet. Sauté the onion until translucent. Add the potatoes and brown them lightly.

3. In a small bowl, combine the sour cream with the dill. Pour the mixture over the potatoes in the skillet and reduce the heat. Reheat the potatoes thoroughly but do not cook. Season with salt and pepper.

Mixed Spring Vegetables with Morels

Leipziger Allerlei

Leipziger Allerlei is one of those dishes whose canned version—usually overcooked peas, carrots and white asparagus—has not the faintest resemblance with the original and has done great harm to the reputation of the dish. The real thing is a very fine mix of crisp spring vegetables. There are many different recipes, from the rather simple, vegetables-only variety given below, to versions with crabmeat and shrimp.

The basic rule for *Leipziger Allerlei*, however, is the same for all recipes: use only fresh and tender vegetables, and cook all of them separately so they keep their unique flavors.

---

1 cup (4 ounces) fresh morels, or $1/2$ ounce dried
1 dozen ($1/2$ pound) fresh white asparagus spears (see page 21)
2 tablespoons unsalted butter, plus more to taste
Salt
Sugar
$1^1/2$ pounds fresh unshelled green peas ($1^1/2$ cups shelled)
$1/2$ small cauliflower, cleaned, trimmed, and cut into small florets
2 small kohlrabi ($1/2$ pound), peeled, halved, and cut into 1-inch slices
$1/2$ pound baby carrots
Freshly milled black pepper

6 to 8 servings

---

1. Wash the morels very carefully in three changes of water. If you use dried morels, place them in a metal bowl and pour boiling water over them. Soak for 20 minutes while you prepare the other vegetables.

2. Peel the asparagus with a vegetable peeler, carefully working your way around the tips; they are the best part and should remain whole. Cut the spears into $1^1/2$-inch chunks. Bring 2 cups water to a boil in a saucepan. Add the asparagus, $1/2$ tablespoon of the butter, and a pinch of salt and sugar. Cook the asparagus over medium heat until just tender, 12 to 15 minutes. Drain and keep warm.

3. Shell the peas. Bring 2 cups water to a boil. Add the peas, $1/2$ tablespoon of the butter, and a pinch of salt and sugar and cook the peas until just tender. Drain and keep warm.

4. Steam the cauliflower florets for 8 to 10 minutes, or until just tender. Keep warm.

5. Bring 1 cup water to a boil. Add the kohlrabi, $\frac{1}{2}$ tablespoon of the butter, and a pinch of salt and sugar. Cook until just tender, about 5 minutes. Drain and keep warm.

6. Steam the carrots for 8 to 10 minutes. Keep warm.

7. If using dried morels, simmer them in their soaking liquid until tender; then, drain. If using fresh morels, melt the remaining $\frac{1}{2}$ tablespoon butter and sauté the morels for 5 to 10 minutes.

8. Toss all the vegetables together and add more butter if desired. Season with salt and pepper and serve hot.

Cucumber Stew

Berliner Schmorgurken

Many Berliners have a tiny green plot in one of the numerous highly organized garden colonies outside the city, which started a century ago. For these *Laubenpieper*, named after their small wooden garden huts (*Lauben*), their garden has always been a welcome escape from crammed living quarters. During wartimes, when food stocks were meager, the gardens were a godsend, supplying vegetables, especially cucumbers.

4 to 6 medium cucumbers (2 pounds)
Salt
1 tablespoon sugar
Freshly milled black pepper
2 tablespoons white wine vinegar
4 thin slices (2 ounces) lean center-cut bacon
1 shallot, peeled and finely minced
½ cup sour cream
2 tablespoons finely chopped fresh dill

6 servings

1. Peel the cucumbers, cut them in half lengthwise and remove the seeds with a small spoon. Cut the cucumbers into ½-inch pieces and put in a bowl. Toss them with salt, sugar, pepper, and vinegar. Cover and let stand for 1 hour.

2. Cut the bacon into small strips. Place them in a large cold saucepan and cook over medium heat until the fat has been drawn out. Add the shallot and cook until translucent.

3. Drain the cucumbers in a sieve and add them to the bacon. Add ½ cup water and cover. Simmer over low heat for 20 minutes, stirring occasionally. Remove the pan from the heat, stir in the sour cream, and reheat the cucumbers thoroughly but do not boil them. Season with salt and pepper and sprinkle with dill. Serve hot.

Glazed Turnips

Teltower Rübchen

Turnips from Teltow are small vegetables with a long name and an intriguing story. *Brassica rapa sativa mima teltoviensis,* commonly known as *Teltower Rübchen,* is a turnip that only grows in the sandy soil of Teltow, a town south of Berlin. In 1711, Teltow was almost completely destroyed by a fire. Its inhabitants searched for new ways of making a living and latched on to the tasty little turnips that had been grown in their area since the Middle Ages. Gourmets all over Europe soon discovered *Teltower Rübchen.* Pope Pius IX had them sent to the Vatican in small barrels, carefully packaged like eggs. In France, where *navets de Teltow* became a delicacy, the nobility ate them with glee, and the turnips from Teltow even found their way onto the tsar's plate in Russia.

All attempts to cultivate *Teltower Rübchen* elsewhere in Germany and other countries failed. Their taste and flavor could simply not be transferred. During the forty years of the German Democratic Republic, growing the turnips in the state-run farm cooperatives was considered too labor-intensive, so they disappeared completely from the market and were only grown in a few backyards. But since the late 1990s, the turnips have been back on the culinary front.

This dish is best re-created with very young, small white turnips.

2 tablespoons unsalted butter
2 tablespoons sugar
1 pound small white turnips, trimmed and peeled
$1/2$ cup chicken broth
Salt and freshly milled black pepper
2 tablespoons finely chopped fresh flat-leaf parsley
4 servings

1. Melt the butter in a saucepan over medium to high heat. Add the sugar and cook until it starts to melt, stirring constantly. Add the turnips and broth and reduce the heat. Cover and simmer for 10 to 15 minutes, or until the turnips are tender and the liquid has been almost completely absorbed.

2. Uncover and continue to cook, shaking the pan and turning the turnips often to glaze them evenly on all sides. Season with salt and pepper and sprinkle with parsley. Serve hot.

Pickled Squash

Eingelegter Kürbis

The many different kinds of pumpkin and winter squash available in the United States make it difficult to decide what to use for this pickled specialty from Berlin, served with virtually any gravy-free meat or poultry. Since I find most squash more flavorful than pumpkin, I recommend you pick a large squash with dense, firm, and preferably colorful orange flesh, such as butternut squash or Blue Hubbard.

2 cups white wine vinegar
2 cups sugar
1 lemon, unpeeled and sliced, preferably organic
1 thumbnail-size piece of peeled fresh ginger
½ cinnamon stick
1 teaspoon black peppercorns
3 whole cloves
Pinch of salt
2¼ pounds (9 cups) peeled and seeded squash, cut into 1-inch cubes

2 (1-quart) jars

1. Bring 2 cups water to a boil in a large pot. Add the vinegar, sugar, lemon slices, ginger, cinnamon stick, peppercorns, cloves, and salt. Cook over low to medium heat for 5 minutes.

2. Add the squash and reduce the heat. Simmer for 10 to 15 minutes, or until the flesh starts to soften. It should still be al dente. Remove the squash with a slotted spoon and put it into 2 sterilized canning jars. To prevent the glass from cracking when you pour hot food into it, place the jars on a wet dishtowel.

3. Reduce the liquid by cooking it uncovered at medium to high heat for 5 to 7 minutes. Pour the syrup over the squash and close the jars with tight-fitting lids. Let them stand for 4 weeks in a cool place. Once opened, the pickles keep for several weeks in the refrigerator.

108   *Spoonfuls of Germany*

Stuffed Potato Dumplings

Thüringer Klöße

There are many different ways to prepare Thuringian dumplings, which are always made of a mixture of raw and boiled potatoes. It works best if you boil the potatoes at least half a day before.

4 pounds starchy potatoes (russet or Yukon Gold)
Salt
$1/4$ to $1/2$ cup hot milk
1 tablespoon unsalted butter
1 cup small unflavored croutons

6 servings

1. A few hours ahead, scrub 1 pound of the potatoes with a brush and boil them in their skins in salted water until tender. Cool, and peel them only right before mashing them.

2. Peel and finely grate the remaining raw potatoes. Drain them in a dishtowel and squeeze out as much liquid as possible and save the liquid in a bowl. The grated potatoes should be very dry.

3. Mash the cooked potatoes and mix them with the raw potatoes in a large bowl. Discard the potato liquid and add only the starch residue that has settled on the bottom. Add salt and as much hot milk as necessary to produce a smooth, but not liquid dough.

4. Heat the butter in a skillet and toast the croutons until golden.

5. Shape 12 dumplings with moistened hands and place a few croutons in the middle of each dumpling. Reshape the dumplings around the croutons.

6. Bring salted water to a boil in a pot that is large enough to hold the dumplings without touching each other. Reduce the heat and gently lower the dumplings into the water. Cover and simmer for 20 minutes. Make sure the water does not boil, or the dumplings will fall apart. Remove the dumplings with a slotted spoon and drain in a colander. Serve at once.

Yeast Dumplings with Blueberry Sauce

Hefeklöße mit Blaubeertunke

Yeast dumplings are a pan-German dish that cannot be attributed to any particular cuisine. There are many different ways to serve them: with a tender roast and gravy for a main course, or for dessert, with compote, or sprinkled with sugar and a little poppy seeds.

The combination of yeast dumplings with blueberry sauce, however, has a distinct regional character. It is considered the signature dish of the Niederlausitz, an area southeast of Berlin that stretches along the Polish border and beyond.

Sauce:
1 quart fresh or frozen blueberries
Sugar

Dumplings:
2 ($\frac{1}{4}$-ounce) envelopes active dry yeast
1 cup lukewarm milk
3 cups all-purpose flour
1 teaspoon salt
1 egg
Unsalted butter, melted

4 to 6 servings

1. For the sauce: Put the blueberries in a small saucepan and cook over low to medium heat until soft and juicy. Add sugar to taste and strain through a fine sieve. Set aside.

2. For the dumplings: Combine the yeast with $\frac{1}{2}$ cup of the milk in a small bowl. Let stand for 10 minutes until frothy.

3. Mix the flour with the salt. In a large bowl, mix the remaining $\frac{1}{2}$ cup milk, the egg, and yeast mixture. Gradually add the flour mixture. Work into a smooth dough, using the kneading attachment of an electric mixer, until the dough easily detaches from the sides of the bowl. Cover with a dishtowel and let rise for 30 minutes in a warm place.

4. Knead the dough with dry hands (coat them with flour if necessary) and shape into 8 to 12 dumplings. Place the dumplings on a large flour-coated platter and let stand for 15 minutes.

5. Fill one, or preferably two, large wide pots one-third to one-half with salted water and bring to a boil—it is important to have enough space in the pot(s) because the dumplings will puff up considerably. Reduce the heat to low; the water should just simmer.

6. Lower the dumplings into the gently simmering water and cover. Cook the dumplings for 20 minutes. Do not remove the lid while the dumplings are cooking or they will collapse.

7. Remove the dumplings with a slotted spoon. Place each dumpling on a plate. To release the steam, gently tear each dumpling open in the middle, using two forks.

8. Melt butter in a small heavy saucepan over medium heat, stirring occasionally. When the butter turns light brown immediately remove from the heat. Spoon a small amount of butter over each dumpling and pour blue-berry sauce over them.

Egg Custard Cake

Dresdner Eierschecke

Most sheet cakes made with yeast dough from Saxony were standard fare for miners and farmers. *Dresdner Eierschecke* is different. Its rich filling of eggs, butter, and quark made it a cake for the wealthy. Today every pastry shop in the city of Dresden makes it.

Dresdner Eierschecke is made with quark, if you can find it. Greek yogurt, however, works as a substitute in this recipe. Because the cake is so rich, I have adjusted it to a smaller size, baked in a round cake pan.

Dough:
¾ teaspoon active dry yeast
¼ cup lukewarm milk
1 cup plus 1 tablespoon all-purpose flour, or more as needed
Pinch of salt
2 tablespoons unsalted butter, room temperature
2 tablespoons sugar
½ beaten egg
1 teaspoon finely grated organic lemon zest

Filling:
1 cup plus 2 tablespoons quark or non-fat Greek yogurt
1 tablespoon plus 1 teaspoon sugar
1 egg yolk
2 tablespoons cornstarch
2 tablespoons milk

1. For the dough: Combine the yeast with the milk in a small bowl and let stand for 10 minutes until frothy.

2. Mix the flour and salt. Pour the yeast mixture into a large bowl and gradually add the flour mixture along with the butter, sugar, egg, and lemon zest. Knead into a smooth dough that easily detaches from the sides of the bowl, using the kneading attachment of an electric mixer. Place the dough in an oiled bowl, cover and let rise for 30 minutes.

3. Roll the dough on a floured work surface to fit a 10-inch round cake pan, or a springform pan plus a 1-inch edge all around. Grease the pan and carefully drop the dough into the pan. Press the dough against the edges and trim the excess with a sharp knife. If the dough does not fit perfectly, and you are a bit short in some spots, use the excess for patching; it will not be visible afterwards. Cover and let rise for 30 minutes.

4. For the filling: Beat the quark or yogurt with the sugar, egg yolk, cornstarch, and milk to a thick, creamy consistency.

Topping:
1 stick unsalted butter,
  softened
¼ cup sugar
2 eggs
⅓ cup raisins, washed and
  drained

Crisp:
2 tablespoons unsalted
  butter, melted
1 tablespoon sugar

16 servings

5. For the topping: Beat the butter with the sugar and eggs until smooth.

6. Preheat the oven to 350 degrees F.

7. Prick the dough with a fork in several places. Pour the filling into the pan. Then very slowly, evenly pour the topping over the filling in a thin, steady stream, making sure not to disturb the filling. Sprinkle with the raisins.

8. Bake in the preheated oven for 35 to 40 minutes, until the filling is set. The filling should still be slightly wobbly but not liquid. If it needs to bake longer and the top is getting too dark, cover with a piece of greased aluminum foil.

9. For the final crisp: As soon as the cake comes out of the oven, drizzle it with the melted butter and sprinkle with sugar so it forms a thin crisp. Cool on a cake rack.

Apple Mousse with Berry Coulis

Berliner Luft

The air of Berlin, a metropolis of 3.4 million people, might not be the healthiest, but it is certainly very inspiring. There are two famous unrelated creations that carry the name *Berliner Luft* (air of Berlin). The first is a march by composer Paul Lincke, written in 1904, and the second is this refreshing dessert. Together with Marlene Dietrich's song *Ich hab noch einen Koffer in Berlin* (I have another suitcase in Berlin), the Lincke march is the most frequently played Berlin tune.

Mousse:
1 organic lemon
3 eggs, separated
1/2 cup plus 2 teaspoons sugar
1 teaspoon vanilla extract
1 cup plus 2 tablespoons apple juice
1 1/2 (1/4-ounce) envelopes unflavored gelatin

Coulis:
1/2 pint mixed fresh or frozen berries (blueberries, raspberries, blackberries)
2 tablespoons sugar, plus more to taste

4 to 6 servings

1. For the mousse: Finely grate the zest and juice the lemon. Mix the lemon zest and lemon juice with the egg yolks, sugar, and vanilla. Stir until the sugar dissolves.

2. Heat the apple juice over very low heat in a small saucepan. Remove the pan from the heat and gradually add the gelatin, whisking vigorously until it dissolves. Let the bowl stand in a cool place for 10 minutes, or until the mixture begins to thicken.

3. Beat the egg whites until they stand in stiff peaks.

4. Mix the gelatin mixture with the egg yolk mixture. Gently fold in the egg whites and chill for several hours until set.

5. For the coulis: Put the berries with 2 tablespoons water and the sugar in a saucepan. If the berries are tart, increase the sugar. Cook over low heat for 10 to 15 minutes. Strain the berries through a fine sieve. Taste and add more sugar if needed. Refrigerate until 30 minutes before serving.

6. To serve, spoon a small amount of coulis on individual dessert plates and top with a few scoops of the mousse, or spoon some coulis over the mousse.

Spice Stollen

Sächsischer Gewürzstollen

This is the almost unknown cousin of the world-famous Christmas stollen from Saxony's capital, Dresden. This Spice Stollen is much less rich. Unlike other recipes, this version does not contain butter. It is as easy, quick, and straightforward to make as it is delicious. Like Dresdner Stollen it keeps for several weeks. Recently, I did not even get to wrapping it in aluminum foil—my family had already eaten it.

3 eggs
1¼ cups sugar
Pinch of salt
1¾ cups unpeeled whole almonds
½ teaspoon ground cloves
2 tablespoons ground cinnamon
2½ cups all-purpose flour, plus more for rolling
1 teaspoon baking powder

10 servings

1. Preheat the oven to 350 degrees F. Line a baking sheet with parchment paper.

2. Beat the eggs with the sugar and salt until light and creamy. Add the almonds, cloves, and cinnamon. Mix the flour with the baking powder. Gradually add to the egg mixture and knead to a smooth dough.

3. Roll the dough on a floured work surface into an 8x12-inch rectangle. Shape it into a Stollen. To get the typical Stollen shape, fold the dough as follows: place the handle of a wooden spoon on each long side, about 1 to 2 inches from the edge; fold the dough by lifting the edges over the handle on each side, towards the center of the loaf; carefully remove the spoon when you are done; gently press the dough together in the middle.

4. Place the Stollen in the middle of the prepared baking sheet. Bake in the preheated oven for 40 minutes. Cool on a cake rack. Wrap in aluminum foil and store in a cool place.

Multi-Layer Cake with Chocolate Frosting

Baumkuchentorte

The traditional preparation of this pastry is a hot affair, and very impressive. Up to 25 ultra thin layers of dough are spread on a huge cylinder that turns over an open fire. The result is a gargantuan cake of up to 3 yards in height, whose weight can easily reach 120 pounds. The sliced cake looks like the annual rings of a tree, hence the name *Baumkuchen* (tree cake).

The center of *Baumkuchen* production is Salzwedel, a town in the state of Saxony, where specialized pastry makers have supplied the world with *Baumkuchen* for centuries.

While the adaptation of the cake for conventional ovens might not produce the same tree trunk look as genuine *Baumkuchen*, it is a delicate cake with a smooth texture.

Dough:
2 1/4 sticks unsalted butter, softened
1 cup sugar
1 tablespoon vanilla extract
6 eggs, separated
1 cup all-purpose flour
1/2 cup plus 2 tablespoons cornstarch
2/3 cup blanched almonds
1 tablespoon rum
Pinch of salt

1. Preheat the oven to 450 degrees F. Line the bottom of a 10-inch springform pan with parchment paper. Grease the parchment paper and the sides of the pan well.

2. For the dough: Beat the butter with the sugar in a large mixing bowl. Add the vanilla and egg yolks. In a separate bowl, combine the flour with the cornstarch and add to the butter mixture.

3. Grind the almonds very finely in a food processor and stir them into the mixture along with the rum.

4. Beat the egg whites with a pinch of salt until they stand in stiff peaks. Fold them into the dough.

5. Spread a thin layer of dough evenly on the bottom of the prepared pan. Bake in the top third of the oven for 3 to 5 minutes, or until golden brown.

6. Continue to add very thin layers, spreading each new layer on top of the previously baked layer, until all the dough is used up. Bake each layer for 3 to 5 minutes, or until golden brown. After the third layer, insert an empty baking sheet of equal size underneath to prevent the dough from getting too dark on the bottom.

7. Remove the cake from the oven and turn it upside-down on a cake rack. Carefully remove the parchment paper and cool.

Glaze:
$3/4$ cup (9 ounces) apricot preserves

8. For the glaze: Warm the apricot preserves in a small saucepan and strain through a fine sieve. Glaze the top and sides of the cake. Let dry.

Frosting:
4 (1-ounce) squares semisweet chocolate
1 tablespoon unsalted butter

12 to 16 servings

9. For the frosting: Melt the chocolate and butter in the top of a double boiler or in a metal bowl set over a pot with boiling water. Stir constantly until smooth. Cool slightly, then spread the frosting evenly over the top and sides of the cake. Set aside for several hours on a cake rack, until the frosting has hardened.

Potato Fritters

Quarkkeulchen

Another staple of Saxony's cuisine, these fritters are served with fruit compote or cinnamon sugar. The original recipe uses quark, but you can substitute Greek yogurt. For best results, cook the potatoes a few hours before, or better, the day before.

3 medium starchy yellow potatoes
$1/3$ cup raisins or currants
1 cup quark or Greek yogurt
$3/4$ cup all-purpose flour
2 tablespoons sugar
2 eggs, lightly beaten
$1/2$ teaspoon finely grated organic lemon zest
Pinch of salt
Pinch of nutmeg
Vegetable oil for sautéing
Sugar and ground cinnamon for sprinkling

12 to 15 pieces

1. Cook the potatoes in their skins. Cool slightly, then peel. Refrigerate for several hours or overnight.

2. Soak the raisins in a small bowl of hot water for 5 minutes. Drain and pat dry with paper towels.

3. Very finely grate the boiled potatoes. Mix with the quark or yogurt, flour, sugar, eggs, lemon zest, salt, and nutmeg, and knead into a smooth dough. Add the raisins and shape into a 2-inch-diameter log with moistened hands. Cut the log into 12 to 15 equal thick slices and form little patties about $3/4$ inch thick.

4. Heat the oil in a large skillet. Sauté the fritters until golden brown on one side; then carefully turn them with a spatula and brown the other side. Serve warm with sugar and cinnamon and some fruit compote.

Chocolate Spice Bars

Berliner Brot

Unlike Labor Day in the United States, Germany does not have a holiday that marks the end of summer, but the appearance of the first boxes of gingerbread in supermarkets is an undeniable sign that fall is upon us. Nibbling on Christmas cookies is as integral to the German Christmas as the Advent wreath or the Christmas tree. Although there is an abundance of new cookie creations, the classics have always been vogue. *Berliner Brot* (Berliner bread) is one of them.

Many recipes tell you to store the bars in a metal jar and let them stand for a few days to develop their full flavor. Well, good luck—mine never last that long.

1 stick unsalted butter, softened
2 eggs plus 1 egg white
$^{3}/_{4}$ cup firmly packed dark brown sugar
$2^{1}/_{2}$ (1-ounce) squares semisweet chocolate, very finely grated
$1^{2}/_{3}$ cups all-purpose flour
1 teaspoon baking powder
2 teaspoons ground cinnamon
1 tablespoon rum
$^{1}/_{2}$ teaspoon ground cloves
$^{3}/_{4}$ cup coarsely chopped unpeeled almonds
1 cup superfine sugar

30 pieces

1. Preheat the oven to 350 degrees F. Grease a baking sheet.

2. Beat the butter with the whole eggs and brown sugar until foamy. Add the chocolate, flour, baking powder, cinnamon, rum, and cloves. Fold in the almonds. You might want to use a very sturdy wooden spoon, as the dough gets very stiff.

3. Spread the dough about $^{1}/_{4}$-inch-thick on the prepared baking sheet. Dipping the blade in water helps to spread it evenly. Beat the egg white and brush it over the dough.

4. Bake for 20 to 25 minutes, or until a toothpick comes out clean. Carefully move the entire uncut block to a large cake rack. When it is slightly cool, return it to the baking sheet.

5. Mix the superfine sugar with 3 tablespoons water in a small saucepan. Simmer until the sugar is completely dissolved. Spread the frosting on the uncut block while still warm and immediately cut it into $1^{1}/_{2}$ x 3-inch bars. Do not remove the bars from the baking sheet until entirely cool and the frosting is set. Store in an airtight container with parchment paper between each layer. The bars keep for up to 4 weeks.

Christmas Stollen

Dresdner Stollen

Stollen (sweet yeast loaves) have a long tradition in German Christmas baking, with *Stollen* from the city of Dresden being the top-of-the-line. In the seventeenth century, a ban on butter during Advent was almost the kiss of death for *Dresdner Stollen*, in which butter is an absolute must. Luckily the ruler, Prince Ernst of Saxony, took it upon himself to write to the Pope and urged him to lift the ban on butter during the four weeks before Christmas. Pope Urban VIII showed leniency. The prince might have intervened to satisfy his own craving for *Dresdner Stollen* as much as for the sake of his *Stollen*-deprived subjects. Because *Stollen* from Dresden was shipped near and far from very early on, it could very well be that the Pope also had a personal interest in getting a delivery from Dresden during Christmastime.

Dresdner Stollen is best aged a few weeks, tightly wrapped in aluminum foil and stored in a cool place. The thick coat of butter and sugar prevents it from drying out.

Dough:
4 ($\frac{1}{4}$-ounce) envelopes active dry yeast
1 cup lukewarm milk
5 cups all-purpose flour
2 teaspoons salt
$\frac{3}{4}$ cup plus 2 teaspoons sugar
1 tablespoon plus 1 teaspoon vanilla extract
Zest of 1 organic lemon, finely grated
Pinch of ground cardamom
Pinch of ground mace
2 sticks plus 7 tablespoons unsalted butter, softened

Continued

1. For the dough: Combine the yeast with the milk in a small bowl. Let stand for 10 minutes until frothy.

2. Mix the flour and salt. Pour the yeast mixture into a large bowl and gradually add the flour mixture and the sugar, vanilla, lemon zest, cardamom, mace, and all but 2 tablespoons of the butter. Work into a smooth dough that easily detaches from the sides of the bowl, using the kneading attachment of an electric mixer. Cover and let rise for 30 minutes.

3. Rinse the raisins in a colander under hot water; drain and dry with paper towels. Mix together the raisins, citron, almonds, almond extract, and orange zest and work into the dough. Cover and let stand at room temperature for 45 minutes.

4 cups (18 ounces) seedless raisins
1 cup (5 ounces) finely chopped candied citron or candied lemon peel
1¼ cups (4½ ounces) slivered and blanched almonds
1 teaspoon almond extract
Zest of 2 organic oranges, finely grated

Glaze:
4 tablespoons unsalted butter, plus more as needed
1 cup confectioners' sugar, plus more as needed

You also need:
1 or 2 plain metal paper clips

30 to 40 servings

4. Preheat the oven to 375 degrees F and grease a baking sheet very well, or line with parchment paper or a baking mat.

5. Roll the dough on a floured work surface to a rectangle, about 1½ inches thick. To get the typical Stollen shape, fold the dough as follows: place the handle of a wooden spoon on each long side, about 1 to 2 inches from the edge; fold the dough by lifting the edges over the handle on each side, towards the center of the loaf; carefully remove the spoon when you are done; gently press the dough together in the middle.

6. Place the loaf on the baking sheet. Melt the remaining 2 tablespoons of the butter and brush the loaf with it.

7. Cut a piece of aluminum foil long enough to wrap around the edge of the entire loaf. Fold the sheet of foil lengthwise until it is a 2-inch-wide strip. Grease the strip on one side and wrap it around the loaf, greased side against loaf. This will help the Stollen maintain its shape during baking. Secure the aluminum foil by attaching metal paper clips at the ends.

8. Bake the loaf for 1 to 1½ hours, or until done. Use a toothpick to test doneness. If the loaf gets too brown before it is ready, cover it with a large sheet of aluminum foil and continue baking. Take the loaf out of the oven and remove the aluminum foil. Place it on a cake rack.

9. For the glaze: Melt the butter and generously brush it over the loaf while still warm. Cover the loaf with a thick layer of confectioners' sugar, using a flour sifter or a fine sieve. Store in a cool, dry place up to 6 weeks.

Custard-filled Cake with Crunch Topping

Bienenstich

This German classic started as a cheap but filling meal for farm workers and coalminers in Saxony. The original was likely less sophisticated than the sheet cake that is made by countless pastry shops all over Germany today. It got its name *Bienenstich* (bee sting) from its golden honey color, and it is said that only a *Bienenstich* that is stung by a bee, meaning made with honey, can claim authenticity.

The Saxonians are not only known for their many scrumptious pastries, but also for their passion for coffee. Was it by coincidence that disposable coffee filters were invented in 1908 by Melitta Benz, a housewife from Dresden? She punched holes in the bottom of a tin cup, lined it with blotter paper from her son's school notebook—and changed the world of coffee brewing forever.

Bienenstich tastes best fresh, the same day it is baked or the next.

Dough:
- 1 (1/4-ounce) envelope active dry yeast
- 1/2 cup lukewarm milk
- 1 3/4 cups all-purpose flour
- 1 teaspoon salt
- 3 tablespoons sugar
- 4 tablespoons unsalted butter, softened
- 1 egg
- Zest of 1/2 organic lemon, very finely grated
- 1 teaspoon vanilla extract

1. For the dough: Combine the yeast with the milk in a small bowl. Let stand for 10 minutes until frothy.

2. Mix the flour and salt. Pour the yeast mixture into a large bowl. Gradually add the flour mixture and the sugar, butter, egg, lemon zest, and vanilla and knead into a smooth dough, using the kneading attachment of an electric mixer. Cover and let stand for 1 hour.

Filling:
$1^3/4$ cups milk
$1^1/2$ teaspoons pure vanilla
    bean paste, or seeds
    scraped from $^1/2$ vanilla
    bean
2 tablespoons sugar
3 tablespoons cornstarch
2 egg yolks
$^1/3$ cup heavy cream

Topping:
$1^1/4$ sticks unsalted butter
$^1/4$ cup light cream
$^1/2$ cup sugar
2 tablespoons honey
$2^1/3$ cups sliced and
    blanched almonds

12 to 16 servings

3. In the meantime, prepare the filling: Bring the milk and vanilla to a boil in a saucepan. In a bowl, whisk together the sugar, cornstarch, and egg yolks. Remove the milk from the heat and whisk in the egg mixture. Bring the custard back to a gentle simmer, stirring vigorously. Remove from the heat and cool, stirring occasionally.

4. Whip the cream in a chilled metal bowl until it stands in soft peaks. Make sure the custard is smooth and free of lumps. If it is not, briefly blend it in a blender or with an immersion stick blender. Fold the whipped cream into the custard. Refrigerate the filling.

5. Preheat the oven to 400 degrees F. Grease an 11x15-inch jellyroll pan. Spread the dough evenly into the pan with a spatula. Cover and let stand for 20 minutes.

6. Meanwhile, prepare the topping: Melt the butter over low heat. Add the cream, sugar, honey, and almonds. Simmer until the almonds become translucent, stirring constantly. Cool for a few minutes, then spread the mixture evenly over the dough with a spatula or a knife.

7. Bake the cake for 20 minutes, or until the cake is done. A toothpick inserted in the cake should come out clean, and the topping should be browned and crunchy. Cool the cake on a cake rack.

8. When the cake is completely cool, slice it in half horizontally. Place the bottom half on a cake plate and spread on the chilled custard. Top with the other half of the cake and refrigerate.

Poppy Seed Loaf

Mohnstriezel

This poppy seed loaf was served for New Year's Eve in Silesia. The idea behind it was the popular belief that serving something with poppy seeds, considered a symbol of wealth and prosperity, would ensure enough money during the New Year.

Dough:
- 1 ($1/4$-ounce) envelope active dry yeast
- $1/2$ cup lukewarm milk
- 2 cups all-purpose flour
- 1 teaspoon salt
- $3 1/2$ tablespoons unsalted butter, melted
- 3 tablespoons sugar
- $1/4$ cup very finely chopped candied citron or candied lemon peel

Filling:
- $1 1/2$ cups (7 ounces) poppy seeds, preferably freshly ground
- $1/2$ cup milk
- $1/3$ cup sugar
- 3 tablespoons unsalted butter
- $1/3$ cup raisins, washed and dried
- $1/3$ cup currants, washed and dried
- $1/3$ cup coarsely chopped blanched almonds
- Pinch of ground cinnamon
- Few drops of almond extract

1. For the dough: Combine the yeast with the milk in a small bowl. Let stand for 10 minutes until frothy.

2. Mix the flour and salt. In a large bowl, mix the melted butter with the yeast mixture. Add the sugar and citron. Add the flour mixture and knead into a smooth dough with the kneading attachment of an electric mixer or the dough blade of a food processor. Cover and let stand for 1 hour.

3. For the filling: Put the poppy seeds in a small saucepan with the milk and enough water to cover. Bring to a boil, then cover and reduce the heat. Cook for 30 minutes, stirring once in a while. Let cool slightly, then transfer the mixture to a food processor and process until the softened poppy seeds start to break apart, scraping down the sides several times.

4. Return the poppy seed mixture to the saucepan or put in a mixing bowl and mix in the sugar and butter. Stir in the raisins, currants, almonds, cinnamon, and almond extract. Let stand for 30 minutes.

5. On a well-floured surface roll the dough into a 5x15-inch rectangle. Spread the filling evenly over the dough, leaving a 1-inch edge on all sides. Roll up the dough lengthwise into a snug log. Pinch the dough firmly together along the edge, and pinch both ends of the loaf together to seal. Place it with the seam-side down on a greased baking sheet and tuck ends under slightly. Cover and let stand for 1 hour.

6. Preheat the oven to 475 degrees F. Put the loaf in the oven and immediately reduce the heat to 375 degrees. Bake for 35 to 40 minutes, or until golden. Place the loaf on a cooling rack.

Glaze:
1 cup confectioners' sugar

12 to 16 servings

7. For the glaze: Mix the confectioners' sugar with $1\frac{1}{2}$ tablespoons water, or a little more as needed to make a shiny and smooth glaze. Brush it thinly over the loaf while still warm. Let the glaze set and store the loaf in a cool place for up to 7 days.

Almond-Apricot Tartlets

Leipziger Lerchen

The invention of *Leipziger Lerchen* (Leipzig larks) is an early case of animal rights. In the eighteenth century, larks were considered a delicacy in the city of Leipzig. Hundreds of thousands of larks were caught and ended up on dining tables in places as far as Spain and Russia. Then animal lovers in Leipzig started to protest, and in 1876 the king of Saxony forbid the merciless lark hunt. But larks are still one of Leipzig's specialties—an ingenious baker who feared for his business simply replaced the larks with a sweet filling.

Dough:
$1^3/4$ cups all-purpose flour
1 stick plus 3 tablespoons unsalted butter, chilled
$1/4$ cup sugar
1 egg yolk
Salt

Filling:
$1^1/4$ cups blanched almonds
1 cup confectioners' sugar
1 tablespoon brandy
3 eggs, separated
A few drops of almond extract
3 tablespoons all-purpose flour
3 tablespoons cornstarch
$1/2$ cup apricot preserves

12 to 16 pieces

1. For the dough: Put the flour in a bowl and cut the butter into it. Work the butter and flour together with your hands until it becomes a coarse meal. This should be done very quickly using only your fingertips, otherwise the butter will soften too much. Add the sugar, egg yolk, and salt and blend well. Shape the dough into a ball, wrap in plastic wrap, and refrigerate for 1 hour.

2. In the meantime, prepare the filling: Grind the almonds very finely in a food processor. Combine them with $1/2$ cup of the confectioners' sugar, the brandy, egg yolks, and almond extract. Mix the flour with the cornstarch. Sift it over the almond paste and combine well.

3. Beat the egg whites until they stand in stiff peaks, gradually adding the remaining $1/2$ cup confectioners' sugar.

4. Preheat the oven to 350 degrees F. Grease a 12-cup muffin pan, or line with paper liners.

5. Roll the dough on a lightly floured work surface about $1/4$-inch thick. Cut out circles slightly larger than the individual tins and fit them snugly into each tin, pressing against the sides. Remove the excess and reserve.

6. Warm the apricot preserves in the microwave or a small saucepan and press them through a fine sieve. Spread an equal amount of the preserves on each tartlet.

7. Fold the egg whites into the filling and place an equal amount on each tartlet. Roll the leftover dough and cut it into thin strips. Place them crosswise over the filling.

8. Bake the tartlets for 25 minutes, or until golden. They should be crisp on the outside but still soft on the inside. Unmold the tartlets at once by gently loosening the sides. Cool on a rack.

Jelly-filled Donuts

Berliner Pfannkuchen

What Berliners call *Berliner Pfannkuchen* (Berliner pancakes) is called simply Berliner in the rest of Germany. In the English-speaking world, John F. Kennedy is often remembered for his famous sentence "*Ich bin ein Berliner*" ("I am a Berliner") in his passionate speech at the Berlin Wall in June 1963. In the rush to press that day, one of the news services translated JFK's statement as "I am a jelly donut." Of course, Kennedy's words were meant to express his solidarity with the people of Berlin in the height of the Cold War, rather than his culinary inclinations.

---

2 ($^1\!/_4$-ounce) envelopes active dry yeast
$^3\!/_4$ cup lukewarm milk
3 cups all-purpose flour
1 teaspoon salt
7 tablespoons unsalted butter, melted
$^1\!/_3$ cup sugar
2 eggs
Zest of 1 organic lemon
$^1\!/_2$ cup raspberry, currant, or plum jelly
Vegetable oil (corn or peanut) for deep-frying
Confectioners' sugar

32 pieces

---

1. For the dough: Combine the yeast with the milk in a small bowl. Let stand for 10 minutes until frothy.

2. Mix the flour and salt. In a large bowl, mix the yeast mixture with the melted butter. Gradually add the flour mixture, then the sugar, eggs, and lemon zest and knead into a smooth dough in a food processor with a dough blade or using the kneading attachment of an electric mixer. The dough should easily detach from the sides of the bowl. Cover and let stand for 1 hour.

3. Divide the dough in half. Roll the first half about $^1\!/_4$ inch thick on a floured work surface. Mark 3-inch circles, using a glass or a cup. Place a teaspoon of jelly in the center of each circle.

4. Roll the other half of the dough and carefully align it neatly on top of the first half. Cut out circles with the 3-inch glass, centering the glass on each protruding jelly filling. Gently press the edges of the circles together to seal. You will have dough left over from in-between the circles and at the edges—roll it again and proceed the same way until all the dough is used.

5. Place the donuts on a large floured board and let them rise for another 30 minutes.

6. Heat the oil to 370 degrees F in a deep-fryer or a large saucepan. The oil needs to be hot enough to sizzle a breadcrumb. Carefully lower the donuts into the hot oil, a few at a time, and fry on both sides until they puff and turn golden brown. Remove with a slotted spoon and drain on paper towels.

7. While still warm, dust the donuts with confectioners' sugar, using a flour sifter or a fine sieve. Serve within a few hours.

Crullers with Lemon Frosting

Eberswalder Spritzkuchen

During the Iron Curtain years, when Germany was divided into two states, these crullers were made by many bakeries in what was then West Germany. Most people ate *Eberswalder Spritzkuchen* for decades with no idea that this pastry originated in an isolated German town at the eastern end of the German Democratic Republic close to the Polish border.

As in the Rhineland, the celebration of carnival (also known as the crazy days before Lent) in Eberswalde is at the origin of this pastry. Before the invention of food additives, the beginning of Lent meant that all animal fat had to be used up, or it would go bad. This is why pastries like *Eberswalder Spritzkuchen* were invented.

Crullers:
3 1/2 tablespoons unsalted butter
1 cup all-purpose flour
1/4 cup cornstarch
2 tablespoons sugar
1 teaspoon vanilla extract
5 eggs
1 teaspoon baking powder
Vegetable oil (corn, peanut) for deep-frying

Frosting:
1 1/2 cups confectioners' sugar
Juice of 1 to 2 lemons

16 pieces

1. For the crullers: Bring 1 1/4 cups water and the butter to a boil in a saucepan. Remove from the heat. Mix the flour and cornstarch together and stir into the liquid until a smooth ball forms. Return the pan to the stove and stir over low heat until a white film appears on the bottom of the pan.

2. Transfer the mixture to a mixing bowl. Combine with the sugar, vanilla, eggs, and baking powder, using an electric mixer.

3. Cut parchment paper into sixteen 3-inch squares. Spread them out on a clean work surface and grease them well. Put the dough into a pastry bag with a large serrated spout and squeeze a 2-inch circle on each piece of parchment paper.

4. Heat the oil to 370 degrees F in a deep-fryer or in a large saucepan. The oil needs to be hot enough to sizzle a breadcrumb. Let the crullers glide into the oil by carefully turning the parchment squares upside down and gently rolling up the two opposite edges. Fry only a few crullers at a time. They should be golden brown and puffy. Remove from the oil and drain on paper towels.

5. For the frosting: Mix the confectioners' sugar with the lemon juice until smooth. Add a few drops of water if necessary. Spread the frosting on the warm crullers and allow them to set at room temperature. Serve within a few hours.

Beer with a Dash of Raspberry Syrup

Berliner Weiße mit Schuss

The signature drink of Berlin is a specialty wheat (white) beer, served chilled with a dash of raspberry or woodruff syrup in glasses that look like an ice-cream bowl with a long stem. That's the recipe.

Berliner Weiße is different from other beers not only in taste but also in its fermentation process. The beer is brewed using yeast that allows the fermentation to take place in the bottle. *Berliner Weiße* is sold solely in bottles and can be stored for up to five years, an unusually long time for beer. When Napoleon and his army invaded Prussia, the French developed such a taste for the fizzy drink that they named it *Champagner des Nordens* (the champagne of the North). While the beer has been brewed since 1642, the addition of syrup is an invention of the nineteenth century.

The two main brands, produced by the Berliner Kindl and Schultheiss breweries, are imported to the United States, but if you cannot find them, you can use any light-bodied wheat beer.

Beer and Wine
Unequal Siblings

"Wine after beer, nothing to fear; beer after wine, that's not so fine" runs a popular German rhyme. There is no sound medical proof behind this advice, but it does shed light on the historic image that these two alcoholic drinks had in Germany. Historically beer was the drink of the common people, while high society preferred the more expensive wine. Despite first appearances, the rhyme does not only refer to stomach pain and headaches, but also to social standing. Once someone has moved "up" to the circle of wine drinkers, he should not revert to drinking beer.

German beer brewing can be traced back almost 2,000 years. In *Germania*, his famous monograph on the ethnography of Germany, first-century Roman historian Cornelius Tacitus wrote with disgust about what he called a horrible fermented brew of barley or wheat. Not all Romans were so opposed to beer. Julius Caesar, for example, praised beer as a nourishing drink and had it served to his guests.

When monks in German monasteries took up brewing in the Middle Ages, they did so for a very good reason. Beer was an ideal way to work around the strict food regulations during Lent because the intake of liquids was not considered breaking the fast. Beer consumption and merriment must have been considerable in those days—each monk was allowed about a gallon of beer per day!

Monks began to produce more beer than they could actually gulp down themselves. Finally the church gave them permission to sell their beer to lay customers in *Klosterschänken*, bars that belonged to the monastery. Weihenstephan, the world's oldest operating brewery in Freising near Munich, started as a monastery brewery in 1040.

The German sense of law and order is legendary. In the case of beer, the strict German Purity Law for beer has helped it maintain its great quality. The law, enacted in 1516 by a Bavarian duke and still in force today, requires that beer be brewed only from barley, hops, yeast, and water. It may have no other additive whatsoever.

There are 1,300 breweries in Germany that produce more than 4,000 brands of beer, including, of course, many regional varieties. Germans have one of the highest per capita beer consumption rates in the world (the greatest per capita beer consumption goes to the Czechs). But still they do not drink quite as much beer as the monks a thousand years ago. Over the past three decades, beer consumption in Germany has been decreasing.

German viticulture is almost as old as beer brewing. The Romans brought winemaking to Germany during their conquests of the lands north of the Alps. As with beer brewing, monasteries were the centers of viticulture, but that is about the only similarity between the two drinks.

There has always been an underlying rivalry between wine and beer in Germany. Although it is known for some of the finest wines in the world—especially its Riesling—most of the world thinks of Germany as a nation of beer drinkers. However, wine consumption continues to rise, as the German wine lobby is proudly reporting. Together with France, Italy, and the United States, Germany ranges among the top wine-consuming nations.

Winegrowing in Germany has never been an easy task, and viticulture had its ups and downs. First, the climate can be rough. Germany is one of the northernmost winegrowing areas of the world. But cold weather is not the only enemy of German vintners. At the end of the nineteenth century, viticulture practically came to a standstill when the vine louse phylloxera, a pest, destroyed vineyard after vineyard, and many indigenous grape varieties disappeared. The country's viticulture was only saved by grafting vines onto American rootstocks, which were resistant to the pest. So the grape varieties grown in Germany today literally have American roots.

Nearly 140 grape varieties are grown in Germany's vineyards, but only two dozen play a role in commercial winemaking. The most important whites are Riesling and Müller-Thurgau, and the best-known red is Spätburgunder (Pinot Noir). There are 13 winegrowing regions, with Rhine Hesse and Palatinate being the largest.

Germany is one of the leading wine exporting nations in Europe, ranking fourth after France, Italy, and Spain. Roughly one-fifth of German wine production reaches goblets outside the country, especially in the United States, which has become the main destination of German wines in terms of export value.

Purity is tantamount in German wines as well as in its beer. Only a Riesling that contains 100 percent Riesling grapes is allowed to carry the Riesling label. In the United States, Riesling can be a blend of up to 25 percent other grapes mixed with Riesling grapes. A German expression for encouraging honesty is "to pour someone a pure glass of wine" (*jemandem reinen Wein einschenken*). If that was a glass of German Riesling, or beer, you could take this quite literally, 100 percent pure. *Prost!*

Western Crossroads

The western region of Germany is a culinary crossroads. The cuisines of North Rhine-Westphalia, Hessia, Rhineland-Palatinate, and the Saarland have been influenced by their western neighbors (the Netherlands, Belgium, Luxemburg, and France) and by one another. For example, a potato dish known as *Dibbelabbes* in the Saarland is known as *Schales* or *Scholet* in Palatinate. Its origin, however, goes back to the Jewish Sabbath dish *Cholent,* a stew that was prepared on a Friday and remained on the lit stove during the Sabbath, when Jewish religious law forbids food preparation.

The West is also the region where one of the oldest German cookbooks, *Ein new Kochbuch,* was published in 1581 by Marx Rumpolt, the personal cook of the Prince of Mainz (the modern capital of the state of Rhineland-Palatinate). Rumpolt's exhaustive collection of two thousand recipes includes many foreign recipes, demonstrating that the culinary border traffic in the western part of Germany was already strong during the Renaissance era—a trend that continues to the present.

The common denominator of the cuisines of the West is the use of potatoes, but otherwise variety reigns. Westphalia is the home of world-famous ham and dark pumpernickel bread that has found its way into many regional dishes, and even desserts. Cooking with wine is no rarity in the winegrowing state of Rhineland-Palatinate. Culinary tastes have dramatically changed since the first century when Roman historian Cornelius Tacitus observed that Germans mainly drank milk and ate meat, cheese, and wild fruit!

Chicken Liver Pâté

Falscher Schnepfendreck

The odd name of this pâté from Hessia is definitely worth a mention. *Falscher Schnepfendreck* means "fake snipe (bird) droppings." Don't be fooled by the name—it is a delicious, easy-to-make spread for fresh bread.

1 tablespoon ghee
2 medium onions, peeled and finely chopped
12 ounces organic chicken livers, sinewy and connective tissue removed
¼ cup chopped fresh flat-leaf parsley
1 teaspoon crumbled dried thyme
¼ cup port
4 tablespoons unsalted butter, softened
1 scant teaspoon salt, or more to taste
Freshly milled black pepper
Pinch of ground cloves

4 servings

1. Heat the ghee in a skillet and cook the onions over low heat until translucent.

2. Chop the livers and add to the skillet. Cook over low heat, stirring, until the livers are cooked through and no longer release liquid. Add the parsley, thyme, and port and bring to a quick boil. Remove from heat and cool slightly.

3. Blend the liver mixture with the butter in a food processor to a fine puree. Season with salt, pepper, and ground cloves.

4. Line a small loaf pan with plastic wrap. Scoop the pâté into it and smooth the top with a spatula. Refrigerate for several hours until set. Serve with fresh wholesome bread.

Limburger Cheese Spread

Kochkäse

Despite the availability of countless cheeses in Germany today, this home-made cheese spread has lived on. It was originally a poor man's dish. Other sour milk cheese can be substituted for the Limburger cheese, such as Hand Cheese or Harzer Cheese.

1 tablespoon unsalted
  butter
1 Limburger cheese (6.4
  ounces), cut into slices
1 egg yolk
2 teaspoons all-purpose
  flour
½ cup milk
1 teaspoon caraway seeds

6 servings

1. Melt the butter in a small saucepan. Add the cheese and stir constantly over low heat until completely melted.

2. Whisk the egg yolk with the flour and milk in a small bowl. Add to the melted cheese and continue cooking over low heat until the mixture thickens, stirring constantly—do not let it boil or the milk will curdle.

3. Stir in the caraway seeds and pour the mixture into a container with a lid. Cool, then refrigerate. Remove from the refrigerator 20 minutes before serving.

Handkäse Cheese Marinated with Onions

Handkäse mit Musik

There are not many dishes where the effect of a food on the human intestinal system is implied by its name as with *Handkäse mit Musik* (hand cheese with music). It is a traditional snack with Frankfurt's signature drink *Äppelwoi* (apple wine), and every apple wine pub serves it. As a native of Frankfurt, I find it perfectly normal to order *Handkäse mit Musik* or *Handkäse ohne Musik* (without music) with a straight face.

Hand cheese is a hand-shaped cheese with a sharp flavor and a strong smell. You can find imported hand cheese from Germany—also sold as *Harzer* cheese—in specialty stores, or substitute with Limburger cheese, which is widely available in many areas.

---

2 (7-ounce) hand cheeses, very ripe
3 tablespoons vegetable oil
2 tablespoons cider vinegar
1 teaspoon caraway seeds
Salt and freshly milled black pepper
1 small yellow onion, peeled and thinly sliced

2 to 3 servings

1. Cut the cheese into ½-inch slices and put them in a shallow serving dish.

2. Whisk the oil, vinegar, caraway seeds, salt, and pepper in a small bowl. Spread the onion slices on the cheese and pour the marinade over all. Marinate for 30 minutes to 1 hour. Serve with thick slices of fresh wholesome bread and butter.

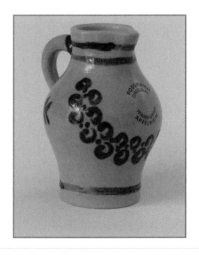

Rye Roll with Gouda and Mustard

Halve Hahn

People from Cologne are known for their great sense of humor, which also reveals itself in the names they have coined for their local specialties. *Kölscher Kaviar* (Cologne caviar) is nothing but blood sausage. When you order a *Halve Hahn* (literally: half a rooster) in a local pub, you should not be surprised that you are served a rye roll with Gouda cheese. *Halve Hahn* is a very popular snack served with the local beer, *Kölsch*.

There is a hilarious anecdote about Bill Clinton and *Kölsch*. When President John F. Kennedy visited Berlin in 1963, he went to the Berlin Wall to make his famous speech, which included the words "*Ich bin ein Berliner*." On a visit to Cologne in 1999, Clinton used what he thought was the JFK standard and uttered "*Ich bin ein Kölsch*" ("I am a Cologne beer") instead of "*Ich bin ein Kölner*" ("I am a citizen of Cologne"). What was meant to evoke strong emotions became a moment of levity and made the crowd roar.

1 rye roll
½ tablespoon unsalted butter, softened
1 teaspoon mustard, plus more to taste
2 thick slices Gouda (preferably aged several months), or any other semi-soft to hard mild cheese
1 serving

Cut the roll in half and butter each half. Spread a thin layer of mustard on each half and top with a slice of cheese. Serve with a glass of beer or wine.

Green Potato Soup

Grüne Kartoffelsuppe

In Palatinate, where this recipe originates, potato soup is often served with yeasted plum cake—not as a dessert but as a side dish. The julienned vegetables—celery leaves, spinach, and leeks—give this light soup a fresh taste.

1 stalk celery with leaves
2 tablespoons olive oil
2 pounds starchy yellow potatoes, peeled and diced
1 carrot, peeled and diced
1 quart canned or homemade beef broth (see page 200)
1 bay leaf
1 leek (white part only), trimmed, washed and julienned
2 cups julienned spinach leaves
Salt and freshly milled black pepper
Pinch of ground nutmeg
Dash of white wine vinegar

4 servings

1. Trim the celery and set aside the leaves. Chop the celery and julienne the leaves.

2. Heat the olive oil in a large pot and add the chopped celery stalk, potatoes, and carrot. Cook over medium heat for 5 minutes, stirring.

3. Add the beef broth and bay leaf. Bring to a boil, cover and reduce the heat. Simmer for 20 minutes. Remove the bay leaf and puree the soup.

4. Add 1 cup water and the leek, spinach, and celery leaves. Cook, uncovered, on medium heat for 10 more minutes, stirring occasionally. If the soup is too thick, add more water. Season with salt, pepper, nutmeg, and a dash of white wine vinegar. Serve hot.

PLAICE ON A BED OF LEEKS AND BACON (page 33)
with POTATO FINGERS (page 219)

SHRIMP SALAD ON MIXED GREENS (page 12)

WINDMILL CAKE (page 56)

RUTABAGA PUREE (page 40)

APPLE DUMPLINGS (page 63)

EGG GROG (page 67)

ONION QUICHE (page 75)

QUICK RYE ROLLS (page 77)

BREADED HAM SLICES (page 90) with
CRUSHED POTATOES WITH ENDIVE (page 164)

POPPY SEED LOAF (page 124)

EGG CUSTARD CAKE (page 112)

POTATO FRITTERS (page 118)

CHRISTMAS STOLLEN (page 120)

ALMOND–APRICOT TARTLETS (page 126)

CHICKEN LIVER PÂTÉ (page 136)

PEA SOUP WITH SEMOLINA DUMPLINGS (page 141)

CREAMY BEET SOUP (page 145)

RICE PUDDING WITH CHERRY COMPOTE (page 171)

POTATO LOAF (page 147)

CHICKEN IN RIESLING WITH WHITE GRAPES (page 162)

CHESTNUT TRUFFLES (page 186)

WESTPHALIAN TRIFLE (page 173)

BAKED MARZIPAN BITES (page 185)

ZWIEBACK PUDDING WITH PRUNES (page 181)

SAGE LEAF FRITTERS (page 196)

SOUP WITH MEAT-STUFFED PANCAKES (page 203)

HAZELNUT-CHOCOLATE COOKIES WITH PISTACHIOS (page 251)

SPINACH BUTTONS (page 226)

GLAZED CHRISTMAS ROUNDS (page 238)

SOFT PRETZELS (page 192)

QUINCE ALMOND TART (page 248)

CAMEMBERT SPREAD (page 197)

Pea Soup with Semolina Dumplings

Erbsensuppe mit Grießklößchen

Most soups served with semolina dumplings are clear. This recipe from Westphalia is different. With the white dumplings floating in the bright green soup, it reminds me of the last patches of snow on the grass—a perfect soup for spring, or, for that matter, any season.

$1\frac{1}{2}$ *tablespoons unsalted butter*

2 medium yellow onions, peeled and chopped

3 cups (1 pound) fresh shelled or frozen green peas

1 ($14\frac{1}{2}$-ounce) can chicken broth, plus more as needed

Salt and freshly milled black pepper

Semolina dumplings (see page 200)

6 to 8 servings

1. Heat the butter in a large saucepan and sauté the onions until translucent. Add the peas, broth, and $2\frac{1}{2}$ cups water. Bring to a boil, reduce the heat to low, and cook for 15 minutes, or until the peas are tender.

2. Puree the soup in batches in a blender and return it to the pan, or puree it with an immersion stick blender in the pan. If the soup is too thick, add more broth. Season with salt and pepper.

3. Drop the semolina dumplings into the simmering soup. Cover and simmer gently for 10 to 15 minutes. The soup should not boil, or the dumplings will fall apart. Serve hot.

Green Bean Soup

Bibbelchesbohnesupp

The proximity to France is palpable in the Saarland, especially in all things culinary. For example, the people of the Saarland have a more elegant name for what in the rest of Germany is simply called *Fleischwurst* (meat sausage); here, it is called *Lyoner* after the French city of Lyon.

But the cuisine of the Saarland has its own distinctive character. It is not uncommon, for example, to serve the following soup with plum pie.

6 thin slices (3 ounces) lean center-cut bacon

1 medium yellow onion, peeled and chopped

2 pounds trimmed fresh or frozen green beans, cut into 1-inch chunks

1 pound red or other low-starch potatoes, peeled and diced

2 (14½-ounce) cans vegetable broth

2 sprigs fresh savory

¼ cup sour cream

Salt and freshly milled black pepper

1 to 2 tablespoons coarsely chopped fresh flat-leaf parsley

6 to 8 servings

1. Cut the bacon into small strips. Place in a cold large saucepan and sauté over medium heat. Add the onions and cook until all the fat has been drawn out of the bacon and the onions are translucent. Add the beans, potatoes, broth, savory, and 3 cups water. Stir and bring to a boil. Reduce the heat and cook over low heat for 45 minutes.

2. Take the soup off the heat. Remove the savory. Puree about one-third in a blender or transfer one-third to a bowl and puree it with an immersion stick blender. Whisk the sour cream into the pureed soup and pour it back into the pan.

3. Return the soup to the heat and stir well. Reheat thoroughly but do not cook. Season with salt and pepper and sprinkle with parsley. Serve hot.

Chestnut Soup

Kastaniensuppe

Dishes with chestnuts have a very long tradition in Germany. A whole collection of chestnut recipes were recorded by eleventh-century abbess Hildegard von Bingen, a much quoted and revered author of authoritative books on natural history and medicine, who was also a composer and mystic.

If you cannot find fresh chestnuts, use canned whole chestnuts, which are available in specialty food stores.

1 pound fresh unpeeled chestnuts (about $2^1\!/_2$ cups peeled)

1 tablespoon unsalted butter

2 ($14^1\!/_2$-ounce) cans beef broth, or 1 quart homemade beef broth (see page 200), plus more as needed

$^1\!/_3$ cup heavy cream

3 tablespoons port

Salt and freshly milled black pepper

Pinch of ground nutmeg

6 servings

1. Make a $^1\!/_2$-inch crisscross at the pointy side of each chestnut. Place the chestnuts flat side down in a large saucepan and add enough water to just cover them. Bring to a simmer. Remove one chestnut at a time to peel, leaving the rest in the water. The colder the chestnuts are, the harder they are to peel. If you cannot remove the shells or the inner skin easily, leave them in the water a little longer. Set the peeled chestnuts aside and discard the water.

2. Heat the butter in the same pan. Sauté the chestnuts until light golden. Add 2 cups of the broth, cover, and simmer gently for 15 to 30 minutes, or until the chestnuts are soft.

3. Puree the chestnuts in a blender or in the pot with an immersion stick blender and add the remaining broth. Bring to a boil while stirring constantly. Reduce the heat and stir in the cream. If the soup is too thick, add more broth. Stir in the port and season with salt, pepper, and nutmeg. Serve hot.

Chervil Soup

Kerbelsuppe

Here is a "true or false" trivia question: Does Germany have its own institute for the promotion and research of soup? True! At first sight, the Deutsches Suppen-Institut (German Soup Institute) might seem like the crazy idea of a rich, eccentric soup aficionado. It is not. In fact, a look at the location of the institute reveals that this initiative was driven by clear economic interest. The institute is located at the same address as the German Association of the Soup Industry. The institute claims that the variety of regional soups in Germany is unparalleled in Europe, even by French cuisine. I cannot verify this, and I do not think the number really matters. What I can confirm is that Germany has a marvelous and highly varied soup repertoire.

Chervil soup, like other green-colored dishes, is traditionally served on the Thursday before Good Friday.

---

3 ($^3/4$-ounce) bunches
 fresh chervil
2 (14$^1/2$-ounce) cans
 chicken broth
1 tablespoon chopped fresh
 flat-leaf parsley
$^1/2$ cup heavy cream
2 egg yolks
Salt and freshly milled
 black pepper

4 servings

---

1. Wash and dry the chervil in a salad spinner. Remove the stems and chop them coarsely. Put the broth in a saucepan and add the stems. Cover and cook for 10 minutes over medium heat.

2. Puree the chervil leaves in a blender with the parsley and cream.

3. Strain the broth and discard the chervil stems. Return the broth to the pan and bring it back to a simmer.

4. Combine the egg yolks with the cream mixture. Remove the broth from the heat and whisk in the cream mixture. Season with salt and pepper and serve right away.

Creamy Beet Soup

Rote-Bete-Suppe

Henriette Davidis is to nineteenth-century German cooking what Irma S. Rombauer, the author of *The Joy of Cooking*, is to twentieth-century American cooking. The daughter of a Westphalian pastor, Davidis wrote the most famous German cookbook of all time. Upon her death in 1876, her *Praktisches Kochbuch* (Practical Cookbook) was in its twenty-first edition and is still being reprinted today. In the German language, the opening phrase of her recipes "*Man nehme…*" ("Take …") has become the synonym for a recipe.

Here is a beet soup in the tradition of Henriette Davidis, adapted to the contemporary palate.

1 pound young beets, unpeeled
1 quart homemade beef broth (see page 200), plus more as needed
5 tablespoons unsalted butter
½ cup all-purpose flour
2 tablespoons red wine vinegar
1 teaspoon sugar
1 leek, thoroughly cleaned, trimmed, and thinly sliced
1 cup crème fraîche (see page 87) or sour cream, plus more for garnish
Salt and freshly milled black pepper

6 to 8 servings

1. Cut the tops off the beets, but leave on about 1 inch of the stem and the roots. Place them in a large saucepan and just cover with boiling water. Cover and cook over low to medium heat for 30 minutes to 1 hour, depending on their size, until the beets are tender. Add more water during the cooking process if necessary. Drain, cool, and slip off the skins. Puree the beets with a small portion of the broth.

2. Melt 4 tablespoons of the butter in the saucepan and add the flour. Cook until it begins to turn beige, stirring constantly with a wooden spoon. Whisk in the remaining broth and simmer for 10 minutes, stirring to avoid lumps. Add the beet puree, vinegar, and sugar and simmer.

3. Melt the remaining 1 tablespoon butter in a skillet and sauté the leek until just translucent.

4. Stir the crème fraîche into the soup. If the soup is too thick, add more broth. Season with salt and pepper. Pour the soup into individual soup bowls, garnish with a little bit of leek and a dollop of crème fraîche.

Snail Soup

Schneckensuppe

Vineyard snails are not only a specialty of France but have also found their way into the regional cuisines of western Germany's winegrowing areas, which are home to such famous grapes as Johannisberg Riesling and Müller-Thurgau. Snail soup is also a specialty in the winegrowing area of Baden in the South of Germany.

You can find canned snails in specialty food stores.

1 clove garlic
1 tablespoon unsalted butter
2 shallots, peeled and finely minced
2 ($14\frac{1}{2}$-ounce) cans chicken broth
$\frac{1}{3}$ cup dry white wine
1 small leek, thoroughly cleaned, trimmed, and very finely chopped
1 small carrot, peeled and very finely chopped
$\frac{1}{2}$ stalk celery, trimmed and very finely chopped
1 bay leaf
1 (7-ounce net weight) can snails, drained and finely chopped
$\frac{1}{2}$ cup crème fraîche (see page 87) or heavy cream
Salt and freshly milled black pepper
Chopped fresh flat-leaf parsley for garnish

4 servings

1. Cut the garlic in half and rub the inside of a large saucepan with the cut side. Melt $\frac{1}{2}$ tablespoon of the butter in the saucepan and sauté the shallots until translucent. Add the broth, wine, leek, carrot, celery, and bay leaf and cook for 10 to 15 minutes.

2. In another saucepan, melt the remaining $\frac{1}{2}$ tablespoon butter and heat the snails. Add them to the soup.

3. Stir in the crème fraîche and reheat thoroughly. Season with salt and pepper and garnish with parsley. Serve hot with fresh white bread or garlic bread.

Potato Loaf

Kastenpickert

This is East Westphalian comfort food par excellence. *Kastenpickert* is cut into thick slices, sautéed as needed, and topped with jam, molasses, or liverwurst (yes, Westphalians like to mix sweet and salty). I still like it best the way we ate it in my family: right from the pan, crisp, topped with an unorthodoxly thick layer of good, creamy butter, and a pinch of salt.

Ideally you should let the *Kastenpickert* stand for a day after baking. Wrapped in aluminum foil and refrigerated, it keeps for 4 to 5 days.

---

2 ($1/4$-ounce) envelopes active dry yeast
$1/2$ cup lukewarm milk
2 pounds russet (Idaho) potatoes
1 tablespoon sugar
2 teaspoons salt
3 cups all-purpose flour
3 eggs
1 cup raisins, washed and dried (optional)
Vegetable oil or unsalted butter for sautéing

12 to 16 servings

---

1. Combine the yeast with the milk in a small bowl. Let stand for 10 minutes until frothy.

2. Peel and very finely grate the potatoes. Put them in a bowl and let stand for a few minutes until liquid builds up in the bottom of the bowl. Discard the excess liquid but keep the white potato starch residue. Combine the potatoes with the yeast mixture, sugar, salt, and flour. Lightly beat the eggs and add them to the mixture. Stir well and beat the dough until bubbles form. Cover and leave to rise for 30 minutes.

3. Stir the raisins into the dough if using. Grease an $8\frac{1}{2}$ x $4\frac{1}{2}$ x $2\frac{1}{2}$-inch loaf pan and fill it with the dough. Cover with a dishtowel and let stand in a warm place to rise again for 20 minutes.

4. Meanwhile, preheat the oven to 400 degrees F.

5. Bake the loaf for 30 minutes, then reduce the heat to 350 degrees and bake for 30 more minutes, or until a toothpick inserted in the center comes out clean. Cover the top with aluminum foil, if it gets too brown.

6. Cool the loaf slightly before removing it from the pan and then cool completely on a rack. Cut it into thick slices and sauté them in vegetable oil or butter on both sides until golden brown and crisp.

Potato and Sour Cream Loaf

Potthucke

Potthucke is a specialty from the Sauerland region of North Rhine-Westphalia. Real *Potthucke* aficionados have their own clubs, whose members gather regularly to eat *Potthucke* and wash it down with beer and schnapps.

Like *Kastenpickert* (*see page 147*), its close relative from Westphalia, *Potthucke* can be kept refrigerated for 4 to 5 days in aluminum foil. Slice and sauté in butter or oil as needed. Popular toppings are ham and pumpernickel.

$2\frac{1}{2}$ *pounds russet (Idaho)*
  potatoes
$\frac{1}{2}$ *cup sour cream*
$\frac{1}{2}$ *cup milk*
4 eggs
Salt and freshly milled
  black pepper
A few dots of unsalted
  butter, plus more for
  sautéing
Vegetable oil for sautéing
  (optional)

12 servings

1. Peel the potatoes. Bring one-quarter of the potatoes to a boil in salted water and cook until tender; then, drain and cool.

2. Grate the remaining potatoes. Put the grated potatoes in a bowl and let them stand for a few minutes, then pour off as much of the liquid as possible, reserving the white potato starch on the bottom.

3. Preheat the oven to 400 degrees F. Grease an $8\frac{1}{2}$ x $4\frac{1}{2}$ x $2\frac{1}{2}$-inch loaf pan.

4. Mash the boiled potatoes and mix with the grated potatoes, sour cream, milk, eggs, salt, and pepper. Incorporate the white starch from the potato liquid into the mixture.

5. Pour the batter into the prepared pan. Dot with butter for a crispier crust. Bake for 45 to 50 minutes, or until crisp and brown. Cool the loaf completely before removing it from the pan.

6. Cut the cooled loaf into thin slices and sauté in butter or oil on both sides. Serve hot.

Herring Salad with Apples and Gherkins

Rheinischer Heringsstipp

Herring has always been the favorite fish of Germans. In the Rhineland with its large Catholic population, this herring salad is an especially popular dish during Lent. Served with small potatoes boiled in their skins, it can make a main course.

8 salted herring fillets
  (1¼ pounds)
1 large white (sweet)
  onion, peeled, halved,
  and thinly sliced
2 large tart apples, cored
  and peeled
1 tablespoon lemon juice
2 cups sour cream
6 white peppercorns
¼ teaspoon powdered
  mustard
1 teaspoon finely chopped
  fresh dill
Pinch of sugar
1 bay leaf
½ cup chopped gherkins

6 to 8 servings

1. Taste the herring for saltiness. If they are too salty, soak them in cold water for several hours. Drain, pat dry with paper towels, and cut into bite-size pieces.

2. Bring water to a boil in a small saucepan. Blanch the onion slices for 1 minute and drain well.

3. Dice the apples and immediately toss them with the lemon juice to prevent them from turning brown.

4. Combine the sour cream, peppercorns, powdered mustard, dill, and sugar, and mix into a smooth dressing. Toss with the herring, onion slices, apples, bay leaf, and gherkins.

5. Put the salad into a container (glass or plastic, not metal) with a lid and marinate in the refrigerator for at least 1 day before serving. Remove the bay leaf before serving.

Buckwheat Pancakes with Bacon

Buchweizenpfannkuchen

In the Westphalian city of Münster and the surrounding Münsterland, buckwheat pancakes are often made with coffee, including some of the coffee grounds. They are served with a special type of dark molasses (*Zuckerrübensirup*) that is also used in baking, especially in Christmas cookies.

Buckwheat pancakes are also made with buttermilk, which gives them a mild flavor. Since buckwheat needs time to rise, and the batter keeps well in the refrigerator for several days, it is a good idea to make it ahead of time.

2¼ cups buckwheat flour
Salt
1 cup cold coffee or
buttermilk
½ cup milk or water
2 eggs
10 thin slices (5 ounces)
lean center-cut bacon
Vegetable oil for baking

4 servings

1. Put the flour and salt in a bowl. Gradually stir in the coffee and milk and add the eggs. Blend well until the batter is smooth and free of lumps. Cover and let the batter rest at room temperature for 4 to 6 hours.

2. Place the bacon in a cold nonstick skillet and cook until all the fat has been drawn out. Drain on paper towels. Leave only a small amount of fat in the skillet to cook the first pancake and reserve the rest.

3. Stir the batter with a whisk before cooking the pancakes. Heat the skillet over medium to high heat. Place little islands of bacon strips in the skillet and pour a small ladle of batter over each so that all pancakes have bacon in them. Cook the pancakes until lightly browned on both sides, turning them once. Proceed the same way with the rest of the bacon and the batter, using a little bit of bacon fat for each portion. If you do not have enough bacon fat, use oil. Keep the pancakes warm until all are cooked, and serve at once.

Potato Pancakes

Reibekuchen

Potato pancakes are eaten all over Germany but their bastion is doubtlessly in the Rhineland, where they are a popular street food with their own regional name: *Rievkooche* ("grated cakes"). In Cologne, potato pancakes are as much a part of the culinary landscape as *Kölsch*, the pale, clear, and refreshing local beer brewed since the fifteenth century and served in its own type of straight narrow glasses, called *Stangen* (sticks).

Potato pancakes are served with applesauce (*see page 48*), steak tartare, or smoked salmon.

2 pounds russet (Idaho) potatoes
1 medium yellow onion, peeled
2 eggs
Salt and freshly milled black pepper
Vegetable oil for baking

16 pieces

1. Peel, halve, and finely grate the potatoes and onion by hand or with the grating disk of a food processor. (Since I prefer potato pancakes with a very fine texture, I first grate the potatoes and onions coarsely and then process them briefly in a food processor.)

2. Let the mixture stand for a few minutes, then remove the excess liquid but do not discard the white potato starch that has built up on the bottom. Lightly beat the eggs and add them to the potatoes. Blend well and add salt and pepper.

3. Cover the bottom of a large nonstick skillet with oil and put it on medium to high heat. Drop a small scoop of the batter into the oil. If it sizzles, the temperature is right. Cook the pancakes until they are golden brown and crisp on both sides, turning once. Use up all the batter and serve immediately.

Boiled Beef with Seven-Herb Sauce

Frankfurter Grüne Soße mit gekochtem Rindfleisch

The most famous of all dishes from Frankfurt, *Grüne Soße*, was most likely invented as a dish for *Gründonnerstag*, the Thursday before Good Friday. It is always made of seven fresh herbs, that vary according to the season: borage, chives, chervil, cress, dill, lemon balm, parsley, pimpernel, sorrel, and tarragon. Many recipes do not use dill because it easily overpowers the other herbs. As long as you keep this in mind and have a good balance between the herbs, it really does not matter which you use. Using dried herbs, however, is an unforgivable sin!

In Frankfurt, the mixture is sold in the unmistakable *Grüne Soße* white paper wrap with green writing. The sauce, served with the boiled beef or hard-boiled eggs, is always accompanied by potatoes.

Beef:
2 pounds top round roast
1 bay leaf
1 teaspoon black peppercorns
Salt
2 medium yellow onions, peeled and quartered
1 carrot, peeled and chopped
1 turnip, peeled and chopped
1 parsnip, peeled and chopped
1 stalk celery, trimmed and chopped
1 leek, thoroughly cleaned, trimmed, and chopped

1. For the beef: Rinse the meat under cold water and put in a stockpot with the bay leaf, peppercorns, salt, onions, carrot, turnip, parsnip, celery, and leek. Add enough water to just cover the meat. Bring to a boil, cover, and reduce the heat. Simmer for 1 hour, or until the meat is tender.

2. Take the meat out of the broth and slice just before serving so it will not dry out. Strain the broth but don't discard it—it makes a great broth for another dish, and homemade broth is so much better than canned broth. Freeze it if you do not intend to use it within the next few days.

Seven-Herb Sauce:

4 packed cups (5 ounces)
mixed fresh herbs: pars-
ley, chives, chervil, cress
(or alfalfa), pimpernel,
sorrel, borage, tarragon,
and lemon balm
$\frac{1}{4}$ cup vegetable oil
4 hard-boiled eggs
1 cup plain yogurt
3 tablespoons white wine
vinegar
1 tablespoon Dijon mustard
Salt and freshly milled
black pepper

6 servings

3. For the sauce: Pick over the herbs for culls and remove the stems. Wash in cold water and dry very thoroughly. In addition to drying the herbs in a salad spinner, I wrap them in a clean dishtowel and pat gently.

4. Chop the herbs briefly in the blender with the oil, but do not overprocess. Peel the eggs and carefully separate the egg yolks from the whites. Add the egg yolks to the herbs and process the mixture very briefly in the blender.

5. Transfer the herbs to a bowl and stir in the yogurt, vinegar, and mustard. Chop the egg whites very finely and incorporate them into the sauce. Season with salt and pepper. Let the sauce stand for 30 minutes before serving. Chill if not serving right away. Stir the sauce before serving it with the hot meat. The sauce is best eaten within a day.

Potato Dumplings Stuffed with Meat

Gefüllte Klöße

Stuffed potato dumplings are a specialty from the Hunsrück, for a long time a rather secluded mountainous area west of the Rhine. It was the home of one of the most famous German robbers of all time: Johannes Bückler, aka *Schinderhannes*, who ended up under the guillotine in 1803. Nowadays he is a celebrity and the area is a tourist attraction.

The dumplings are rather large and therefore are served as a main course. They require some preparation the previous day: half of the potatoes must be boiled ahead of time.

3 pounds starchy yellow potatoes (Yukon Gold)
1 (4- to 5-inch) dry roll, or 3 slices dry white bread, cut into 1-inch cubes
6 thin slices (3 ounces) lean center-cut bacon
1 medium yellow onion, peeled and finely chopped
$\frac{1}{2}$ pound ground meat (half lean ground beef/ half pork, or all beef)
1 clove garlic, crushed
1 leek, thoroughly cleaned, trimmed, and finely chopped
Salt and freshly milled black pepper
$\frac{1}{2}$ teaspoon paprika

Continued

1. The day before, scrub 1$\frac{1}{2}$ pounds of the potatoes with a brush and boil them in their skins until tender. Drain and refrigerate to give them a firmer consistency.

2. If the rolls are still soft, place them on a baking sheet and put them in the oven at 350 degrees F until dry.

3. Cut the bacon into tiny strips. Place in a large cold skillet and cook until the fat has been drawn out. Add the onion and sauté until translucent. Add the ground meat and cook until brown. Add the bread cubes, garlic, and leek and cook for 10 minutes, stirring constantly. Season with salt, pepper, and paprika. Set aside to cool.

4. Peel the boiled potatoes and pass them through a potato ricer or mash them very well. Grate the remaining 1$\frac{1}{2}$ pounds raw potatoes and put them in a clean dishtowel. Pick up the four corners of the towel and carefully squeeze the liquid from the potatoes by twisting the towel. Place them in a large bowl along with the mashed potatoes.

4 eggs
1½ cups all-purpose flour,
* plus more as needed*
Pinch of ground nutmeg
6 tablespoons unsalted
* butter*
3 tablespoons dry
* breadcrumbs*

8 servings

5. Beat 2 of the eggs and mix them thoroughly with the mashed and grated potatoes. Stir in the flour. The dough should not stick to your hands. If it does, add more flour, a teaspoon at a time, until it does not stick to your hands any more. Season with salt, pepper, and nutmeg.

6. Beat the remaining 2 eggs and blend them well with the meat filling.

7. Moisten your hands (have a bowl of cold water standing by) and divide the dough and the meat filling into 8 equal portions. Form a round dumpling with one portion of the dough and insert a portion of the filling into the center. The stuffing should be very well covered with the dough. Place the finished dumplings on a wet plate to prevent them from sticking.

7. Bring a large pot of salted water to a boil and slide the dumplings into the water. Immediately reduce the heat, cover, and simmer for 30 minutes. Remove the dumplings with a slotted spoon and drain them in a colander.

8. Melt the butter in a small saucepan and brown the breadcrumbs in it. Drizzle over the hot dumplings and serve at once.

Sauerbraten with Raisins

Rheinischer Sauerbraten

In the 2000 census, 57 million Americans claimed some degree of German ancestry. I believe that German immigrants must have done a good job telling their children about their cravings for home-style Sauerbraten, because the dish, although it is almost exclusively served in German-style restaurants, is even listed in Webster's dictionary.

The most famous version is from the Rhineland, although other regions, like Swabia and Bavaria, claim their own variations of marinated beef. There is thus no shortage of recipes and legends about Sauerbraten. My favorite story attributes the dish to Julius Caesar, who sent amphoras filled with beef marinated in wine over the Alps to the newly founded Roman colony of Cologne. According to this legend, this inspired residents of Cologne to imitate the Roman import.

Marinating the beef for three to four days is crucial. In today's fast-paced life, this might seem long. But in view of two thousand years of Sauerbraten history, I do not think we are in a position to complain about the length of the marinating time. It's well worth the wait.

$2\frac{1}{2}$ to 3 pounds top
round roast

Marinade:
1 cup dry red wine
1 cup red wine vinegar
1 bay leaf
2 whole cloves
$\frac{1}{2}$ teaspoon crushed black
 peppercorns
$\frac{1}{2}$ teaspoon crushed
 juniper berries

---

1. Wash the meat and pat it dry with paper towels. Put in a glass, plastic, or ceramic dish (not metal!) with a cover. The dish should be only slightly larger than the meat.

2. For the marinade: Bring the wine, vinegar, bay leaf, cloves, peppercorns, and juniper berries to a boil in a small saucepan. Cool completely.

3. Pour the marinade over the meat. Cover and marinate in the refrigerator for 3 to 4 days, turning the meat once every day.

Sauerbraten:

Salt and freshly milled black pepper

1 tablespoon clarified butter

1 medium to large yellow onion, peeled and sliced

1 turnip, peeled and sliced

1 stalk celery, trimmed and chopped

1 large carrot, peeled and sliced

$\frac{1}{3}$ cup raisins, preferably seedless

$\frac{1}{4}$ to $\frac{1}{2}$ slice authentic (imported) pumpernickel, crumbled

1 cup light cream

1 cup milk, plus more as needed

$\frac{1}{2}$ teaspoon sugar, plus more as needed

6 to 8 servings

4. For the sauerbraten: Remove the meat from the marinade, drain, and pat dry with paper towels. Reserve the marinade. Rub the meat with salt and pepper. Heat the clarified butter in a large saucepan and brown the meat on all sides. Take the meat out of the saucepan and sauté the onion, turnip, celery, and carrot.

5. Transfer the meat back to the saucepan and arrange the vegetables around it. Add a quarter of the marinade, the raisins, and pumpernickel. Reduce the heat, cover, and simmer for 1½ to 2 hours, or until the meat is very tender. Check the liquid frequently to be sure that the roast is cooking in marinade but not entirely immersed in it. Gradually add the rest of the marinade and 1 to 1½ cups water, as needed.

6. Take the meat out of the saucepan and keep it warm. Remove the bay leaf and puree the vegetables with the liquid. Add the cream, milk, and sugar. Taste for sourness; if the gravy is too sour, add a little more sugar or milk. Return the gravy to the heat and simmer until it thickens. Slice the roast and pour the hot gravy over it. Serve at once.

Tender Beef and Onion Stew

Potthast

There are conflicting stories about the origin of this dish but there is consensus over the fact that it has a long tradition. One story connects the invention of *Potthast* with one of Germany's many wars. During a siege of the city of Dortmund, a woman who lived in the city but was sympathetic to the enemy managed to distract the hungry soldiers by telling them where they could find a *Pott* (pot) with tasty *Hast* (sautéed meat). Luckily the woman's ruse was discovered before the soldiers had the chance to abandon their posts and head for the food, and the city was saved.

Mashed potatoes are a good accompaniment.

2 bay leaves
Salt
3 tablespoons vegetable oil
2 pounds top round roast, cut into $1^{1}/_{2}$-inch cubes
3 large yellow onions, peeled and thinly sliced
1 ($14^{1}/_{2}$-ounce) can beef broth, or 2 cups homemade beef broth (see page 200)
2 whole cloves
6 black peppercorns
4 slices organic lemon
2 tablespoons dry breadcrumbs
Freshly milled black pepper

6 servings

1. Crush the bay leaves with some salt with a mortar and pestle.

2. Heat the oil and brown the meat in a large saucepan. Add the onions and cook until they are translucent. Add the broth, cloves, peppercorns, lemon slices, and crushed bay leaves. Stir and cook over low heat for 45 minutes. Check for liquid every so often and add water as necessary.

3. Remove the lemons slices and cook the meat for $1^{1}/_{4}$ more hours, or until tender. Add the breadcrumbs to thicken the sauce and season with salt and pepper.

Veal Ragout

Töttchen

This ragout is a specialty from the Münsterland in Westphalia. Traditionally it is served on two occasions: the Monday following a wedding, and the *Schützenfest* (annual shooting competition). The competition has a long history, and in many towns and villages, it continues to be a major social event. It goes back to the shooting guilds, which received permission from the king or the local authorities to train their members in weapon handling. For the shooting guilds, the *Schützenfest* was the highlight of the year. During the competition, a wooden bird is the target, and the best shooter to hit the bird is declared the *Schützenkönig* (the Shooting King), a highly prized title. Nowadays, the event is often held in conjunction with a carnival.

Originally, *Töttchen* was prepared with head of veal, tongue, and/or heart, but modern recipes use ingredients that are easily available and fit a more general taste. The dish is often served with rolls and beer.

---

2 pounds veal shoulder with bones
2 medium yellow onions, peeled and quartered
2 bay leaves
1 whole clove
½ teaspoon white peppercorns
Salt
1 tablespoon unsalted butter
1 tablespoon all-purpose flour
1 to 2 tablespoons white wine vinegar
2 tablespoons medium dry sherry
Freshly milled white pepper

4 servings

1. Put the veal in a large saucepan and barely cover it with water. Bring to a boil and add the onions, bay leaves, clove, peppercorns, and salt. Skim the foam off the top. Cover and simmer for 1½ hours, or until tender, turning occasionally. Strip the meat from the bones and cut it into bite-size pieces. Keep warm.

2. Strain the broth and reserve 2 cups for the sauce and reserve the onions. Do not discard the leftover broth, but save it for another use, such as Bavarian stuffed breast of veal (*see page 214*) or soup. Pour the reserved broth back into the saucepan and let it simmer until reduced by about one-third. Puree the reserved onions and mix them with the broth.

3. In a small saucepan, melt the butter. Add the flour and cook until the mixture is pale golden, stirring constantly with a wooden spoon. Whisk in 1 cup of the broth and simmer until the sauce thickens. If the sauce gets too thick, add the remaining reduced broth. Add the vinegar and sherry and season with salt and pepper. Reheat the meat thoroughly in the sauce and serve.

Potatoes and Apples with Bratwurst

Himmel und Erde

This is a hearty dish with a poetic name. *Himmel und Erde* (heaven and earth) is made with apples from heaven and potatoes from the earth. For the sake of accuracy, I need to add that this dish is traditionally served with sautéed blood sausage. That, of course, is optional. The sweetness of the apples and the mashed potatoes are a delicious counterpoint to any well-seasoned frying sausage.

2 pounds russet potatoes, peeled and quartered
2 pounds tart cooking apples, cored, peeled, and cut into chunks
1 tablespoon sugar
1 tablespoon cider vinegar
6 thin slices (3 ounces) lean center-cut bacon
2 medium yellow onions, peeled, halved, and thinly sliced
2 tablespoons vegetable oil
1 pound sausage (blood sausage, bratwurst, or other)
$\frac{1}{4}$ cup hot milk
1 tablespoon unsalted butter
Salt and freshly milled black pepper
Pinch of ground nutmeg

6 servings

1. Bring the potatoes to a boil in salted water and cook until tender. Drain.

2. In a separate pot, cook the apples with the sugar, vinegar, and 2 to 3 tablespoons water until tender but not falling apart, 10 to 15 minutes.

3. Place the bacon in a cold skillet. Cook over medium to high heat until crisp. Add the onions and sauté until golden brown. Remove from the skillet and set aside.

4. Heat the oil in the same skillet and sauté the sausage until brown and crisp. Cut the sausage into $\frac{1}{2}$-inch slices.

5. Combine the potatoes and the apples and mash them coarsely. Stir in the milk and butter and season with salt, pepper, and nutmeg.

6. Put the potato mixture in a serving bowl and top with the onions, bacon, and sausage. Serve at once.

Lentil Stew with Frankfurter Sausages

Linseneintopf mit Frankfurter Würstchen

When Frankfurter sausages were introduced internationally at the Chicago World's Fair in 1883, they were such a success that producers from Frankfurt wanted to prevent culinary plagiarism. In 1929, a court in Berlin decided that only sausages made in the Frankfurt area could legitimately be labeled *Frankfurter Würstchen* (Frankfurter sausages). Ever since, producers in other areas of Germany have had to give their sausages slightly different names, for example "Frankfurt-style sausages." Outside Germany, however, it is a different story.

Most sausages sold as frankfurters in America are made of a mixture of pork and beef, unlike the original frankfurters, which consist only of pork. American frankfurters also lack the particular casing that produces a crackling sound when you bite into it.

Authentic frankfurters or not, this lentil stew makes a yummy and easy meal that is also great for reheating.

1 tablespoon vegetable oil
1 medium yellow onion, peeled and finely chopped
$1\frac{1}{2}$ cups brown or green lentils
2 ($14\frac{1}{2}$-ounce) cans beef broth, or 1 quart homemade beef broth (see page 200)
1 leek, thoroughly cleaned, trimmed, and sliced
1 medium turnip, peeled and chopped
1 medium parsnip, peeled and chopped
1 stalk celery, trimmed and chopped
1 large russet potato, peeled and cut into cubes
1 carrot, peeled and chopped
1 tablespoon white wine vinegar
Salt and freshly milled black pepper
4 to 6 frankfurters

6 servings

1. Heat the oil in a large saucepan and sauté the onion until translucent. Rinse the lentils in a colander under cold water and add to the onions along with the broth, leek, turnip, parsnip, and celery. Stir, bring to a boil, and reduce the heat. Simmer for 1 hour. Check for liquid every so often and add water as necessary. The vegetables should always be just covered with water.

2. Add the potato and carrot and cook for 30 more minutes.

3. Stir in the vinegar and season with salt and pepper. Add the frankfurters, either whole or sliced, and heat them thoroughly but do not boil. If you use "real" frankfurters, boiling will make the casings burst.

Chicken in Riesling with White Grapes

Woihinkelche

This is a dish from the Rheingau winegrowing area, north of the city of Mainz. You can substitute Riesling with another fruity, dry white wine.

1 chicken (3 to $3\frac{1}{2}$
  pounds), cleaned and
  most of the skin removed
Salt and freshly milled
  black pepper
Generous pinch of dried
  tarragon
2 tablespoons vegetable oil
1 medium yellow onion,
  peeled and chopped
1 clove garlic, crushed
1 cup dry white wine
$\frac{1}{2}$ cup light cream
1 teaspoon unsalted butter
12 medium white
  mushrooms, cleaned,
  trimmed, and thinly
  sliced
$\frac{3}{4}$ cup (4 ounces) halved
  seedless white grapes

4 to 6 servings

1. Cut the chicken into 8 parts and rub with salt, pepper, and tarragon. Heat the oil in a large saucepan and brown the chicken on all sides. Add the onion, garlic, and wine and cook over low heat for 45 minutes, stirring occasionally.

2. Take the chicken out of the pan and keep warm. Whisk the cream into the sauce and let it thicken.

3. Heat the butter in a large skillet and sauté the mushrooms until they start to soften. Add the mushrooms to the sauce along with the chicken. Stir carefully and simmer for 10 minutes.

4. Add the grapes and heat them briefly in the sauce. Season with salt and pepper. Serve hot with plain white rice.

Oven–Baked Potato-Leek Hash

Dibbelabbes

If southern Germany is the land of dumplings, then the West is the kingdom of potatoes. The following dish from the Saarland is considered the state's signature dish. Even for German speakers, the name *Dibbelabbes*, in the regional dialect, needs translation. It means "something large in the pot."

16 thin slices ($^1/_2$ pound) lean center-cut bacon
2 leeks, thoroughly cleaned and trimmed
1 medium yellow onion, peeled and finely chopped
2 pounds russet potatoes, peeled
2 eggs
Salt and freshly milled black pepper
1 teaspoon marjoram
Pinch of ground nutmeg
$^1/_2$ cup finely chopped fresh flat-leaf parsley

6 to 8 servings

1. Cut the bacon into small strips and place them in a cold skillet. Cook until the fat has been drawn out. Halve the leeks lengthwise and then slice them very thinly. Add the leeks and onion to the skillet and sauté in the bacon fat. Set aside to cool.

2. Preheat the oven to 375 degrees F and grease a 2-quart gratin dish.

3. Grate the potatoes. Beat the eggs and combine them with the potatoes, bacon, leeks, and onions. Add salt, pepper, marjoram, nutmeg, and parsley and place in the prepared dish.

4. Bake for 45 minutes, or until done, stirring the hash several times with a spatula to crisp it evenly. Serve hot.

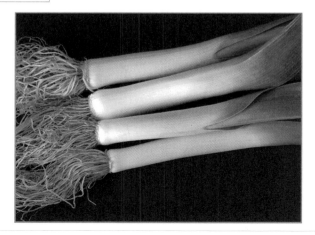

Crushed Potatoes with Endive

Stampfkartoffeln

Stampfkartoffeln (crushed potatoes), not to be confused with *Kartoffelbrei* (mashed potatoes), was one of those dishes from the German home cooking repertoire at which people would turn up their noses. That was the case until celebrity cooks such as TV host Alfred Biolek and best-selling cookbook author Wolf Uecker put it on their menus. *Stampfkartoffeln* can be combined with virtually any kind of flavorful greens, such as curly endive or dandelion, or a bunch of finely chopped herbs—common varieties like parsley, basil, dill, and chives, or more unusual ones such as lovage, chervil, and borage.

2 pounds russet potatoes, peeled and quartered
1/4 cup vegetable oil
Salt
Freshly milled white pepper
2 tablespoons white wine vinegar
1 small yellow onion, peeled and finely chopped
1 small head curly endive (about 1/2 pound), washed, dried, and stems removed
2 tablespoons unsalted butter
Pinch of ground nutmeg

6 servings

1. Bring the potatoes to a boil in salted water and cook until tender. Drain.

2. Whisk the oil with some salt and pepper and the vinegar. Add the onion. Cut the endive into very fine strips and toss with the dressing.

3. Crush the hot potatoes with a potato masher or a fork and stir in the butter. Season with salt and nutmeg. Fold in a portion of the endive.

4. Heap the potatoes in the middle of a large shallow serving platter, and arrange the rest of the endive in a circle around the potatoes. Serve at once.

Apple Cider Potato Gratin

Bäckerkartoffeln

This potato dish is called "baker's potatoes" because in former times, housewives brought it to their local baker for baking. There are a number of variations of *Bäckerkartoffeln* from different regions; in most recipes the potatoes are cooked with a piece of pork. In Rhineland-Palatinate, white wine is added to the dish, while the Hessia version incorporates apple wine, the specialty drink from Frankfurt.

Without meat, *Bäckerkartoffeln* makes a tasty side dish. With a bit of luck you might find imported apple wine, otherwise you can substitute French cider or nonalcoholic sparkling apple cider.

---

*2 pounds red or other
low-starch potatoes
2 tablespoons vegetable oil
2 medium yellow onions,
peeled and finely
chopped
$\frac{1}{2}$ cup apple cider
1 cup heavy cream
Pinch of ground nutmeg
Salt and freshly milled
black pepper*

6 to 8 servings

---

1. Preheat the oven to 375 degrees F and grease a 2-quart gratin dish.

2. Wash and peel the potatoes and cut them into thin slices.

3. Heat the oil in a skillet and sauté the onions until golden.

4. Whisk the cider and cream in a bowl. Add the nutmeg and season with salt and pepper.

5. Layer the potatoes in the prepared dish overlapping like fish scales and spread some onions over each layer. Pour the cream mixture over the potatoes and bake for 1 hour, or until the potatoes are soft and the top has a nice brown crust. Make sure the upper layer of the potatoes does not get dry. If necessary, push the potatoes into the liquid with a large spoon or spatula. Serve hot.

Fresh Fava Beans with Potatoes

Dicke Bohnen

Fava beans, also known as broad beans, are one of the oldest cultivated crops. They were a staple in central Europe long before green beans and dried beans were introduced from Latin America. But unlike in Italian cuisine, fava beans are an ugly duckling in German cooking, and this reputation is certainly reflected in the names that the German language has coined for them: *Dicke Bohnen* (thick beans), *Saubohnen* (sow beans), or *Pferdebohnen* (horse beans). If you eat them with an unprejudiced mindset, you will find them very tasty, and to top it off, they are extremely high in protein and other nutrients.

Not all fava beans need to be peeled after shelling. If you can find small, crisp pods—the size of the shelled beans not larger than a thumbnail—you do not have to remove the skins. Otherwise blanch the shelled beans for 1 minute, drain them, and remove the skins.

Some Westphalian fava bean recipes call for bacon, but I do not think that is necessary, as fresh fava beans have enough flavor on their own.

---

3 pounds fresh fava beans (yields 1 pound shelled but not peeled beans)
2 tablespoons vegetable oil
1 large yellow onion, peeled and coarsely chopped
2 medium russet potatoes, peeled and cubed
1 ($14\frac{1}{2}$-ounce) can vegetable broth
1 to 2 sprigs fresh savory, or $\frac{1}{4}$ to $\frac{1}{2}$ teaspoon dried
Salt and freshly milled black pepper
$\frac{1}{2}$ cup coarsely chopped fresh flat-leaf parsley

4 to 6 servings

1. Shell the beans, discarding the blemished ones, and blanch and peel if necessary.

2. Heat the oil in a large saucepan and sauté the onion until translucent. Add the fava beans, potatoes, broth, and savory. Stir, cover, and cook over low heat for 20 to 25 minutes, or until the beans and potatoes are tender.

3. Season with salt and pepper. If you used fresh savory, remove the sprigs before serving. Garnish with parsley and serve hot.

Sauerkraut with Wine and Apples

Weinkraut

The derogatory English term for Germans, "Krauts," was coined after World War I because the food rations of German soldiers included canned sauerkraut, a food rich in vitamin C, lactobacilli, and other nutrients, that also keeps well.

Today the tables are turned. The French and the Americans eat more sauerkraut per capita than the Germans. And in contemporary German cuisine, sauerkraut is moving away from being an accompaniment to heavy, hearty meat dishes, and becoming a healthy ingredient in lean, vegetarian, and even vegan cuisine.

Many traditional German recipes add white wine to sauerkraut.

$1\frac{1}{2}$ *teaspoons clarified butter*
1 medium yellow onion, peeled and chopped
1 medium sweet apple, such as Red Delicious
1 pound sauerkraut
$\frac{1}{4}$ *teaspoon juniper berries*
$\frac{1}{4}$ *teaspoon black peppercorns*
1 bay leaf
$\frac{1}{2}$ *cup dry white wine*

4 servings

1. Melt the clarified butter and sauté the onion until translucent.

2. Core and peel the apple and cut it into thin, julienne-style strips. Add the apple, sauerkraut, juniper berries, peppercorns, and bay leaf to the onions. Add $\frac{1}{2}$ cup water and the wine and stir well.

3. Cover and cook over low heat for 45 minutes. Check for liquid occasionally and add a little bit more water, as necessary. The sauerkraut should be neither too dry nor have a soupy consistency. Remove the bay leaf before serving.

Puree of Green Peas

Erwes

Puree of peas is traditionally served with pigs' feet, but if that is not your cut of meat, one goes well without the other. In the Rhineland, puree of peas is prepared from green peas and called *Erwes*. In Berlin, on the other hand, it is made from yellow split peas.

I like it best made from frozen or fresh green peas, which make a very delicate and light puree.

2 tablespoons unsalted butter
1 medium yellow onion, peeled and finely chopped
1 pound fresh shelled or frozen green peas
Pinch of ground nutmeg
Salt and freshly milled black pepper

4 servings

1. Melt the butter in a large saucepan. Sauté the onions until translucent. Add the peas and 1 cup water and cook until just tender. Drain in a sieve, reserving the liquid.

2. Puree the pea mixture and add a few tablespoons of the liquid, or as much as needed to reach a smooth consistency. Season with nutmeg, salt, and pepper and serve hot.

Spinach Dumplings

Grüne Knepp

Grüne Knepp are dumplings from the Saarland and Rhineland-Palatinate. The word *Knepp* (dialect for "dumpling") has found its way to America. A popular dish in Pennsylvania Dutch cuisine is *Schnitz un Knepp* (apples and dumplings).

3 tablespoons unsalted butter, plus more for drizzling
1 yellow onion, peeled and finely chopped
2 cloves garlic, crushed
1 pound spinach, washed, dried, stemmed, and coarsely chopped
2 cups dry breadcrumbs
2 eggs
1 tablespoon all-purpose flour
Salt and freshly milled black pepper
Pinch of ground nutmeg

10 dumplings

1. Heat the butter in a large saucepan and sauté the onion until translucent. Add the garlic and cook for 1 minute. Reduce the heat and add the spinach. Cook until the spinach is tender, 3 to 5 minutes. Set aside to cool.

2. Combine the cooled spinach mixture, breadcrumbs, eggs, flour, salt, pepper, and nutmeg and work into a dough. Form into a ball, wrap in plastic wrap, and refrigerate for 1 hour.

3. Bring salted water to a boil in a large pot. With wet hands, shape small dumplings of about $1\frac{1}{2}$ inches in diameter. Reduce the heat and drop the dumplings into the simmering water. Let simmer until they float on the top, 15 to 20 minutes. Drizzle with browned butter and serve hot.

Note: Leftover dumplings can be sautéed in butter or oil.

Apple-Pumpernickel Betty

Apfelbettelmann

Westphalia is the home of pumpernickel, a very dark rye bread baked for 16 to 36 hours at a low temperature. Pumpernickel is added to many regional dishes, including some desserts that taste so good that you can easily imagine having them as a full meal. Obviously the name *Bettelmann* (beggar man) is a reference to the leftover bread in the dish. But served hot with chilled vanilla sauce (*see page 51*) or vanilla ice-cream, it seems more like a royal treat to me.

*4 (2-ounce) slices very
dry authentic (imported)
pumpernickel, crumbled
into small bits*
*4 tablespoons unsalted
butter*
*$1/3$ cup plus 2 tablespoons
sugar*
*$1/2$ teaspoon ground
cinnamon*
Pinch of ground ginger
Pinch of ground cloves
$1/2$ cup chopped hazelnuts
*$1/2$ cup currants, washed
and dried*
*2 pounds tart cooking
apples, cored and peeled*
$1/2$ cup dry white wine
*1 teaspoon finely grated
organic lemon zest*

6 to 8 servings

1. If the pumpernickel is not completely dry, put it on a baking sheet and place in the oven at 350 degrees F until it reaches the desired dryness.

2. Melt the butter in a large skillet and add the pumpernickel with 2 tablespoons of the sugar, the cinnamon, ginger, cloves, and hazelnuts. Caramelize and remove from the heat. Combine with the currants and set aside.

3. Preheat the oven to 375 degrees F and grease a 2-quart gratin dish.

4. Slice the apples very thinly and put them in a large saucepan. Add the remaining $1/3$ cup sugar, the wine and lemon zest and cook until the apples are soft.

5. Spread a layer of apples on the bottom of the prepared dish and sprinkle a layer of the pumpernickel mixture on top. Repeat until the apples and pumpernickel mixture are all used, ending with a layer of pumpernickel mixture. Bake for 30 minutes and serve warm.

Note: Leftover *Bettelmann* keeps in the refrigerator for 2 days. It can be reheated in the oven, or eaten at room temperature.

Rice Pudding with Cherry Compote

Milchreis mit Kirschkompott

Unlike the typical *Kaffee und Kuchen* (coffee and cake), in the Bergisches Land north of Cologne, the staples of the *Bergische Kaffeetafel* (coffee table) are rice pudding, freshly baked waffles, raisin bread, and even sausage and ham.

I learned this old farmwife's trick to make creamy rice pudding from my aunt. After cooking it briefly, the rice is left to swell in bed under a warm comforter—a duvet works best!

Pudding:
3 cups milk (2% or whole)
2 tablespoons sugar
Pinch of salt
¾ cup arborio rice

Compote:
1 (14½-ounce) can red tart pitted cherries
1 tablespoon cornstarch
1 tablespoon sugar, plus more to taste

6 servings

1. For the pudding: Mix the milk with the sugar and salt in a heavy pot with a tight-fitting lid and slowly bring to a boil. Add the rice and stir. Bring back to a boil and cook for 5 minutes, stirring constantly. Remove the pan from the heat. Cover.

2. Place the pot on a level, empty bed, preferably in a corner. Cover completely with a folded thick comforter or a down duvet and let sit for about 1½ hours.

3. Carefully remove the duvet. Using potholders (the pot is still very hot!) return the pot to the kitchen. Uncover and stir well, scraping over the bottom of the pan. Initially the milk will be on top and the rice on the bottom but the rice will absorb all the milk as it cools.

4. For the compote: Drain the cherries and reserve the juice. Heat the juice in a small saucepan. Mix the cornstarch with 3 tablespoons cold water in a small bowl until the cornstarch is completely dissolved. Whisk it into the hot juice and bring to a boil. The mixture will clear up while thickening. Add the cherries and reheat. Add sugar to taste and serve hot or cold with the rice pudding.

Bread Pudding with Cherries

Kirschmichel

The personification of Germany (the equivalent of the charming French Marianne) is the *Deutscher Michel* (German Mike), a narrow-minded, slow, and rather stupid fellow. The origins of the Michel with his typical pointed hat go back as early as the sixteenth century. Michel still appears in German and foreign cartoons today.

Michel's culinary namesake, the *Kirschmichel* on the other hand, is a pure delight. It is served warm with a chilled fruit sauce.

Cherry sauce:
- 1 (14$\frac{1}{2}$-ounce) can red tart pitted cherries
- 2 tablespoons strained cherry preserves

Pudding:
- 1 dry baguette
- 1 cup milk
- 2 tablespoons dry bread-crumbs
- Pinch of ground cloves
- $\frac{1}{2}$ teaspoon ground cinnamon
- 6 tablespoons unsalted butter, softened
- $\frac{1}{2}$ cup plus 1 tablespoon sugar
- 2 tablespoons sour cream
- 3 eggs, separated
- $\frac{1}{2}$ teaspoon finely grated organic lemon zest
- 1 teaspoon vanilla extract
- $\frac{1}{2}$ cup chopped and blanched almonds
- Pinch of salt

6 to 8 servings

1. For the sauce: Drain the cherries in a sieve, reserving the juice. Set the cherries aside. Mix the cherry preserves with the juice and $\frac{1}{2}$ cup water. Cook over low heat until it thickens, stirring constantly. Chill. Stir well before serving.

2. For the pudding: If the bread is too soft, place it in the oven at 350 degrees F until dry. Cut it into thin slices and place them in a large bowl. Bring the milk to a boil and pour it over the bread. Soak until the milk is entirely absorbed.

3. Preheat the oven to 375 degrees F. Grease a 2-quart gratin dish and coat it with breadcrumbs.

4. Mix the drained cherries with the cloves and cinnamon. Beat the butter with $\frac{1}{2}$ cup of the sugar, the sour cream, and egg yolks. Add the lemon zest and vanilla. Combine with the soaked bread and almonds. Fold in the cherries.

5. Beat the egg whites with a pinch of salt until they stand in stiff peaks. Fold them into the bread mixture.

6. Pour the bread mixture into the prepared dish and sprinkle the remaining 1 tablespoon sugar on top. Bake for 40 minutes, or until crisp and light brown. Serve warm with chilled cherry sauce.

Westphalian Trifle

Westfälische Quarkspeise

This is a pumpernickel dessert that requires minimum preparation, although it needs to stand for at least half a day to develop its full flavor. *Westfälische Quarkspeise* is made with a mixture of German quark (*see next page*) and whipped cream. Greek yogurt is an excellent substitute for quark in this recipe.

3 (2.5-ounce) slices authentic (imported) pumpernickel 1 cup heavy cream 2 cups quark or Greek yogurt ½ cup plus 2 tablespoons sugar 2 teaspoons vanilla extract 1 (24-ounce) jar pitted sour cherries, drained ¼ cup kirsch 2 (1-ounce) squares semi-sweet chocolate, coarsely chopped 6 to 8 servings	1. Crumble the pumpernickel. Put it in a large skillet and toast over medium-high heat until completely dry and crunchy. Set aside to cool. 2. Whip the cream until it stands in stiff peaks. Whisk the quark or Greek yogurt with ½ cup of the sugar and the vanilla. Fold in the whipped cream. Pour three-quarters of this mixture in a glass serving dish with a flat bottom. 3. Distribute the cherries on top and spread with the remaining yogurt mixture. 4. Mix the toasted pumpernickel with the remaining 2 tablespoons sugar and drizzle with the kirsch. Toss with the chocolate and sprinkle over yogurt-cream mixture. Chill until serving.

Ode to Quark

If there is one German food that I seriously miss living in America, it's quark, the very smooth, wonderfully creamy dairy product that is a staple of German (and Austrian) cuisine. Why quark is not made in the United States, especially with the abundance of dairy farms and other dairy products, is a mystery to me.

I have seen imported *fromage blanc*, the French equivalent of quark, in some specialty food stores but it is quite pricey and rare. But in many recipes, you can use Greek yogurt instead of quark, or you can make your own quark (*see next page*).

Unlike cottage cheese, quark has no curds. It has a mild, slightly sour flavor and is easy to digest. There is hardly any meal of the day during which quark cannot be served. A German classic is quark with chives, served with potatoes boiled in their skins. Quark is also incorporated into pies or used as a cheese-cake filling. Because of its high moisture content, quark keeps baked goods moist.

Quark can be prepared from whole milk, reduced-fat milk, or low-fat milk. The higher the fat content, the smoother and more flavorful the quark. *Sahnequark* (creamy quark) has 40 percent fat. During my first years in the United States, I lived in Manhattan, and whenever I walked into a new specialty food store I kept my eyes open for quark. I realized that the object of my desire was not available because it was not likely to pass the city's almost impenetrable low-fat/no-fat border.

On our first trip together to Berlin, I enjoyed seeing my American husband helping himself every morning to several servings of herb quark from the breakfast buffet. He spread it with great relish on the freshly baked multigrain rolls. "Aha, another quark convert," I thought. I am convinced that quark is like Nile water in the old Egyptian proverb: someone who drinks it will return to it ever after. If you get the chance to taste quark, snow-white quark clouds will most likely appear in the sky of your culinary dreams, as they do in mine.

Recipe for homemade Quark

You can make your own quark with rennin, a coagulating enzyme that is used to curdle milk. The most common brand is Junket®, which is available in health food and specialty food stores. The result might not be quite as firm as the store-bought product, but it is very creamy and well worth the time and effort.

Homemade quark can be refrigerated for up to a week, or frozen in an airtight container.

1 gallon whole, 2-percent, or 1-percent milk (fat-free milk will not work)
1 quart buttermilk, at room temperature
¼ Junket (rennet) tablet

4½ to 5 pounds

1. Heat the milk to 70 degrees F. Mix the milk with the buttermilk in a covered but not tightly sealed large plastic or glass container (not metal!) and let stand at room temperature for about 12 hours.

2. Dissolve the rennet in ¼ cup cold water and stir into the milk. Cover and let stand at room temperature until set, 8 to 12 hours.

3. Drain the quark for 8 to 12 hours to remove the whey. I find it convenient to make a "filter bag" by placing a large clean kitchen towel over a big pot, such as a stockpot. Fasten the towel securely with small kitchen or laundry clips around the rim of the pot, but do not tighten the towel too much— the bag must be at least 5 inches deep so that it will hold all the quark. Pour the quark into the towel. Cover the top loosely with plastic wrap and let it drain in the refrigerator or a cool place.

4. When set, ladle the quark off the towel, including the firm white residue on the bottom. Discard the liquid (whey) that has accumulated in the pot. Put the quark in containers and refrigerate. Stir well or whisk before serving.

Chocolate Pumpernickel Pudding

Pumpernickelpudding

This is a very old recipe that has only recently been rediscovered by German chefs. The spices give it a distinct Christmas flavor, but it is a wonderful dessert for a festive meal any time in fall or winter.

Serve the pudding warm with chilled whipped cream or red wine sauce (*see page 178*).

3 (2-ounce) slices authentic (imported) pumpernickel
7 tablespoons unsalted butter, softened
$1/3$ cup sugar
6 eggs, separated
$3 1/2$ (1-ounce) squares unsweetened chocolate
$2/3$ cup blanched almonds
3 tablespoons golden rum
$1/2$ teaspoon ground cinnamon
$1/2$ teaspoon ground allspice
$1/2$ teaspoon ground cloves
$1/2$ teaspoon ground ginger

8 to 10 servings

1. Process the pumpernickel in the blender to crumble it evenly. Place on a baking sheet in the oven at 300 degrees F for 20 minutes, or until dry. Set aside to cool.

2. Increase the heat to 350 degrees F. Grease a 2-quart gratin dish.

3. Beat the butter with half of the sugar and add the egg yolks one at a time. Grind the chocolate and almonds very finely in a food processor and stir them into the mixture. Add the pumpernickel crumbs, rum, cinnamon, allspice, cloves, and ginger.

4. Beat the egg whites until soft peaks form. Add the rest of the sugar and continue beating until the egg whites stand in stiff peaks. Fold into the pudding.

5. Pour the pudding into the prepared dish. Place the dish in another ovenproof dish that leaves at least 2 inches of space all around. Pour hot water into the larger dish up to two-thirds of the sides of the gratin dish. Cover the dish with the pudding tightly with aluminum foil and bake for 1 hour, or until set. Cool slightly before slicing.

Covered Apple Pie

Appeltaat

*A*ppeltaat is the Rhineland's version of apple pie. It can also be filled with plums or other seasonal fruit.

7 tablespoons unsalted butter, chilled
2 cups all-purpose flour
$\frac{1}{2}$ cup plus 1 tablespoon plus 1 teaspoon sugar
2 eggs
2 tablespoons sour cream
Zest of $\frac{1}{2}$ organic lemon
2 pounds tart cooking apples, cored and peeled
2 tablespoons dry white wine
2 teaspoons vanilla extract
$\frac{1}{2}$ cup washed and dried raisins
$\frac{1}{2}$ cup chopped blanched almonds
Pinch of ground cinnamon

12 servings

1. Cut the butter into small chunks and quickly work it into the flour adding $\frac{1}{2}$ cup of the sugar, the eggs, sour cream, and lemon zest and work into a ball of moist but not sticky dough. If the dough is sticky, add a little bit of flour, a teaspoon at a time, until it does not stick to your hands any more. If it is too dry, add a few drops of ice-cold water. Wrap the dough in plastic wrap and refrigerate for 1 hour.

2. Preheat the oven to 400 degrees F. Grease a 9-inch pie pan.

3. Thinly slice the apples and simmer them with the wine, vanilla, and 1 teaspoon of the sugar until they soften, stirring occasionally. Cool.

4. Roll two-thirds of the dough thinly on a floured work surface. Carefully drop the dough into the pan and let it flop over the edges. Press the dough against the edges and trim the excess with a sharp knife.

5. Spread the apples on the bottom crust and cover evenly with the raisins and almonds. Roll the remaining dough to a 9-inch circle and cover the pie with it and seal the edges. Prick the top crust in several places with a fork to release the steam during the baking process. Bake for 25 minutes, or until the top is golden brown.

6. Mix the remaining 1 tablespoon sugar with the cinnamon and sprinkle over the warm pie.

Spiced Bread Pudding with Red Wine Sauce

Frankfurter Pudding mit Bischofssoße

Of all the recipes in this book, this is my biggest discovery. To my surprise, I had never heard of *Frankfurter Pudding* before, nor had any of my fellow Frankfurt natives. How could this outstanding dish have been overlooked? The only piece of information I found is that the recipe dates back to the days of Goethe in the late seventeenth or early eighteenth century. Fortunately we still have the recipe.

Frankfurter Pudding is a grand finale to a festive Christmas dinner. Since the wine sauce should be served chilled with the warm pudding, making the sauce the day before is a good idea.

Red wine sauce:
1/2 organic orange
1/2 organic lemon
2 cups plus 2 tablespoons dry red wine
1/4 cup red currant jelly
1/4 cup sugar
Pinch of ground cinnamon
Pinch of ground cloves
Pinch of ground nutmeg
Seeds from 1 cardamom pod
1 tablespoon cornstarch

1. For the sauce: Peel off the zest of the orange and lemon in spirals as thinly as possible, using a peeler or a sharp knife, without removing the white pith. Put the zest, 2 cups of the red wine, the jelly, sugar, cinnamon, cloves, nutmeg, and cardamom in a small saucepan. Bring to a boil and cook over medium heat for 5 to 7 minutes. Strain.

2. Dissolve the cornstarch in the remaining 2 tablespoons wine and whisk into the hot sauce. Simmer until the sauce becomes clear again. Remove from the heat and chill.

Pudding:
$\frac{1}{2}$ cup raisins
1 tablespoon golden rum
12 thin slices baguette
Dry breadcrumbs for
the pan
1 stick unsalted butter
5 eggs
$1\frac{1}{2}$ cups milk
$\frac{1}{4}$ cup plus 1 tablespoon
dry red wine
$\frac{1}{3}$ cup sugar
Pinch of ground cinnamon
Pinch of ground cloves
Zest of $\frac{1}{2}$ organic lemon,
finely grated
Zest of $\frac{1}{2}$ organic orange,
finely grated
$\frac{1}{3}$ cup chopped and
blanched almonds
$\frac{1}{4}$ cup finely chopped
candied citron or candied
lemon peel
$\frac{1}{4}$ cup finely chopped
candied orange peel

6 to 8 servings

3. For the pudding: Rinse the raisins in a colander under cold water and pat them dry with paper towels. Mix them with the rum in a small bowl and set aside.

4. Cut the bread into $\frac{1}{2}$-inch cubes; you should have about 6 cups. Spread the bread on a large baking sheet and set the oven to 350 degrees F. Leave the bread cubes in the oven until dry and light brown. Leave the oven on when you take the bread out.

5. Grease a 2-quart gratin dish and coat it with breadcrumbs. Remove the excess breadcrumbs by holding the dish upside down over the kitchen sink and gently knocking on the bottom of the pan.

6. Melt half of the butter in a large skillet and sauté half of the bread in it until golden. Repeat with the remaining butter and bread.

7. Lightly beat the eggs in a large bowl and combine with the milk, red wine, sugar, cinnamon, cloves, and lemon and orange zest. Add the cooled toasted bread, raisins, almonds, citron, and candied orange peel, and toss well.

8. Pour the pudding into the prepared dish and cover it tightly with aluminum foil.

9. Place the dish with the pudding in a roasting pan or a large ovenproof dish and fill the larger dish with water to about two-thirds up the sides of the dish with the pudding. Put in the oven and cook for 1 hour, or until set.

10. Carefully unmold the pudding from the gratin dish by placing it upside down on a serving plate. Serve the chilled red wine sauce over the warm pudding.

Dark Chocolate Pudding

Schlackenkohle

The Ruhr Valley was once Germany's most important coal-mining region. Today most coal mines are closed, and the region had to reinvent itself with a new diversified industrial structure.

The name of this pudding is a remnant of the coal-mining days—*Schlackenkohle* means "clinker." It is served warm with chilled vanilla sauce (*see page 51*).

---

1 cup milk
3 (1-ounce) squares semi-sweet chocolate, broken into pieces
1 tablespoon unsweetened cocoa powder
4 tablespoons unsalted butter
1 teaspoon vanilla extract
Salt
½ cup all-purpose flour
4 eggs, separated
⅓ cup sugar

4 to 6 servings

1. Preheat the oven to 350 degrees F and grease a 2-quart round or oblong baking dish.

2. Heat the milk in a saucepan. Add the chocolate and stir until melted. Add the cocoa, butter, vanilla extract, and a pinch of salt. Bring to a boil, then whisk in the flour. Whisk vigorously until the mixture forms a thick paste that detaches from the bottom of the pan. Remove from the heat.

3. Beat the egg yolks with the sugar with an electric mixer until pale and creamy. Gradually add the chocolate mixture and mix well.

4. In a separate bowl, beat the egg whites with a pinch of salt until they stand in stiff peaks. Fold them into the pudding.

5. Pour the pudding into the prepared dish. Place the dish in a roasting pan or a large ovenproof dish and fill the larger dish with water to about two-thirds up the sides of the dish with the pudding. Put in the oven and bake for 90 minutes, or until set. Serve warm with chilled vanilla sauce.

Zwieback Pudding with Prunes

Schwarzer Magister

Funny names abound in German regional recipes. *Schwarzer Magister* (Black Master) sounds like something straight from a Harry Potter novel. *Schwarzer Magister* is made with zwieback, the classic German twice-baked teething rusks. If you cannot find zwieback, use white toast.

13 ounces pitted prunes
1 large strip organic lemon peel
½ cup plus 2 teaspoons sugar
¼ cinnamon stick
16 to 18 slices zwieback or toasted white bread, crust removed
4 eggs, separated
¼ teaspoon ground cinnamon
⅛ teaspoon almond extract
3 tablespoons lemon juice
1 teaspoon finely grated organic lemon zest
Pinch of salt
½ cup heavy cream

6 servings

1. Place the prunes in a saucepan with 2 cups water, the strip of lemon peel, 2 teaspoons of the sugar, and the cinnamon stick. Bring to a boil, reduce heat and cook covered for 20 to 30 minutes, stirring occasionally and adding more water to prevent scorching. Transfer to a sieve placed on top of a bowl to collect the cooking liquid. Measure out ½ cup plus 1 tablespoon liquid and mix the rest back into the prunes. Remove the lemon peel and cinnamon stick and cool.

2. Preheat the oven to 350 degrees F.

3. Spread the ½ cup of reserved prune liquid in an oblong 3-quart baking dish. Place a layer of zwieback on top, trimming the rusks as needed to fit them snugly. Spread with a layer of cooked prunes and top with another layer of zwieback. Repeat until all the prunes and zwieback have been used, ending with a layer of zwieback. Push it down gently with your flat hands.

4. Beat the egg yolks with the remaining ½ cup sugar, cinnamon, almond extract, lemon juice, grated lemon zest, and the remaining tablespoon prune liquid until creamy. Beat the egg whites with a pinch of salt in one bowl, and the heavy cream in another bowl, until they stand in stiff peaks. Fold them both into the batter. Spoon the batter onto the last layer of zwieback.

5. Bake in the preheated oven for 30 minutes, until golden. Serve warm or at room temperature.

Buttercream Ring Cake

Frankfurter Kranz

Why this omnipresent festive cake was named after the city of Frankfurt is one of the unsolved mysteries of pastry history. In many recipes, it is cut twice and filled only with buttercream, but I think that the tartness of an additional thin layer of raspberry preserves gives it a more refined taste.

This cake requires a $9\frac{1}{2}$-inch savarin mold.

Batter:
- 2 tablespoons dry bread-crumbs for the pan
- $1\frac{3}{4}$ sticks unsalted butter
- Zest of $\frac{1}{2}$ organic lemon, finely grated
- 1 cup sugar
- 3 eggs
- 1 tablespoon golden rum
- 2 cups all-purpose flour
- 1 tablespoon baking powder

Crunch Topping:
- 1 tablespoon unsalted butter
- $\frac{1}{2}$ cup coarsely chopped blanched almonds
- $\frac{1}{3}$ cup sugar

1. Preheat the oven to 350 degrees F. Grease a $9\frac{1}{2}$-inch ring mold (savarin mold) and sprinkle it with breadcrumbs. Turn it over and shake to remove excess breadcrumbs.

2. For the batter: Beat the butter with the lemon zest and sugar until fluffy. Add the eggs and rum. Mix the flour with the baking powder and gradually sift it into the mixture, mixing well after each addition.

3. Pour the batter into the prepared mold and even out the top with a spatula or knife. Bake for 40 minutes, or until a knife comes out clean and the cake has a golden color. Let the cake stand for a few minutes, then unmold and cool completely on a cake rack.

4. While the cake is baking, prepare the crunch topping: Heat the butter in a small saucepan. Add the almonds and sugar and let them caramelize over medium heat, stirring constantly. Spread the hot mixture on a well-greased sheet of aluminum foil and cool. Grind the caramelized almonds to small bits in a mortar.

Buttercream:
1 (4.6-ounce) package vanilla-flavored pudding and pie filling (not instant)
2 cups milk
1¾ sticks unsalted butter, softened
¾ cup confectioners' sugar
2 tablespoons golden rum

¼ cup strained raspberry preserves

16 servings

5. For the buttercream: Stir the pudding mix into the milk in a small saucepan and cook over medium heat until the mixture comes to a full boil, stirring constantly. Remove from the heat. Cool while stirring to prevent a skin from forming.

6. Beat the butter and confectioners' sugar until fluffy and then gradually add to the cool pudding. Stir in the rum.

7. Cut the cake horizontally into 3 layers. A neat and easy way of doing this is to first use a sharp knife to make two equidistant ¼-inch-deep incisions around the cake. Then take a piece of heavy twine or dental floss the diameter of the cake plus enough to twist around your fingers. Pull the twine taut between your fingers and slide it into each incision. Using the twine like a saw, cut slowly through the cake.

8. Spread a layer of raspberry preserves on the bottom layer and some buttercream on the second layer. Reassemble the cake and use the remaining buttercream to cover the cake all around. Sprinkle the cake evenly with the cool almond crunch and chill. Remove from the refrigerator 30 minutes to 1 hour before serving.

Deep-Fried Almond Pastry

Mutzen

*F*astnacht, the carnival in the Rhineland, is something that many non-natives do not care much for, to say the least. The general rule is: you either go whole hog and become part of the carnival experience, or you seek refuge out of town. The special carnival goodies, however, are the smallest common denominator of those who love carnival and those who abhor it. In other words: you do not have to like carnival to crave this pastry.

2 cups all-purpose flour
¾ cup cornstarch
⅓ cup sugar
1 teaspoon baking powder
3 eggs
Pinch of salt
Zest of ½ organic lemon,
  finely grated
2 tablespoons sour cream
⅓ cup blanched almonds
7 tablespoons unsalted
  butter, chilled
Vegetable oil (peanut or
  corn) for deep-frying
Confectioners' sugar for
  dusting

40 pieces

1. Mix the flour and cornstarch with the sugar and baking powder. Make a well in the middle and add the eggs, salt, lemon zest, and sour cream. Mix well. Grind the almonds very finely in a food processor and stir them into the dough.

2. Cut the butter into little chunks and add it to the dough. Quickly knead the dough into a moist but not sticky ball. Add a few more teaspoons flour if the dough is too wet, or a few drops of water if it is too dry. Cover and refrigerate for 30 minutes.

3. Roll the dough about ½ inch thick and cut out shapes of your choice with large cookie cutters.

4. Heat the oil in a deep-fryer or a large saucepan to 370 degrees F. The oil needs to be hot enough to sizzle a breadcrumb. Fry the *Mutzen* until golden brown, turning them once. Remove them with a slotted spoon and drain on paper towels.

5. Sprinkle a thick layer of confectioners' sugar over the hot pastry, using a flour sifter. Serve within the next hour or two.

Baked Marzipan Bites

Bethmännchen

Bethmännchen are named after the Bethmanns, a prominent banker family in Frankfurt. The invention of the fine marzipan candy goes back to the year 1838. Originally, there were four almonds on each piece, one for each of the Bethmann sons, but when one of them died, the almonds were reduced to three. *Bethmännchen* were not the only contribution of the Bethmanns to German civilization and culture. The bank also financed the trip of Johann Wolfgang von Goethe to Italy in 1786, a critical phase in the life of Germany's most famous literary figure.

Marzipan:
2 cups blanched almonds
2⅓ cups confectioners'
  sugar
1 tablespoon rose water

Topping:
½ cup blanched almond
  halves
1 egg white

45 pieces

1. For the marzipan: Grind the almonds in the food processor to a very fine powder. Add the confectioners' sugar and rose water and keep grinding until a thick, smooth paste forms. Add drops of water to get the desired consistency but do not overdo it, otherwise your marzipan will become difficult to shape. Scrape down the sides of the food processor bowl frequently to ensure that all the paste is smooth.

2. Preheat the oven to 275 degrees F. Grease a baking sheet.

3. Spread the marzipan 1-inch thick. Cut the marzipan into 1-inch cubes and roll them into cylinders slightly rounded at the top. Garnish each with 3 almond halves, in equal distance from each other, with the tips pointing up.

4. Brush the candies with the egg white and place them on the prepared baking sheet. Bake in the upper third of the oven for 15 minutes; then broil at low heat until the tops are just lightly browned. Gently remove from the baking sheet and cool.

Note: *Bethmännchen* can be kept in an airtight container in a cool place for 1 to 2 weeks.

Chestnut Truffles

Kastanienkugeln

Sweet, edible chestnuts have been grown in Palatinate since Roman times, when every soldier of the Legion received a chestnut ration instead of bread. The natives also used the chestnuts collected in the forest as a substitute for bread or potatoes. In Palatine, Germany's second-largest winegrowing region, chestnut trees were also valued for their wood, which was used for poles in vineyards.

I like to roll these truffles in sugar, vanilla sugar, or cocoa just before serving. This is merely for appearance—the truffles still taste excellent even if the moisture from the chestnuts has soaked through. To make vanilla sugar, mix 1 teaspoon pure vanilla powder with 1 cup sugar.

⅓ cup unpeeled raw
  almonds
4 cups peeled chestnuts
  (about 1 pound)
½ stick unsalted butter
½ cup sugar
2 (1-ounce) squares semi-
  sweet chocolate, grated
1 tablespoon finely diced
  candied lemon peel
1 tablespoon finely diced
  candied orange peel
1 to 2 tablespoons rum
Confectioners' sugar,
  unsweetened cocoa, or
  vanilla sugar for rolling

20 to 24 pieces

1. Toast the almonds in an ungreased skillet. Cool, then finely grind them in a food processor.

2. Steam the chestnuts over boiling water until they break apart when pierced with a knife. Cool and finely grind them in a food processor.

3. Melt the butter in a saucepan. Add the ground almonds, sugar, chocolate, lemon peel, and orange peel. Cook over very low heat until the chocolate is melted. Add the ground chestnuts and mix well. Remove from the heat and stir in the rum. Cool.

4. Shape round walnut-size truffles with moistened hands. Store them in an airtight container in the refrigerator.

5. Just before serving, roll the truffles in confectioners' sugar, unsweetened cocoa, or vanilla sugar, and place in paper candy cups.

Baked Stuffed Apples

Winzeräpfel

Whole baked apples (*Bratäpfel*) are a traditional fall and winter dessert that has seen a renaissance in Germany. New recipes abound with all sorts of stuffings, and there is even baked-apple tea! I'd rather have these simple, unpretentious stuffed baked apples with white wine from Palatinate, and drink a cup of good tea with them.

Choose baking apples that hold their shape, such as Stayman, Winesap, Jonathan, or Goldrush.

4 medium baking apples
Lemon juice
2 tablespoons golden raisins
2 tablespoons coarsely chopped walnuts, toasted
1 tablespoon dark brown sugar
1 teaspoon vanilla extract
½ teaspoon ground cinnamon
1 cup dry white wine
4 servings

1. Preheat the oven to 350 degrees F.

2. Peel and core the apples and brush them with some lemon juice.

3. Mix the golden raisins with the walnuts, brown sugar, vanilla, and cinnamon. Stuff the apples with this mixture. Place them in a small ovenproof dish. Pour the wine over the apples.

4. Bake for 20 to 30 minutes, until the apples can be pierced with a sharp knife, basting them every now and then with the wine. Serve warm with chilled vanilla sauce (*see page 51*).

Strawberry and White Wine Punch

Erdbeerbowle

The rule for Cold Duck (*opposite page*) also applies to fruit punch: make sure to use only good quality wine. *Bowle*, which you can also prepare with nice ripe peaches, is undeniably a German summer party classic.

2 pounds strawberries, washed, dried, and hulled
1 bottle chilled dry white wine
1 bottle chilled champagne or sparkling wine
A few leaves of fresh lemon balm

12 to 16 servings

1. Cut the strawberries into halves or quarters, depending on size, and place them in a punch bowl or a large glass bowl. Pour the wine over them and chill for at least 2 hours.

2. Add the champagne and lemon balm and serve chilled, using a decorative ladle to fill individual glasses with the punch.

Cold Duck

Kalte Ente

In North America, this drink is often made with sparkling Burgundy. The original recipe from Germany is different: a mixture of white wine and champagne. I recommend you stick to a very dry white wine and use no sugar at all to avoid a hangover.

Cold Duck is a great drink for a summer party, served with seafood, poultry, or salad.

1 organic lemon
2 bottles chilled dry white wine
1 bottle chilled champagne or good sparkling wine

12 to 16 servings

1. Wash and dry the lemon. Peel off the zest in spirals as thinly as possible, using a peeler or sharp knife, and without removing the white pith. Put the zest in a large pitcher and pour the wine over it. Place the pitcher in an ice bucket and let stand for 15 minutes.

2. Taste the wine every so often—when it has a slight lemon flavor, remove the peel. Pour the champagne into the pitcher just before serving and keep the drink chilled in an ice bucket.

Southern Peaks

Bavaria and Baden-Württemberg are the two southern states. Bavaria, Germany's largest state, views itself as very different from the rest of Germany. There is an invisible line called *Weißwurstäquator* (white sausage equator) that delineates the psychological border between Bavaria and the North. It is a striking paradox that of the four German regions, Bavaria has played the strongest role in creating the stereotype of German food. How many people think of German food as pork roast and dumplings, eaten by men in lederhosen and women in dirndl dresses in an Alpine setting. This cliché, I hope, is dispelled by the depth and variety of dishes in this book.

Bavaria itself has a cuisine that is far from the stereotype and not at all homogeneous. Franconia in northern Bavaria has its own culinary traditions. White sausages (*Weißwürste*) are a mainstay of southern Bavaria, while Nuremberg in Franconia is the place where the original and true German gingerbread is made.

Bavarian cuisine traditionally includes many different soups and meat dishes, and, of course, dumplings. Cabbage is the most popular vegetable, either cooked or raw in salads. When it comes to desserts and pastries, the choices are endless, and many of the sweets have close relatives in the Austro-Hungarian cuisine.

The state of Baden-Württemberg in the South has two distinct cuisines. Swabia, home of spaetzle (noodles), is known for its simple (and tasty) hearty foods. Then there is the refined cuisine of Baden, influenced by nearby France. Baden is also Germany's southernmost winegrowing area, which is why wine is an important ingredient in many of its recipes.

Soft Pretzels

Laugenbrezeln

Pretzel baking in Germany goes back at least to the early twelfth century, when the pretzel first appeared on the coat of arms of the baker's guild. The pretzel has been the symbol of the baker's guild ever since, so if you are ever trying to locate a bakery in Germany, especially in a small town or village, just look for the pretzel symbol.

There are conflicting stories about how pretzels got their typical shape. One theory is that they show hands crossed in prayer. Another legend says that a baker who had been sentenced to death for shortchanging his customers, was promised remission if he could come up with a pastry through which the sun could shine three times. He invented the pretzel and saved his life.

---

*2 ($\frac{1}{4}$-ounce) envelopes
active dry yeast*
$\frac{1}{2}$ teaspoon sugar
*$\frac{1}{2}$ cup plus $\frac{1}{3}$ cup
lukewarm water*
*$2\frac{1}{2}$ cups plus $\frac{1}{3}$ cup
all-purpose flour*
1 teaspoon salt
2 teaspoons baking soda
*Coarse (kosher) salt for
sprinkling*

10 pretzels

1. Combine the yeast and sugar with the lukewarm water in a small bowl. Let stand for 10 minutes until frothy.

2. Mix the flour and salt. Put the yeast mixture in a large bowl and gradually add the flour. Knead thoroughly for several minutes, using the kneading attachment of an electric mixer or your hands, until the dough is elastic and easily detaches from the bottom of the bowl. If it is too dry and crumbly, add more water, 1 tablespoon at a time. Shape into a ball, cover with a clean damp dishtowel, and let stand for 2 hours at room temperature.

3. Briefly knead the dough again and shape it into a long roll. Cut it into 10 equal pieces and roll each piece into a rope about 12 inches long. The ropes should be thin on both ends and thick in the center. Twist each rope into the typical pretzel shape and press the joints together to make them stick (*see illustration*). Place the pretzels on a greased $17\frac{1}{2}$ x 14-inch baking sheet, cover with the dishtowel, and let stand for 15 minutes.

4. Dissolve the baking soda in 3 quarts water and bring to a boil in a large pot. Reduce the heat. Drop one pretzel at a time into the water and cook for 30 seconds or until the pretzel rises to the surface. Take it out immediately with a slotted spoon and drain.

5. Return the pretzels to the baking sheet and sprinkle with coarse salt. If the salt does not stick well, brush the pretzels with baking soda water.

6. Place the pretzels on the middle rack in a cold oven and set the oven to 425 degrees F. Bake for 25 minutes, or until brown and crisp on the outside. Serve at once.

Roll into a rope ...

and twist ...

then fold over.

Sweet and Savory Bologna Salad

Bayerischer Wurstsalat

Salads made with boiled sausage are popular in Bavaria, Swabia, and Franconia, with recipes varying from region to region. This Bavarian recipe is a sweet-and-savory version with apple. In the original recipe the onion is added raw; I prefer to blanch it to make it less pungent.

1 large white onion, peeled, halved, and thinly sliced
3 tablespoons canola oil
2 tablespoons white wine vinegar
3 tablespoons pickling liquid, or more as needed
Salt and freshly milled black pepper
3 medium carrots, trimmed, peeled, and diced
2 large apples, peeled, cored, and diced
1 large pickle, diced
12 ounces Bologna sausage, cubed
Snipped chives

6 servings

1. Bring water to a boil in a small saucepan. Blanch the onion slices for 1 minute, drain and immerse in ice water. Drain again.

2. Whisk the oil with the vinegar, pickling liquid, and some salt and pepper.

3. Toss the blanched onion slices, carrots, apples, pickle, and sausage in a large bowl. Mix with the dressing until evenly coated. Season with salt and pepper and add more pickling liquid to taste. Refrigerate until serving. Serve sprinkled with snipped chives.

Cottage Cheese with Herbs and Caraway

Luckeles Käs

In Germany, like in many other countries, the natives of each region have their stereotypes. The Swabians are known to be very diligent and economical. This simple but tasty spread is a part of the *Vesper*, the sacred mid-morning or mid-afternoon snack of handymen and other hard-working Swabians.

1 cup cottage cheese
1 tablespoon sour cream
1 teaspoon caraway seeds
1 tablespoon snipped
  chives
2 teaspoons finely chopped
  fresh dill
Salt and freshly milled
  black pepper

4 servings

Mix the cottage cheese with the sour cream, caraway seeds, chives, and dill. Season with salt and pepper. Serve within a few hours with freshly baked country-style bread or warm pretzels.

Sage Leaf Fritters

Salbeiküchle

This is a specialty from Swabia. It is served plain as an appetizer, or dusted with confectioners' sugar and accompanied with compote as a dessert.

1 cup all-purpose flour
$^{1}/_{2}$ teaspoon baking powder
Pinch of salt
2 eggs
$^{1}/_{3}$ cup milk, plus more if needed
25 to 30 large fresh sage leaves
Vegetable oil for deep-frying

6 servings

1. In a medium bowl with an electric mixer, combine the flour, baking powder, salt, eggs, and as much milk as needed to make a thick yet still liquid batter. Cover and let stand at room temperature for at least 1 hour.

2. Heat the oil in a deep-fryer or a large saucepan to 370 degrees F. The oil needs to be hot enough to sizzle a breadcrumb.

3. Stir the batter with a spatula. Dip each sage leaf into the batter, using a fork, and drop it into the hot oil. Fry until golden on all sides and remove with a slotted spoon. Drain on paper towels and serve warm.

Camembert Spread

Obatzta

This Bavarian spread has performed the feat of crossing the northern border of Bavaria—without even changing its tongue-twisting name. *Obatzta* is popular all over Germany. For example, Bavarians and Prussians are notorious for their disregard for each other, but when it comes to *Obatzta*, this historic antagonism is forgotten. Today, Prussians eat the spread as happily as the rest of the country.

Obatzta tastes best the same day it is made.

1 (8- to 10-ounce) very ripe Camembert
$\frac{1}{2}$ small yellow onion, peeled and very finely chopped
2 tablespoons unsalted butter, softened
1 teaspoon paprika
3 tablespoons sour cream
Salt and freshly milled black pepper

4 servings

1. Mash the Camembert with a fork.

2. Mix Camembert with the onion, butter, paprika, and sour cream in a bowl. Season with salt and pepper and refrigerate.

3. Take the spread out of the refrigerator 1 hour before serving to bring to room temperature.

Cheese Soup

Allgäuer Käsesuppe

You can be almost sure that any dish with Allgäu in the name contains cheese. The Allgäu Alps are a dairy region with picturesque green pastures and brown Allgäu cows. The cattle population in the Allgäu is the densest in all of Germany.

1 (4- to 5-inch) roll, or 4 slices white bread, cut into cubes
7 tablespoons unsalted butter
1 medium yellow onion, peeled and thinly sliced
$1/3$ cup all-purpose flour
2 ($14^1/2$-ounce) cans beef broth, or 1 quart homemade beef broth (see page 200), plus more as needed
$1^3/4$ cups (7 ounces) shredded Swiss cheese
$1/4$ cup lager beer
3 tablespoons heavy cream
Pinch of ground nutmeg
Salt and freshly milled black pepper

6 servings

1. Set the oven to 350 degrees F. Spread the bread on a baking sheet and put it in the oven until dry and light brown. Set aside.

2. Heat 1 tablespoon of the butter in a skillet and sauté the onion until lightly browned. Set aside.

3. Melt the remaining 6 tablespoons butter in a large saucepan and blend in the flour. Cook for 5 minutes over low heat, stirring frequently, until it begins to turn beige. Add the broth and simmer for 15 minutes, stirring occasionally.

4. Slowly stir in the cheese and bring to a simmer. Add the beer. Remove the saucepan from the heat. Stir in the cream. If the soup is too thick, add more broth. Add the nutmeg and season with salt and pepper.

5. Place some of the browned onions and croutons in individual soup bowls and ladle the soup over them. Serve at once.

Creamy Onion Soup

Badische Zwiebelsuppe

The cuisine of Baden ranks among the most sophisticated German regional cuisines, and the influence of neighboring France is unmistakable. However, it has its own distinct character, as you can see in this creamy onion soup, which is very different from French onion soup.

2 ($14\frac{1}{2}$-ounce) cans chicken broth, plus more as needed
3 tablespoons unsalted butter
2 large Vidalia onions, peeled and thinly sliced
3 tablespoons all-purpose flour
Salt and freshly milled black pepper
1 egg yolk
$\frac{1}{3}$ plus $\frac{1}{4}$ cup dry white wine
$\frac{1}{4}$ cup light cream
Snipped chives for garnish

4 to 6 servings

1. Heat the chicken broth in a saucepan.

2. Melt the butter in another large saucepan and sauté the onions until translucent. Add the flour and cook over low heat just until it begins to turn beige. Whisk in the heated chicken broth. Season with salt and pepper and simmer for 15 to 20 minutes.

3. Mix the egg yolk with the wine and cream. Remove the soup from the heat and stir in the egg-wine mixture. Reheat for 2 to 3 minutes but do not boil. Garnish with chives and serve hot.

Semolina Dumpling Soup

Grießnockerlsuppe

This traditional Bavarian soup looks like matzo ball soup, but the similarity ends right there. The dumplings in *Grießnockerlsuppe* are made from semolina, a coarsely ground durum wheat. Semolina, or its soft version, farina (*see page 16*), is incorporated into many popular dishes all over Germany.

The beef broth should be prepared at least a few hours ahead so you can easily remove the layer of fat from the surface when the broth is cold. Broth can be refrigerated for several days, or frozen.

Beef broth:
1 piece beef chuck or shin meat (1 pound)
1 to 1½ pounds beef bones
1 large yellow onion, peeled and halved
1 bay leaf
¼ teaspoon black peppercorns
1 leek, thoroughly cleaned, trimmed, and chopped
1 carrot, peeled and sliced
1 parsnip, peeled and quartered
1 stalk celery, trimmed and sliced
1 turnip, peeled and sliced
Freshly milled black pepper
Salt

Makes 2 quarts

Semolina dumplings:
½ cup milk
4 tablespoons unsalted butter
¾ cup semolina
2 eggs
Salt
Pinch of ground nutmeg

6 to 8 servings

1. For the beef broth: Rinse the meat and bones under cold water and put them in a stockpot. Add 2 quarts cold water, the onion, bay leaf, and peppercorns. Bring to a boil and remove the foam from the top during the first 30 minutes of cooking. Reduce the heat and let simmer for 1 more hour.

3. Add the leek, carrot, parsnip, celery, and turnip. Cook for another hour.

4. Strain the broth through a fine sieve and return it to the pot. Season with pepper. Salt the broth only when ready to use it; salted broth can turn sour, especially in hot weather. Cool the broth and refrigerate.

5. For the dumplings: Heat the milk in a small saucepan and melt the butter in it. Gradually stir in the semolina, stirring constantly with a wooden spoon. Lightly beat the eggs and add them to the mixture. It should be smooth and lump-free. Season with salt and nutmeg and let stand for at least 30 minutes in a cool place.

6. Remove the layer of fat from the broth. Bring broth to a boil and add salt to taste. Shape small dumplings, using two spoons or your (wet) hands. Drop the dumplings into the hot broth and simmer for 15 minutes. Do not boil, or the dumplings will fall apart. Serve at once.

Liver Dumpling Soup

Leberknödelsuppe

Liver dumpling soup is to Bavaria what clam chowder is to New England. The very large liver dumplings are often also served with sauerkraut.

4 (4- to 5-inch) dry rolls
½ cup lukewarm milk
1 tablespoon unsalted butter
1 medium yellow onion,
  peeled and finely chopped
¼ cup finely chopped
  fresh flat-leaf parsley
2 eggs
½ pound fresh calves' liver
2 teaspoons dried marjoram
1 teaspoon organic lemon
  zest
Salt and freshly milled
  black pepper
Dry breadcrumbs
2 quarts homemade beef
  broth (see page 200)
Snipped chives for garnish

8 servings

1. If the rolls are soft, slice them, place them on a baking sheet, and put them in the oven at 350 degrees F until dry. Cut the rolls into ¼-inch cubes. Pour the milk over the bread and soak.

2. In the meantime, melt the butter in a skillet. Sauté the onion until translucent. Add the parsley and cook for 1 more minute.

3. Squeeze any excess liquid from the bread and mix the bread with the onion. Lightly beat the eggs and incorporate them into the paste.

4. Wash the liver and pat it dry with paper towels. Chop it very finely with a sharp knife or grind it in a meat grinder and add it to the mixture. Add the marjoram and lemon zest and season generously with salt and pepper.

5. Bring a large pot of salted water to a boil. Reduce the heat to a simmer. Shape a tiny test dumpling and drop it into the water to check for the right consistency. If the dumpling falls apart, add breadcrumbs, a teaspoon at a time, and test again.

6. Shape 8 large round dumplings and lower them into the simmering water. Cook covered for 25 minutes without boiling.

7. In the meantime, heat the beef broth thoroughly. Remove the dumplings from the water with a slotted spoon, drain, and place them in individual soup plates or a large soup bowl. Ladle hot beef broth over them, garnish with chives, and serve very hot.

Pancake Soup

Flädlesuppe

The Swabians love diminutives, and countless words end with the diminutive suffix -le. In Swabia, pancakes are called *Flädle* (from *Fladen*, flatbread). The refined variation is *Kräuterflädle* (pancakes with herbs), which simply have fresh herbs in the batter; a great taste for pancakes that are "small" in name only.

3/4 cup all-purpose flour
2/3 cup soda water
Pinch of salt
2 eggs
2 tablespoons vegetable oil
1 1/2 quarts homemade beef broth (see page 200)

6 to 8 servings

1. Combine the flour with the soda water, salt, and eggs and mix well until smooth.

2. Lightly coat a nonstick skillet with oil and cook thin, crisp pancakes. Cut them into small strips, or roll them up tightly and thinly slice them.

3. Reheat the beef broth thoroughly. Add the warm pancakes and serve immediately.

Soup with Meat-Stuffed Pancakes

Brätstrudelsuppe

Butcher shops in the south of Germany sell seasoned ground veal (called *Brät* or *Kalbsbrät*) that is used for various traditional dishes, mainly as a stuffing. Mildly flavored breakfast sausage is a widely available substitute that works well in this soup.

Pancakes:
¾ cup all-purpose flour
⅔ cup soda water
Pinch of salt
2 eggs
2 tablespoons vegetable oil

Filling:
6 ounces breakfast sausage
1 tablespoon finely chopped fresh flat-leaf parsley
3 tablespoons heavy cream
½ teaspoon finely grated organic lemon zest
¼ teaspoon crumbled dried thyme

1½ quarts homemade beef broth (see page 200)

6 servings

1. For the pancakes: Prepare and cook the pancakes as described on page 202.

2. For the filling: Mix the breakfast sausage with the parsley, cream, lemon zest, and thyme until well combined.

3. Evenly spread the filling onto the pancakes. Roll them up tightly. Let the stuffed pancakes rest in the refrigerator for 20 minutes.

4. Cut the stuffed pancakes into ¾-inch-wide slices using a small serrated knife.

5. Bring the beef broth to a simmer. Add the pancakes and cook over low heat for 7 to 10 minutes. Serve soup hot.

Sorrel Soup

Sauerampfersuppe

Only in the last decade has sorrel gained culinary recognition in Germany. Before that, it was only foragers and quirky naturists who went for sorrel. Today it is not unusual to find sorrel soups, sauces, and salads on the menus of upscale restaurants.

The distinctive sour flavor comes from oxalic acid. The acid is also the reason why you should not prepare sorrel in copper pots, but use stainless steel or enamel pots instead.

This soup is rather mild, made with a small amount of young, light green sorrel leaves, which are most tender in the spring.

---

1 tablespoon unsalted butter
2 shallots, peeled and minced
2 packed cups sorrel (about 2 ounces), washed and stemmed
2 tablespoons all-purpose flour
2 (14½-ounce) cans chicken or veal broth
1 egg yolk
½ cup heavy cream or crème fraîche (see page 87)
Salt and freshly milled black pepper

6 servings

1. Melt the butter and sauté the shallots until translucent. Coarsely chop the sorrel and add to the shallots and sauté until just wilted.

2. Whisk in the flour and cook until it begins to turn beige. Slowly add the broth and stir until the flour is entirely incorporated. Cover and simmer for 15 minutes.

3. Puree the soup and reheat it. Remove it from the heat. Mix the egg yolk with the cream and stir into the soup. Season with salt and pepper and serve hot.

Bread Soup with Browned Onions

Aufgeschmalzene Brotsuppe

As the most important food in the Bible, bread had an almost sacred status for a long time, and discarding dry old bread came close to a sin—hence bread soup was invented. Bread soup with sautéed onions is a specialty from Bavaria. It is as simple as it is delicious.

3 thin slices rustic dark country or rye bread
1½ quarts homemade beef broth (see page 200)
½ teaspoon dried marjoram
Salt and freshly milled black pepper
1 tablespoon plus 2 teaspoons clarified butter
2 medium yellow onions, peeled and thinly sliced
½ teaspoon ground caraway
Snipped chives for garnish

6 servings

1. Cut the bread into 1-inch strips and place them on a baking sheet. Set the oven to 350 degrees F and leave the bread in the oven until crisp.

2. Bring the broth to a boil and season with marjoram, salt, and pepper. Simmer over very low heat.

3. Heat the clarified butter in a large skillet. Add the onions and sauté until golden brown. Add the caraway and combine with the broth. Season with salt and pepper.

4. Place the bread in individual soup plates or in a large soup bowl and pour the steaming hot soup over it. Sprinkle with chives and serve at once.

Cheese Spaetzle

Käsespätzle

Spaetzle (little sparrows) have long been a topic of culinary debate. The origin of the name is unclear—is it really derived from the Italian word *spezzato* ("torn into pieces")? Another hot topic is the best preparation method. Should one manually scrape them off a spaetzle board, or use one of the many variants of spaetzle makers? Hardcore spaetzle cooks shun anything other than the spaetzle board as the lazybones method. What is unquestioned is that spaetzle is the Swabians' most popular comfort food.

The recipe below is for spaetzle with cheese and onions. Plain spaetzle are also a good accompaniment for meat stews.

Spaetzle:
3 cups all-purpose flour,
plus more as needed
1 teaspoon salt
4 eggs
½ cup lukewarm water
½ cup soda water

Topping:
3 tablespoons unsalted
butter or vegetable oil
2 medium yellow onions,
peeled and thinly sliced
Freshly milled black pepper
2 cups (½ pound) shredded
Swiss cheese

6 servings

1. For the spaetzle: Put the flour and salt in a bowl. Make a well in the middle. Beat the eggs and pour into the well. Mix using the kneading attachment of an electric mixer, starting from the middle of the bowl and work your way to the edges. Gradually add the water and soda water. Depending on the size of eggs you are using, you might have to add a few tablespoons more flour. Knead the dough until it produces bubbles and easily detaches from the sides of the bowl. Be patient; it takes 10 minutes or more to get there. Cover the bowl with a dishtowel and let the dough rest for 30 minutes.

2. Preheat the oven to 400 degrees F. Grease an ovenproof dish.

3. For the topping: Melt the butter in a large skillet and sauté the onions until brown and crisp. Set aside.

4. Bring salted water to a boil in a large pot. Reduce the heat. Spread about one-sixth of the dough on the short end of a large cutting board and scrape it off the board into the boiling water, using a large knife. Make sure that you cook only small batches at a time; the spaetzle must be floating freely in the water and should not stick together. You can also use a spaetzle press or a potato ricer, which will provide you with very evenly shaped little knots. Simmer until the spaetzle float on the surface.

5. Remove the spaetzle with a slotted spoon and place in a colander. Rinse with cold water and immediately place in the prepared dish. Sprinkle with pepper and a little cheese. Cover with aluminum foil and place the dish in the oven. Process the rest of the dough the same way and place each layer on top of the previous one, sprinkling it with pepper and cheese and returning dish to oven.

6. Increase the oven temperature to 450 degrees F.

7. Top the last layer of spaetzle with the sautéed onions and the remaining cheese and bake, uncovered, for 5 to 7 minutes. Serve hot with a salad of mixed greens.

Lentils, Sausage and Spaetzle

Linsen und Spätzle

Swabian comfort food: Lentils, boiled sausages, and spaetzle, homemade if you have the time. Some recipes contain smoked beef, for which I substituted the non-smoked and less salty Canadian bacon.

Traditionally, additional vinegar and mustard are served at the table.

1 tablespoon olive oil
1 medium onion, peeled and finely chopped
3 garlic cloves, peeled and crushed
1 large bay leaf
1¼ cups brown lentils, rinsed and drained
2 tablespoons unsalted butter
2 tablespoons all-purpose flour
2 ounces Canadian bacon, finely diced
½ cup dry red wine
2 tablespoons dry red wine vinegar
Salt and freshly milled black pepper
4 precooked boiling sausages, such as frankfurters, knackwurst, or wieners
2 cups (9 ounces) dried spaetzle or fresh home-made (see page 206)
4 to 6 servings

1. Heat the oil in a large pot and sauté the onion until translucent. Add the garlic and cook for 1 more minute. Add the bay leaf, lentils, and 4 cups water. Bring to a boil, then reduce the heat and cook, covered, for 45 minutes, until the lentils are soft.

2. Heat the butter in a small saucepan over low heat. Blend in the flour and cook until the mixture begins to turn brown, stirring constantly. Add to the lentils and stir well. Add the bacon, wine, vinegar, salt, and plenty of pepper. Add the sausages and heat thoroughly.

3. Cook the spaetzle according to package instructions, or use homemade. Serve with the lentils and sausage.

Spinach Pockets

Schwäbische Laubfrösche

The bright green color of tree frogs served as inspiration for this Swabian dish: *Schwäbische Laubfrösche* (Swabian tree frogs). It can be served as a main course or appetizer.

24 large spinach leaves (about $\frac{1}{2}$ pound), stemmed and thoroughly washed and dried
1 (4- to 5-inch) dry roll
2 tablespoons vegetable oil
1 small yellow onion, peeled and finely chopped
$\frac{1}{4}$ cup finely chopped fresh flat-leaf parsley
1 clove garlic, crushed
$\frac{1}{2}$ pound lean ground beef
1 egg
$\frac{1}{4}$ teaspoon ground nutmeg
Salt and freshly milled black pepper
$\frac{1}{2}$ cup canned or home-made beef broth (see page 200)
1 tablespoon sour cream or crème fraîche (see page 87)

4 servings

1. Bring water to a boil in a large pot. Plunge the spinach leaves into the water one by one and remove them immediately with a slotted spoon. Spread them out on several large platters or a clean work surface.

2. If the roll is too soft, slice it, place on a baking sheet and put in the oven at 350 degrees F until dry. Soak the roll in a small bowl with hot water.

3. Heat 1 tablespoon of the oil in a large skillet and sauté the onion until translucent. Add the parsley and garlic and cook for 2 minutes. Add the ground beef and cook until browned. Set aside to cool.

4. Squeeze the excess liquid from the roll and combine it with the meat. Mix in the egg. Season with nutmeg, salt, and pepper and stir well until evenly moistened and smooth.

5. Divide the filling into 12 equal portions. For each spinach pocket, place two leaves on top of each other. Put a portion of the filling in the middle, tuck in the edges over the meat, and roll up the leaves to make tight little pockets.

6. Heat the remaining 1 tablespoon oil in a large saucepan and sauté the pockets on all sides. Pour the broth over them, cover, and simmer for 20 minutes. Remove the pockets from the skillet and keep warm.

7. Strain the broth, whisk in the sour cream, and season with salt and pepper. Pour the sauce over the pockets and serve hot with potatoes or rice.

German Ravioli with Meat or Spinach Filling

Maultaschen

One of the most popular Swabian dishes, *Maultaschen,* has found its way into food stores and restaurant kitchens all over Germany. Apart from the standard meat or spinach filling, you can find these ravioli filled with mushrooms, seafood, sweetbreads, vineyard snails, vegetables of all kinds, and much more.

There are many legends about the origin of *Maultaschen.* My favorite story goes like this: During the Thirty Years War in the seventeenth century, a time of great depravation, the monks in the Maulbronn monastery got a hold of a nice, large piece of meat. Unfortunately, it was Lent. Still, the monks' appetite outweighed their religious fervor. They managed to sneak the meat on their empty dinner plates. Since there was an abundance of spinach and herbs in the monastery garden, the monks simply mixed the meat with the greens for disguise. Believing that God sees everything, they took another precautionary measure and wrapped dough around it.

Below is the recipe for *Maultaschen* filled with meat or spinach. *Maultaschen* are served in beef broth as a soup, or sautéed as a main course. If you want to make both fillings at once, double the dough, or prepare half of each filling.

Dough:
2 cups all-purpose flour
1/2 teaspoon salt
3 eggs
1 teaspoon vegetable oil

Meat filling:
1 (4- to 5-inch) dry roll
1 tablespoon vegetable oil
1 small yellow onion, peeled and chopped
3 to 4 small scallions including some of the greens, trimmed and chopped

Continued

1. For the dough: Put the flour and salt in a mixing bowl. Add the eggs one at a time. Stir in the oil. Knead all the ingredients into a smooth dough, using the kneading attachment of an electric mixer. Add water, 1 teaspoon at a time, until you get a smooth dough that does not stick to your hands. Wrap the dough in plastic wrap and let it rest in a cool place for 1 to 2 hours.

2. For the meat filling: If the roll is too soft, slice it, place on a baking sheet and put in the oven at 350 degrees F until it has the desired dryness. Soak the roll slices in a small bowl with hot water for 10 minutes. Squeeze out the excess water and set aside.

$3/4$ pound lean ground beef
Salt and freshly milled
  black pepper
1 tablespoon finely chopped
  fresh flat-leaf parsley
Pinch of ground nutmeg
$1/2$ teaspoon ground
  marjoram
1 egg

Spinach filling:
1 (4- to 5-inch) dry roll
2 tablespoons vegetable oil
1 medium yellow onion,
  peeled and finely chopped
1 clove garlic, crushed
3 to 4 small scallions
  including some of the
  greens, trimmed and
  chopped
$1^1/2$ pounds spinach,
  thoroughly washed,
  trimmed, and chopped
Salt and freshly milled
  black pepper
Pinch of ground nutmeg

For main course:
2 tablespoons unsalted
  butter
1 cup (4 ounces) shredded
  Swiss cheese

For soup:
$1^1/2$ quarts homemade beef
  broth (see page 200)

6 servings

3. Heat the oil in a large skillet and sauté the onion until translucent. Add the scallions and cook for 3 minutes. Add the ground beef and cook until browned and cooked through. Combine with the roll, salt, pepper, parsley, nutmeg, and marjoram. Cool. Crack the egg into the mixture and combine well until a paste forms.

4. For the spinach filling: Prepare roll as explained in step 2. Heat the oil and sauté the onion and garlic. Add the scallions and cook for 3 minutes. Add the spinach and cook until just wilted. Mix the spinach with the roll, salt, pepper, and nutmeg until well combined.

5. Divide the dough into equal halves. Roll the first half on a floured work surface to an 18-inch square. Place a heaping tablespoon of filling every 3 inches. Roll the second half of the dough to a square of equal size and neatly place it on top of the first square. Press the dough together around each mound of filling using your index and middle fingers. Cut out 3-inch squares around each filling, using a sharp knife or a square ravioli cutter. Pinch the edges to seal.

6. For a main course: Bring 2 to 3 quarts water to a boil in a large pot. Reduce the heat and lower the ravioli into the simmering water. Cook for 10 minutes and drain well. Heat the butter in a large skillet and sauté the ravioli on both sides until crisp. To serve them topped with Swiss cheese, preheat the oven to 400 degrees F. Place them in a greased 2-quart gratin dish, sprinkle with cheese, and bake until the cheese is melted and bubbly.

7. For soup: Bring the broth to a simmer in a large pot. Add the ravioli, cook for 10 minutes, and serve.

Pot-au-Feu with Potatoes and Spaetzle

Gaisburger Marsch

Gaisburger Marsch is named after a suburb of Stuttgart, the capital of Swabia. Spaetzle are an indispensable ingredient in this dish. *Gaisburger Marsch* tastes great reheated. It is just the kind of dish to have in the refrigerator during the cold season, when you want a hot nourishing meal but don't feel like cooking.

1/2 pound beef bones
3 medium yellow onions, peeled
1 carrot, peeled and chopped
1 turnip, peeled and sliced
1 parsnip, peeled and chopped
1 leek, thoroughly cleaned, trimmed, and sliced
Salt
1/2 teaspoon black peppercorns
1 1/2 pounds top round roast
1 1/4 pounds red or other low-starch potatoes, peeled and cubed
1 1/2 tablespoons unsalted butter
1/2 recipe plain homemade spaetzle (see page 206)
Freshly milled black pepper
Pinch of ground nutmeg
1/4 cup coarsely chopped fresh flat-leaf parsley

6 servings

1. Rinse the bones under cold water and put them in a stockpot. Cut 1 of the onions in half and add it to the pot along with the carrot, turnip, parsnip, leek, salt, and peppercorns. Add 6 cups water and bring to a boil. Add the meat and reduce the heat. Simmer for $1\frac{3}{4}$ to 2 hours. Remove the foam during the first 30 minutes of cooking.

2. Strain the broth, reserving the meat and discarding the bones. Pour the broth back into the pot and add the potatoes. Cook for 15 minutes, or until tender. Cut the meat into bite-size pieces.

3. Heat the butter in a large skillet. Thinly slice the remaining 2 onions and sauté them in the butter until brown and crisp.

4. Add the spaetzle and meat to the broth. Reheat thoroughly. Season with salt, pepper, and nutmeg. Top with onions and parsley just before serving.

Note: This dish keeps in the refrigerator for 2 days.

Pork Roast with Beer Glaze

Schweinsbraten

In Bavaria, the gravy for a pork roast has to be brown and translucent. Thickening it with flour or cornstarch is considered culinary sacrilege. The traditional accompaniment to pork roast is bread dumplings (*see page 220*). Pork roast also makes a great cold cut for a picnic or buffet.

3 pounds boneless pork shoulder roast
Salt and freshly milled black pepper
2 cloves garlic, crushed
1 tablespoon clarified butter
1 teaspoon caraway seeds
Generous pinch of ground marjoram
2 medium yellow onions, peeled, halved, and thinly sliced
1 (12-ounce) bottle lager beer
6 to 8 servings

1. Preheat the oven to 375 degrees F.

2. Wash the pork and pat dry with paper towels. Cut a diamond pattern (each diamond should be about 1 inch long) into the fat side using a sharp knife. This will produce a crispier crust. Rub the pork with salt, pepper, and garlic.

3. Heat the clarified butter in a large skillet and brown the pork on all sides. Place fat side down in a roasting pan and pour the fat from the skillet plus 1 cup hot water over it. Sprinkle with caraway seeds and marjoram. Arrange the onion slices around the meat. Cover and roast for 1 hour.

4. Uncover and turn roast fat side up. Increase the oven temperature to 425 degrees F and cook for another 30 to 45 minutes, basting frequently with beer. Check for doneness with a meat thermometer; the meat is ready when the internal temperature reaches 165 degrees F and the crust is browned and crunchy. Let the roast rest for 10 minutes before carving.

5. Deglaze the pan with the remaining beer and, if necessary, with ½ cup hot water or more. Strain the gravy into a small saucepan. Simmer to thicken. Season with salt and pepper. Cut the meat into thin slices and serve the gravy separately.

Stuffed Breast of Veal

Gefüllte Kalbsbrust

Munich-style breast of veal is stuffed with seasoned dry rolls or soft pretzels. You can make it ahead of time as it tastes good hot or cold.

Stuffing:
3 (4- to 5-inch) dry rolls,
  cut into small cubes
½ cup hot milk
3 tablespoons unsalted
  butter
1 medium yellow onion,
  peeled and finely chopped
2 tablespoons finely chopped
  fresh flat-leaf parsley
3 eggs
Salt and freshly milled
  black pepper
½ teaspoon dried thyme
Pinch of ground nutmeg
1 teaspoon organic lemon
  zest

1. For the stuffing: If the rolls are still soft, slice them, place on a baking sheet, and put in the oven at 350 degrees F until dry. Soak the roll slices in the hot milk.

2. Meanwhile, heat the butter in a large skillet and briefly sauté the onion and parsley. Remove from the heat.

3. Squeeze the rolls to remove excess liquid. Beat the eggs lightly and add them to the bread together with the onions. Add the salt, pepper, thyme, nutmeg, and lemon zest and blend all the ingredients well.

4. Preheat the oven to 400 degrees F.

Veal:
$3^{1}/_2$ pounds boned veal breast, with a pocket cut into it
3 tablespoons clarified butter
1 carrot, peeled and finely chopped
1 medium yellow onion, peeled and finely chopped
1 bay leaf
1 ($14^{1}/_2$-ounce) can chicken or veal broth
2 tablespoons all-purpose flour

8 to 10 servings

5. For the veal: Rinse the meat under cold water and pat dry with paper towels. Rub with salt and pepper and stuff the pocket loosely with the bread mixture. Make sure not to overstuff it. Mold the surface with your hands for an even shape. Sew up the pocket with a trussing needle and twine, or close with small skewers.

6. Heat the clarified butter in the skillet and evenly brown the stuffed breast. Move it to a roasting pan large enough to hold the meat with the vegetables around it. Pour the clarified butter from the skillet over the meat. Cover the pan with a lid or aluminum foil and braise in the oven for 1 hour.

7. Arrange the carrot, onion, and bay leaf around the meat. Pour the broth over the meat and vegetables. Reduce the heat to 375 degrees and braise, uncovered, for about 1 hour, basting frequently, until the meat is tender.

8. Remove the meat from the oven and keep warm. Deglaze the pan with $1/2$ cup hot water or more, if necessary. Strain the juices and pour them into a small saucepan. Mix the flour with $1/4$ cup water. Whisk into the gravy and simmer until the sauce thickens. Season with salt and pepper. Remove the twine from the meat. Slice the roast and serve the gravy separately.

Trout in Sorrel Sauce

Forelle mit Sauerampfersoße

Native German trout (*Bachforelle*) is an endangered species today. Most trout consumed in Germany today is rainbow trout, a cross of different North American species that was introduced to Germany in the 1880s. Rainbow trout, which can also be farm raised, is more adaptable to environmental changes and there is concern it might drive out the remaining population of native trout.

There are many regional recipes for trout, and even music composed for the fish, such as the famous *Trout Quintett* by nineteenth-century German composer Franz Schubert, written during a summer vacation in Austria.

---

2 tablespoons unsalted butter
4 whole rainbow trout, gutted but including head and tail
Salt and freshly milled black pepper
1 cup dry white wine
2 packed cups (about 2 ounces) fresh sorrel
1/4 cup packed fresh flat-leaf parsley
1/4 cup heavy cream

4 servings

1. Preheat the oven to 450 degrees F. Use 1 tablespoon of the butter to grease an ovenproof dish large enough to hold the trout in a single layer.

2. Wash the trout under cold running water and pat dry with paper towels. Season with salt and pepper. Place the trout in the prepared dish. Pour the wine over the trout. Cover the dish well with aluminum foil and cook for 10 to 15 minutes, or until the fish flakes easily with a fork. Keep warm.

3. While the fish is baking, finely chop the sorrel and parsley by hand or briefly in a food processor. Heat the remaining 1 tablespoon butter in a small saucepan and sauté the herbs.

4. Carefully pour the liquid off the cooked fish and add it to the herbs. Cook over medium to high heat until the sauce thickens. Reduce the heat. The sauce should only simmer at this point. Whisk in the cream and reduce the sauce a little more. Season with salt and pepper. Pour the sauce over the trout and serve at once.

Pike Quenelles in Dill Sauce

Hechtklößchen mit Dillsoße

This delicate fish specialty originated in the southern state of Baden-Württemberg. Although the original recipe calls for freshwater pike, you can substitute farm-raised tilapia, which you should have no problem finding. The quenelles can be served with linguine or plain white rice.

Quenelles:
*2 slices soft white bread,
  crust removed*
1 cup heavy cream, chilled
*1 pound pike or tilapia
  fillet*
1 egg white, cold
*Salt and freshly milled
  white pepper*
Pinch of ground nutmeg
*5 teaspoons canned
  seafood base (to make
  1 1/4 quarts liquid)*
1 cup dry white wine

Dill sauce:
1 tablespoon unsalted butter
*1 shallot, peeled and
  minced*
1/2 cup dry white wine
1/2 cup heavy cream
*1 tablespoon finely
  chopped fresh dill*
*Salt and freshly milled
  white pepper*

6 servings

1. For the quenelles: Place a metal mixing bowl in the freezer. Put the bread in a separate bowl and pour the cream over it. Mash with a fork to a smooth consistency and chill.

2. Grind the fish very finely in a food processor. Place it in the chilled metal bowl and stir in the egg white. Season with salt, pepper, and nutmeg and mix with the bread mixture. Chill.

3. Dissolve the seafood base in $1\frac{1}{4}$ quarts water. Add the wine and bring to a boil in a wide saucepan. The pan needs to be big enough to hold the quenelles in a single layer. Reduce the heat; the liquid should just simmer, or the quenelles will fall apart.

4. Using two coffee spoons, shape small dumplings and gently lower them into the broth. Cover and simmer for 15 to a maximum of 20 minutes.

5. In the meantime, make the sauce: Melt the butter in a small saucepan and sauté the shallot until translucent. Add the wine and simmer for 10 to 15 minutes. When the sauce is slightly reduced, stir in the cream and dill and reheat but do not boil. Season with salt and pepper.

6. Remove the quenelles from the broth with a slotted spoon and place in a warmed shallow serving dish. Pour the sauce over them and serve immediately.

Perch with Capers in Wine Sauce

Goldbarsch auf badische Art

Baden is Germany's southernmost and third largest winegrowing area. It is the only region in Germany classified as a "B" winegrowing area by the European Union, a particularly high standard for winegrowing and winemaking. The elaborate circle of "B" winegrowing areas also includes Alsace, Champagne, and the Loire Valley in France.

Ocean perch is also known as rockfish, rosefish, or (golden) redfish.

6 to 8 skinned ocean perch fillets (about 2 pounds)
Juice of 1 lemon
Salt
4 large or 6 medium ripe tomatoes
$1/4$ cup drained capers
2 tablespoons finely diced tart cooking apple
2 tablespoons finely chopped yellow onion
2 tablespoons finely chopped seedless cucumber
2 tablespoons finely diced Black Forest ham
2 tablespoons unsalted butter, chilled
$1/2$ cup dry white wine
4 slices Swiss cheese
Freshly milled black pepper
2 tablespoons coarsely chopped fresh flat-leaf parsley
6 servings

1. Briefly rinse the fish fillets under running water and pat dry with paper towels. Put them on a large platter and sprinkle with the lemon juice and salt. Set aside.

2. Bring water to a boil in a large pot and blanch the tomatoes for 1 minute to loosen their skins. Take them out with a slotted spoon, drain, and cool. Core, peel, halve, and seed the tomatoes. Cut into $1/4$-inch slices.

3. Preheat the oven to 350 degrees F. Grease an ovenproof dish large enough to hold the fish in a single layer. Spread the tomato slices on the bottom of the dish and place the fish on top.

4. Mix the capers, apple, onion, cucumber, and ham and spread the mixture evenly on the fillets. Cut the butter into small chunks and sprinkle it over the fish. Bake for 15 minutes.

5. Pour the wine over the fish and top with the cheese. Bake for 10 minutes, or until the fish is opaque and cooked through.

6. Season with salt and pepper and garnish with parsley. Serve immediately with plain rice.

Potato Fingers

Schupfnudeln

Swabians call them *Schupfnudeln*, Bavarians *Fingernudeln*, and in Baden they are called *Bubespitzle*. The formula for these crisp potato fingers, however, is the same everywhere.

In Swabia, *Schupfnudeln* are often served with sauerkraut. For a firmer consistency, the potatoes have to be cooked a few hours ahead.

1½ pounds russet potatoes
2 eggs
1 cup all-purpose flour
Salt and freshly milled
*   black pepper*
Pinch of ground nutmeg
¼ cup butter or vegetable
*   oil*

6 servings

---

1. Boil the potatoes in their skins until tender. Drain and cool for several hours.

2. Peel the cooked potatoes and pass them through a potato ricer or mash with a potato masher. Mix with the eggs and flour. Season with salt, pepper, and nutmeg.

3. Using your hands, shape the potato mixture into fingers with two pointy ends. If the dough sticks to your hands, moisten them with cold water.

4. Bring water to a boil in a large pot and reduce the heat. Drop small batches of the fingers into the just simmering water. Cook until they float on the top. Take out of the water with a slotted spoon and drop into a bowl of cold water. Remove them with the slotted spoon and drain in a colander.

5. Heat the butter and sauté the fingers until golden brown and crisp on all sides. Drain on paper towels and keep warm until all fingers are done.

Bread Dumplings with Mushroom Ragout

Semmelknödel mit Pilzragout

If Thuringia and Bavaria held a contest for the largest variety of dumplings, I do not know who would win. I counted more than ten varieties for each state, and they all taste and look different.

Semmelknödel are dumplings made from dry rolls. They are Bavaria's most famous dumplings. *Semmelknödel* are typically served with mushroom ragout. The ragout tastes best when made with different kinds of mushrooms, and even better with wild mushrooms, but you can always mix easily available varieties such as white and portobello mushrooms.

Dumplings:
6 (4- to 5-inch) dry rolls
1 cup lukewarm milk
1 tablespoon vegetable oil
1 medium yellow onion, peeled and finely chopped
3 tablespoons finely chopped fresh parsley
3 eggs
Salt
Freshly milled black pepper
1/8 teaspoon ground nutmeg
All-purpose flour to thicken the dough (optional)

1. For the dumplings: Cut the rolls into very thin slices. If the rolls are soft, spread the slices on a large baking sheet, set the oven to 350 degrees F and leave them in the oven until dry. Put the rolls in a large bowl and pour the milk over them. Stir and let stand at least 20 minutes.

2. Meanwhile, heat the oil and sauté the onion until translucent. Add the parsley and cook for another 3 minutes.

3. Lightly beat the eggs. Add to the bread with the onion mixture, salt, pepper, and nutmeg. Mix thoroughly.

4. Bring salted water to a boil in a large, wide pot. Reduce the heat and drop a small test dumpling into the simmering water—if it falls apart, add 1 tablespoon flour and test again. Repeat until the consistency is right.

5. Divide the dough into 8 equal parts and shape round dumplings with moistened hands. Bring the water back to a boil, reduce the heat, and lower the dumplings into the simmering water. Make sure that you do not overfill the pot—the dumplings should float freely in the water. Cook for 20 minutes, partially covered. Remove with a slotted spoon. Keep warm in a covered dish.

Ragout:

1 tablespoon vegetable oil

2 shallots, peeled and finely minced

1 pound mixed mushrooms, cleaned and trimmed

1 cup light cream

1 tablespoon cognac or any other good brandy

Salt and freshly milled white pepper

8 servings

6. For the ragout: Heat the oil in a large skillet and sauté the shallots until translucent. Cut the mushrooms into very thin slices and add to the shallots. Cook over low to medium heat for 15 minutes, or until the mushrooms are soft, stirring occasionally.

7. Reduce the heat, pour in the cream, and add the cognac. Season with salt and pepper and simmer for 5 minutes, or until the sauce thickens. Serve the dumplings topped with the mushrooms.

Note: Leftover *Semmelknödel* can be sautéed in butter or vegetable oil.

White Radish Salad

Rettichsalat

The large white radish is an indispensable ingredient of a typical Bavarian *Brotzeit* (hearty snack), which many outdoor beer gardens allow their patrons to bring along. For that occasion, the radish is simply cut into very thin slices and sprinkled with a bit of salt. Here is the recipe for radish salad, a Bavarian classic that requires minimum preparation.

1 large white radish
1 tablespoon plus 1 teaspoon white wine vinegar
2 tablespoons plus 1 teaspoon vegetable oil
Salt and freshly milled black pepper
1 tablespoon snipped chives

4 servings

1. Peel the radish and slice it into thin disks, using a mandoline or the proper slicing disk of a food processor.

2. Whisk the vinegar with the vegetable oil, salt, and pepper. Toss the radish slices with the vinaigrette and sprinkle with chives.

Cabbage Salad with Caraway and Crunchy Bacon Bits

Krautsalat mit Kümmel und Speck

This most popular of all Bavarian salads is usually served with pork roast or suckling pig. It should stand for a day to develop its full flavor. Most original recipes do not call for blanching the cabbage but I recommend doing so, as it makes the cabbage easier to digest.

1 small young (white) cabbage (1½ pounds)
¼ cup vegetable oil
¼ cup white wine vinegar
2 teaspoons salt
Freshly milled black pepper
½ teaspoon coarsely ground caraway
4 thin slices (2 ounces) lean center-cut bacon

6 servings

1. Remove the outer green leaves from the cabbage and discard them. Quarter the cabbage, remove the core, and finely shred. Bring water to a boil in a large pot and blanch the cabbage for 1 minute. Drain very well in a colander.

2. Whisk the oil, vinegar, salt, pepper, and caraway together in a large bowl. Toss the cabbage with the vinaigrette so that it is evenly coated. Cover and refrigerate for several hours to 1 day.

3. Place the bacon in a cold skillet and cook until crisp. Drain on paper towels and toss with the cabbage just before serving.

Spiced Red Cabbage with Apples

Rotkraut

Red cabbage is a traditional German accompaniment for many holiday dishes, such as Christmas goose, duck, pork roast, or game. The ultimate refinement is to add red currant jelly at the end. Red currants are much more popular in Germany than in North America, where you can find red currant jelly in specialty food stores.

Red cabbage is very well-suited for freezing and lends itself to preparation ahead of time—it tastes better reheated.

1 small red cabbage (2 pounds)
1 tablespoon honey
1 cup red wine vinegar
Salt
2 tablespoons clarified butter
2 shallots, peeled and finely minced
3 medium tart cooking apples, cored, peeled, and cut into small chunks
1 bay leaf
Freshly milled black pepper
1 medium yellow onion, peeled
3 whole cloves
2 tablespoons red currant jelly

6 servings

1. Remove the outer leaves of the cabbage and discard. Quarter and remove the core with a sharp knife. Wash the cabbage and shred finely.

2. Mix the honey, vinegar, and salt in a large bowl. Toss the cabbage with the vinegar mixture and let stand for 1 hour so the cabbage can release its juice.

3. Heat the clarified butter in a large saucepan and sauté the shallots until translucent. Add the apples and cook until they start to soften. Add the cabbage, bay leaf, pepper, and 1 cup cold water.

4. Stud the onion with the cloves and place it right in the middle of the cabbage. Cover and cook over low heat for 1 hour, or until the cabbage is soft. Stir occasionally and check frequently for consistency, adding water if necessary.

5. Stir in the jelly. Remove the onion and bay leaf before serving.

Potato Dumplings

Seidene Klöße

I only started to make dumplings from scratch after I moved to the United States. As most people in Germany, I had always used packaged dumplings, which come in a wide array of flavors, tastes, and brands. But making dumplings from scratch is easy, and the result is infinitely better. It only requires a little bit of planning, as the cooked potatoes have to stand for several hours before processing them.

When making dumplings, use only yellow potatoes; otherwise you end up with grayish dumplings that look less appealing although they still taste good.

These dumplings are a great fit for meat dishes with sauce or gravy.

---

2 pounds starchy yellow potatoes (Yukon Gold)
$\frac{1}{2}$ cup dry breadcrumbs
$\frac{1}{4}$ cup all-purpose flour
3 eggs
Salt
Pinch of ground nutmeg

6 servings

---

1. Boil the potatoes in their skins until tender. Drain and cool. Peel and pass through a potato ricer. Put in a container and refrigerate for 6 to 8 hours.

2. Mix the breadcrumbs and flour with the mashed potatoes. Lightly beat the eggs and mix them thoroughly with the potato mixture. Season with salt and nutmeg.

3. Bring salted water to a boil in a pot large enough for all dumplings to float freely.

4. Shape a small test dumpling and drop it into the water. If it falls apart, add 1 tablespoon flour at a time and test another dumpling.

5. Shape the dough into 12 round dumplings with moistened hands. Reduce the heat—the water should only simmer—and carefully lower the dumplings into the water. Simmer for 20 to 25 minutes. Remove the dumplings with a slotted spoon and drain. Serve immediately or cover well and keep warm until serving.

Spinach Buttons

Spinatknöpfli

Even for Germans who are not familiar with this dish, its geographic origin is easy to determine. In the dialect of southwestern Germany, many nouns are used in a special diminutive form. Not that Baden-Württemberg is a miniature state; on the contrary, it is the third largest German federal state. The diminutive is just a homey way of speaking. *Spinatknöpfli* are indeed very small noodles. A potato ricer does a great job in producing their typical knot-shape.

$1/2$ pound spinach, stemmed, trimmed, washed, and dried
$2 3/4$ cups all-purpose flour
1 teaspoon salt
3 eggs
$1/4$ teaspoon ground nutmeg
Unsalted butter for sautéing

6 to 8 servings

1. Puree the spinach in a food processor. Start with a small batch, adding up to $1/2$ cup water to keep the blade from running dry. Then add the rest of the spinach and puree, frequently scraping down the sides of the food processor bowl.

2. Mix the flour and salt in a large bowl and make a well in the middle. Crack the eggs into the well and stir them into the flour, starting in the middle and working your way outward. Slowly add $1/2$ cup water, the nutmeg, and the spinach paste. Work into a smooth dough with the kneading attachment of an electric mixer. The dough should form bubbles and detach easily from the bottom of the bowl. If it is too sticky, add a few teaspoons of flour, one at a time. Cover and let stand for 15 minutes.

3. Bring salted water to a boil in a large pot. Spread a small portion of the dough on the small side of a wet cutting board and scrape thin stripes off with a long, sharp knife, or press small portions of the dough into the water through a potato ricer. Reduce the heat and simmer until the noodles rise to the surface.

4. Remove the noodles with a slotted spoon and place them in a colander. Rinse with cold water, drain, and keep warm. Process the rest of the dough the same way. If you have to use your hands, make sure that they are moist so the dough does not stick to them (I always have a bowl of cold water standing by).

5. Melt butter in a large skillet and sauté the noodles for 3 to 5 minutes. Serve immediately.

Red Currant Meringue Pie

Träublestorte

Tart red currants are fantastic in pies. *Träublestorte* is a classic from Swabia. This is an adaptation of my grandmother's recipe, with a less buttery dough.

Butter is used quite freely in German baking. Recipes calling for almost half a pound of butter are not uncommon. Unless butter is needed for texture, I do not think it is worth using in large amounts because butter in the United States and Canada contains an average of 81% milk fat, while most German butter has up to 85% milk fat. Without German butter, you cannot match results. This recipe is plenty tasty with just one stick of butter.

Dough:
2 cups plus 2 tablespoons all-purpose flour
1 stick plus 2½ tablespoons unsalted butter, softened
¼ cup plus 2 tablespoons sugar
Pinch of salt

Filling:
5 large egg whites
1 cup sugar
1 pound plus 2 ounces red currants, fresh or frozen

12 servings

1. For the dough: Process the flour, butter, sugar, and salt in a food processor or with a pastry blender, until the dough holds together in a ball. Wrap in plastic foil and refrigerate for 30 minutes.

2. Preheat the oven to 350 degrees F. Grease a 10-inch springform pan.

3. Roll the dough on a floured work surface to fit the pan plus a 1-inch edge. Carefully drop the dough into the pan. Press the dough against the edges and trim the excess with a sharp knife. Pierce the dough in several places with a fork.

4. For the filling: Beat the egg whites, gradually adding the sugar, until they are shiny and stand in stiff peaks. Fold in the red currants, taking care not to smash them, especially if they were frozen. Pour the filling into the pan and even it out with a spatula.

5. Bake in the preheated oven for 60 minutes. If the top gets too dark, loosely cover it with a greased sheet of aluminum foil and continue baking until the meringue is lightly browned. Let cool for a few minutes, then carefully run a knife around the crust and remove the rim of the springform pan. Cool completely on a cake rack.

Currants vs. Currants

Red and black currants are tart berries and a signature ingredient in many traditional German recipes. They grow on shrubs and are not to be confused with dried currants, which come from a small seedless grape, the Corinth grape. In Germany, dried currants are called *Korinthen* so there is no confusion there.

Unlike red currants, black currants are less palatable raw and are usually made into jams and jellies.

Bavarian Cream with Raspberry Coulis

Bayerische Crème mit Himbeersoße

Bavarian cream is as famous as its origin is mysterious. It might have been invented by French cooks at the court of the Wittelsbacher, the powerful dynasty that ruled Bavaria for more than seven centuries until the last Bavarian king abdicated in 1918. Or possibly, it was first made by Isabeau de Bavière, daughter of a Bavarian duke who married King Charles VI of France in 1385. Whichever version you prefer, one thing is clear: Bavarian cream is deeply entrenched in history and a royal treat in the true sense of the word.

Bavarian cream:
$1\frac{1}{2}$ cups heavy cream
3 ($\frac{1}{4}$-ounce) envelopes
  unflavored gelatin
6 egg yolks
1 cup plus 2 tablespoons
  confectioners' sugar
2 cups milk
Seeds from 2 vanilla
  beans, or 2 tablespoons
  pure vanilla bean paste

1. For the Bavarian cream: Chill a metal bowl and the whisk attachment of an electric mixer in the freezer for a few minutes. Then whip the cream until it stands in soft peaks. Chill until needed.

2. Soak the gelatin in $\frac{2}{3}$ cup cold water for 10 minutes.

3. Beat the egg yolks with the confectioners' sugar in a large metal bowl until they are pale yellow and have a thick, creamy consistency.

4. Bring the milk and vanilla seeds to a boil in a saucepan, stirring occasionally to make sure the milk does not scorch at the bottom of the pan. Remove from the heat and slowly pour the milk into the egg yolk mixture, stirring constantly.

5. Transfer the egg mixture to the top of a double boiler, or place the metal bowl over a pot of gently boiling water. Continue stirring over simmering water until the mixture coats a wooden spoon.

6. Gradually stir in the dissolved gelatin and place the bowl over a large bowl of ice water. Make sure that the mixture is lump-free. If you discover any lumps, quickly strain the cream through a fine sieve. Continue stirring vigorously until the cream starts to cool and stiffen. This is the time to fold in the whipped cream.

7. Immediately pour the Bavarian cream into a large glass serving bowl or individual serving dishes and chill for several hours until set.

Raspberry coulis:
1 1/2 pints fresh raspberries, or 2 (12-ounce) packages frozen raspberries
1/2 cup confectioners' sugar

8 to 10 servings

8. For the raspberry coulis: Cook the raspberries and the confectioners' sugar over low heat for 10 to 15 minutes, stirring occasionally. Strain through a fine sieve to remove any seeds and chill.

9. Take the Bavarian cream and coulis out of the refrigerator 30 minutes before serving so they can develop their full flavor. Top each serving of Bavarian cream with a few spoonfuls of coulis.

Honey Parfait with Kirsch

Honigparfait

Honey from trees typically growing in the forest, such as fir, pine, and spruce, is quite popular in Germany. It has a dark color and a unique flavor. In Germany, only honey from white spruce may be called spruce honey (*Tannenhonig*). One of the areas where fine spruce honey is collected is the Black Forest, where this frozen custard dessert originates. It is sublime with a slice of warm fruit pie.

You can use any kind of dark golden honey except buckwheat honey, as its flavor is too pungent for this delicate parfait.

2 eggs, separated
$\frac{1}{3}$ cup golden honey
2 tablespoons kirsch
$\frac{3}{4}$ cup heavy cream
Fresh fruit or ground
cinnamon for garnish

6 servings

1. Put the egg yolks and honey in the top of a double boiler or a metal bowl placed over a pot of gently boiling water. Whisk until the egg yolks develop a very foamy consistency. Place the bowl over a bowl of ice water and continue stirring. Add the kirsch.

2. Whip the cream until it forms soft peaks. In a separate bowl, beat the egg whites until they stand in stiff peaks. Fold the whipped cream and the egg whites into the egg yolk mixture. Pour the parfait into a round container and freeze for at least 4 hours, or until firm.

3. To release the parfait from the container, hold the closed container upside down under hot running water for a few seconds. Unmold the parfait onto a plate and cut it into thick slices. Serve with slivers of fresh fruit, or dust with a little bit of ground cinnamon.

Snowballs in Vanilla Sauce

Schneeeier in Vanillesoße

This is the Bavarian version of Floating Islands.

4 eggs, separated
Pinch of salt
1/3 cup plus 1/4 cup plus
* 3 tablespoons sugar*
1 teaspoon vanilla extract
4 cups plus 1/2 cup milk
Seeds of 1 vanilla bean,
* or 1 tablespoon pure*
* vanilla bean paste*
2 teaspoons cornstarch

6 servings

1. Beat the egg whites with a pinch of salt until they form soft peaks. Gradually add 1/3 cup plus 1/4 cup of the sugar and the vanilla extract and continue beating until the egg whites stand in stiff peaks.

2. Bring 4 cups of the milk and the vanilla seeds or paste to a boil in a large saucepan, stirring occasionally to make sure the milk does not scorch at the bottom. Remove from the heat.

3. Using two small spoons, form the egg whites into 1½-inch football-shaped dumplings, a few at a time. Return the pan to the heat. Gently lower a few of the dumplings into the milk and simmer for 1 to 2 minutes on each side. The dumplings should be poached in small batches so they do not touch. Remove the dumplings with a slotted spoon and place on a large platter in a single layer.

4. Strain the milk through a fine sieve and return it to the saucepan. In a small bowl, combine the remaining ½ cup milk with the remaining 3 tablespoons sugar and whisk in the egg yolks and cornstarch. Add this to the milk in the saucepan and bring to a gentle boil and cook until the sauce thickens, stirring constantly.

5. Transfer the sauce to an ovenproof glass dish, set the snowballs on top, and turn on the broiler. Place the dish on the rack in the top third of the oven. When the dumplings are lightly browned on top immediately remove the dish from the oven. Watch it carefully as this only takes a couple of minutes. Chill before serving.

Steamed Dumplings with Wine Sauce

Dampfnudeln mit Weinschaumsoße

When I asked my family and friends in Germany and German expatriates about their favorite regional dishes, *Dampfnudeln* was a clear winner, usually expressed with a nostalgic undertone. My grandmother prepared *Dampfnudeln* for me, and the prospect of having them for lunch made me rush on my 30-minute walk home from school to her place. When I asked her for her recipe, she did not want to believe at first that anybody in this time and day would have the time and patience for this sort of cooking. I disagreed—with a little bit more than an hour of preparation, *Dampfnudeln* are really not that time-consuming, and definitely worth the effort.

Dampfnudeln can be served warm with wine sauce, vanilla sauce (*see page 51*), or fruit compote.

Wine sauce:
4 eggs
Pinch of salt
$\frac{1}{4}$ cup sugar
1 tablespoon cornstarch
$\frac{1}{2}$ cup milk
1 cup dry white wine,
    at room temperature

Dumplings:
1 ($\frac{1}{4}$-ounce) envelope
    active dry yeast
4 tablespoons plus
1 teaspoon sugar
$1\frac{1}{2}$ cups lukewarm milk,
    plus more as needed
$1\frac{3}{4}$ cups all-purpose flour
1 teaspoon salt
4 tablespoons unsalted butter
1 egg

8 servings

1. For the wine sauce: Separate 2 of the eggs. Beat 2 whole eggs with 2 eggs yolks, the salt, sugar, and cornstarch until foamy. Pour the mixture into a small saucepan. Add the milk and cook over low heat until the sauce thickens and the cornstarch becomes clear, stirring constantly. Whisk in the wine and remove from the heat.

2. Beat the remaining 2 egg whites until they stand in stiff peaks. Fold them into the hot sauce and chill.

3. For the dumplings: Combine the yeast and 1 teaspoon sugar with $\frac{1}{2}$ cup of the milk in a small bowl. Let stand for 10 minutes until frothy.

4. Mix the flour and salt in a large bowl. Melt 2 tablespoons of the butter and add to the yeast mixture. Add the mixture to the flour along with the egg and 2 tablespoons of the sugar. Work all ingredients into smooth dough, using the kneading attachment of an electric mixer. Cover with a damp dishtowel and let stand for 40 minutes in a warm place.

5. Place the dough on a floured work surface and form a roll about 10 inches long. Cut into 8 equal portions and shape into small round dumplings with floured hands. Cover and let stand for 10 minutes in a warm place.

6. Slowly heat the remaining 1 cup milk with the remaining 2 tablespoons sugar and remaining 2 tablespoons butter in a large, wide saucepan with a tight-fitting cover. The milk should fill the pan at least ½ inch deep. Place the dumplings in the milk, about ½ inch apart. Cover the pan immediately with a warmed lid (hold the lid under hot running water for a few seconds and dry it thoroughly afterward). Cook over medium heat for about 30 minutes—opening the pan during the cooking process is an absolute no-no or your dumplings will collapse.

7. Open the pan only when you hear a sizzling sound, which indicates that the dumplings have a nice brown crust on the bottom and are light and shiny on the top—this is exactly the way they should be. Remove the dumplings with a metal spatula one by one and place them bottom up on a large serving platter. Serve the dumplings warm with chilled wine sauce.

Bavarian French Toast with Prune Filling

Zwetschgenpavesen

The name *Zwetschgenpavesen* is believed to come from the Italian word *pavese*, designating a shield used to protect the archer. This Bavarian version of a refined French toast will certainly shield you against hunger for a while—it is quite filling. Originally, *Zwetschgenpavesen* were only served during the days immediately following the Roman Catholic holiday of *Lichtmeß* (Maria Candlemas) on February 2. This day marks the beginning of a new farm year, when farm workers were allowed to change their employer. Farmer's wives would serve *Zwetschgenpavesen* to bid farewell to the parting workers and to welcome new ones. Today, bakeries in Bavaria make *Zwetschgenpavesen* year-round.

The filling can be made with dried prunes as described below, or with Plum Butter made from fresh plums (*see page 56*). The prune preserves can be prepared in advance, as they keep for 3 to 4 weeks.

Prune preserves:
*$1\frac{1}{4}$ cups ($\frac{1}{2}$ pound)
   pitted prunes
$\frac{1}{4}$ cinnamon stick
1 strip organic lemon peel
Sugar*

1. For the prune preserves: Puree the prunes with $\frac{1}{4}$ cup water in a food processor. Put them in a small saucepan and add the cinnamon stick, lemon peel, and sugar to taste. Check for sweetness—if the prunes are already sweet, you might not want to add any sugar at all.

2. Stir in $\frac{1}{4}$ cup water, cover, and simmer until the prunes develop a thick consistency, stirring frequently. If the prunes are too dry, add water, a teaspoon at a time. Remove the cinnamon stick and lemon peel. Cool and refrigerate in an airtight container. It will keep for several weeks.

Toast:
12 slices soft white bread
1 cup milk
3 eggs
1 to 2 tablespoons unsalted
  butter or vegetable
  shortening
Sugar for sprinkling
Ground cinnamon for
  sprinkling

6 servings

3. For the toast: Evenly spread a generous amount of preserves on half the slices of bread and place a matching slice on top of each.

4. Pour the milk in a shallow plate. Lightly beat the eggs and pour them in another shallow plate.

5. Melt the butter in a large nonstick skillet. Dip each sandwich into the milk and drain on a platter. Then, dip each sandwich into the eggs on both sides and sauté until golden brown and crisp on both sides.

6. Mix the sugar with a few pinches of cinnamon and sprinkle on the toast.

Note: *Zwetschgenpavesen* are best right from the stovetop but they can also be eaten cold. Just don't reheat them in the microwave—they will get soggy.

Glazed Christmas Rounds

Elisenlebkuchen

If the abbots in Franconian monasteries had been stricter, the finest of German gingerbreads would not have been invented. Nuns and monks started to use holy hosts (Eucharist wafers) to produce gingerbread according to their own secret recipes. But the word and the formula spread quickly, and soon a whole new industry of specialized gingerbread bakers (*Lebküchner*) developed in and around the city of Nuremberg, which became the world gingerbread capital and remains so today. It was no coincidence that Nuremberg played this important role. The city was at the center of many important medieval trade routes, including an old spice route, so the necessary ingredients were available.

Only gingerbread made in Nuremberg can legitimately be labeled *Nürnberger Lebkuchen*. The finest of those gingerbreads are the flourless *Elisenlebkuchen*, the masterpiece of the trade since the early nineteenth century.

In Germany, precut edible paper, also called rice paper, is readily available, especially around Christmas. In the United States, you can find sheets of it in baking supply stores.

Elisenlebkuchen come glazed with sugar or chocolate, or plain. This recipe glazes one half of the rounds with sugar glaze and the other half with chocolate glaze. If you want only one kind of glaze, double the desired glaze ingredients.

---

4 eggs
$1\frac{1}{4}$ cups confectioners' sugar
Pinch of ground mace
Pinch of ground cloves
Pinch of ground allspice
2 teaspoons ground cinnamon
Pinch of salt
Grated zest of 1 organic lemon
$1\frac{1}{4}$ cups shelled unpeeled almonds
$1\frac{1}{4}$ cups chopped hazelnuts
$\frac{1}{3}$ cup ($2\frac{1}{2}$ ounces) candied orange peel

Continued

1. Beat the eggs with the sugar until foamy. Add the mace, cloves, allspice, cinnamon, salt, and lemon zest.

2. Preheat the oven to 350 degrees F.

3. Grind the almonds and hazelnuts very finely in a food processor and combine with the eggs. Chop the orange peel and citron very finely and add to the mixture.

4. Place the edible paper disks on a baking sheet and spread each with the mixture about $\frac{1}{2}$ inch thick, leaving about $\frac{1}{4}$ inch all around. Bake for 20 minutes. The rounds should still be moist and soft. You can check this by gently pressing on the bottom (paper) side. Place the rounds on a cake rack and glaze while warm.

$1\frac{1}{4}$ cups (6 ounces) diced candied citron or candied lemon peel
20 to 24 edible paper disks (3 to $3\frac{1}{2}$ inches in diameter)

Sugar glaze:
$\frac{3}{4}$ cup confectioners' sugar
1 to 2 tablespoons hot water

Chocolate glaze:
4 (1-ounce) squares semisweet chocolate
$1\frac{1}{2}$ teaspoons unsalted butter

20 to 24 pieces

5. For the sugar glaze: Mix the confectioners' sugar with the hot water until the sugar is completely dissolved, adding just as much water as needed for a thick but spreadable consistency. Coat the warm rounds with the glaze and let it dry completely.

6. For the chocolate glaze: Melt the chocolate and butter in the top of a double boiler or in a metal bowl set over a pot with boiling water. Stir constantly until smooth. Cool slightly, then spread the glaze evenly over the warm rounds and let it dry completely.

7. Store the cookies in an airtight, preferably metal, container. They keep for up to a month.

Mini-Soufflés with Berry Compote

Pfitzauf

Pfitzauf is a soufflé-like pastry from Swabia that should be eaten right out of the oven. You can serve it with mixed berry compote, strawberries in syrup, or any other fresh, juicy fruit. There are special *Pfitzauf* molds made of terracotta or metal, but a muffin pan, preferably with a nonstick finish, will work just fine.

Compote:
1/2 pint fresh red raspberries
1 pint blueberries
1/4 cup sugar
1 tablespoon port

Soufflés:
2/3 cup all-purpose flour
Pinch of salt
1 cup milk
2 eggs, lightly beaten
4 tablespoons unsalted
* butter, softened*

12 soufflés

1. For the compote: Pick over the berries and remove any culls and put the berries in a small saucepan. Add 2 tablespoons of water. Cover and simmer for 3 to 5 minutes, or until the blueberries pop and release their juice. Stir in the sugar and port and chill.

2. For the soufflés: Preheat the oven to 375 degrees F. Generously grease a 12-cup muffin pan.

3. Mix the flour with the salt. Add the milk and eggs. Melt the butter and stir into the batter.

4. Pour the batter into the prepared muffin pan and bake for 30 minutes, or until golden brown. Serve warm with whipped cream and the chilled compote.

Dried Fruit Loaf

Hutzelbrot

This Swabian Christmas specialty is packed with dried fruit and nuts. The name comes from the Swabian word for dried pears, *Hutzeln*.

The preparation of the dried fruit has to be started the day before. The bread is very suitable for freezing.

2 cups ($\frac{1}{2}$ pound) whole dried pears
$1\frac{1}{4}$ cups ($\frac{1}{2}$ pound) pitted prunes
$1\frac{1}{3}$ cups ($\frac{1}{2}$ pound) dried figs, stems removed
$\frac{1}{2}$ cup raisins
$\frac{3}{4}$ cup (5 ounces) dried apricots
1 cup (5 ounces) dried and pitted dates
$\frac{1}{3}$ cup diced candied citron or candied lemon peel
$\frac{1}{3}$ cup candied orange peel
$\frac{1}{4}$ cup kirsch or dry red wine
3 ($\frac{1}{4}$-ounce) envelopes active dry yeast
$3\frac{1}{4}$ cups bread flour
$\frac{1}{3}$ cup sugar
1 teaspoon salt
1 teaspoon ground cinnamon
1 teaspoon ground aniseed
$\frac{1}{4}$ teaspoon ground cloves
1 cup coarsely chopped hazelnuts
1 cup coarsely chopped blanched almonds, plus additional whole almonds for garnish

2 loaves

1. Put the pears and prunes in a bowl and pour cold water over them so they are just covered. Soak for 3 hours. Cook them in their soaking water over low heat for about 20 minutes, or until soft. Drain in a sieve and reserve the liquid.

2. Wash the figs, raisins, and apricots and pat dry. Chop the pears, prunes, figs, apricots, and dates. Mix together with the raisins, citron, and candied orange peel. Pour kirsch over the mixture, cover, and let stand for 8 to 12 hours.

3. Combine the yeast with ¼ cup of the reserved fruit liquid in a small bowl and let stand for 10 minutes until frothy.

4. Mix the flour, sugar, and salt in a large bowl. Add the yeast mixture and knead into a firm dough, using the kneading attachment of an electric mixer. Gradually add about 1 cup of the fruit liquid until the dough reaches a smooth consistency. Cover and let rise in a warm place for at least 1 hour.

5. Work the cinnamon, aniseed, cloves, hazelnuts, chopped almonds, and chopped and soaked fruit into the dough well. Divide the dough into two equal portions and shape each portion into an oblong loaf about 8 inches long. Place the loaves on a greased baking sheet, and let rise for 20 minutes.

6. Preheat the oven to 375 degrees F. Garnish the loaves with whole almonds and brush with the fruit liquid. Bake for 1 to 1½ hours, or until brown.

Lemon-Rice Cake

Augsburger Reistorte

Sophie Juliane Weiler, cookbook author and creator of this cake, was a pastor's wife in the Bavarian city of Augsburg. In the 1780s, she published the *Augsburgisches Kochbuch*, which went through numerous printings in the following decades and was even released in an expanded edition by her descendants in 1844.

When I initially prepared this cake, I was surprised by the amount of lemons, which seemed quite extravagant for the time. Lemons certainly do not grow in Germany, so they had to be imported from a Mediterranean country, most likely Italy. But how could a pastor's wife in the late-eighteenth century get ahold of several of these exotic fruits for just one cake? I found the answer when I served the cake to history-savvy friends. Augsburg had been a leading center of worldwide trade and finance since the Middle Ages, and was home to the Fugger family, powerful merchants. In a privileged city like this, lemons must have been so readily available that Frau Weiler felt encouraged to include this cake in her cookbook.

Dough:
2¼ cups all-purpose flour
1 stick plus 2⅔ tablespoons unsalted butter, chilled
2 teaspoons vanilla extract
⅓ cup sugar
1 egg

1. For the dough: Put the flour in a mixing bowl. Cut the butter into small chunks and work into the flour using a pastry cutter or food processor. Add the vanilla, sugar, and egg, and work into a smooth, thick dough.

2. Immediately roll two-thirds of the dough to a circle about 10 inches in diameter. Place the dough in a 9-inch springform pan and push it up the sides. With the remaining dough, roll a 9-inch circle and a small rope for the edge. Refrigerate.

3. For the filling: Heat the wine in a saucepan and add

Filling:

*2 cups plus 2 tablespoons
   dry white wine*
1¼ cups arborio rice
4 whole organic lemons
1¼ cups sugar
*¾ cup finely chopped
   candied citron or candied
   lemon peel*
1 egg

12 to 16 servings

the rice. Cover and cook over very low heat for 30 to 40 minutes, stirring frequently. If the rice starts to cook dry, add water 2 tablespoons to ¼ cup at a time, to prevent it from scorching.

4. Meanwhile, finely grate the zest of 2 of the lemons and juice the same 2 lemons. Heat the lemon juice with the lemon zest in a small saucepan and add the sugar. Stir until the sugar is entirely dissolved. Set aside.

5. Peel the 2 remaining lemons and remove the white pith and seeds. Finely chop the lemons. Stir them into the cooked rice along with the lemon syrup. Cook over low heat for 15 minutes, stirring occasionally. Add the candied citron. Let cool for 30 minutes.

6. Preheat the oven to 425 degrees F.

7. Evenly spread the filling on the shell in the spring-form pan. Place the dough circle on top and snugly fit the rope around the edge. Gently pinch waves into the edge using two fingers. Lightly beat the egg and brush it over the cake. Bake for 25 minutes, or until golden. Remove from the pan and cool.

Note: When stored in an airtight container or wrapped in aluminum foil, *Augsburger Reistorte* can be kept refrigerated for more than a week.

Seven–Layer Chocolate Cake

Prinzregententorte

This cake is laden with history, symbolism, and chocolate. The personal chef of the Bavarian prince regent Luitpold created the *Prinzregententorte* in 1886. The seven layers represent the seven districts of the former Kingdom of Bavaria.

Batter:
2 sticks unsalted butter, softened
$1\frac{1}{4}$ cups sugar
$\frac{2}{3}$ cup milk
Pinch of salt
3 eggs, separated
$\frac{1}{3}$ cup cornstarch
2 teaspoons vanilla extract
$1\frac{3}{4}$ cups all-purpose flour
2 teaspoons baking powder
$\frac{1}{2}$ teaspoon lemon juice

Filling:
4 (1-ounce) squares unsweetened chocolate
4 tablespoons unsalted butter, softened
1 cup confectioners' sugar

1. For the batter: Beat the butter with the sugar until light. Stir in the milk, salt, egg yolks, cornstarch, and vanilla. Mix the flour and baking powder and gradually add to the batter until well combined.

2. Beat the egg whites with the lemon juice until they stand in stiff peaks. Fold them into the batter.

3. Preheat the oven to 350 degrees F. Grease the bottom of a 9-inch springform pan (don't clip the rim on).

4. Divide the batter into 7 equal portions. Evenly spread the first batch of batter on the bottom. Bake for 6 to 8 minutes, or until golden. Bake the remaining 6 layers the same way, cleaning and greasing the pan between baking each layer. Cool each layer on a cake rack for several minutes, then place on a cake plate and put a paper towel between each layer as well as on top. Put a heavy dinner plate on top to keep all the layers nice and flat.

5. For the filling: Melt the chocolate in the top of a double boiler or in a metal bowl placed over a pot with boiling water. Remove the chocolate from the heat shortly before it is completely melted. Beat the butter with the confectioners' sugar in a separate bowl until light and gradually add the chocolate until well blended.

6. Spread an equal amount of filling on each cake layer and place the layers neatly on top of each other. Leave the top layer plain.

Glaze:
6 (1-ounce) squares
  semisweet chocolate
3 tablespoons unsalted
  butter

12 to 16 servings

7. For the glaze: Melt the chocolate and butter in the top of a double boiler or in a metal bowl set over a pot with boiling water. Stir constantly until smooth. Cool slightly. Brush any crumbs off the cake and spread the glaze thinly and evenly over the entire cake. Let dry on a rack for several hours.

8. The cake should stand in a cool place for at least 24 hours before serving. The cake keeps for 3 to 4 days in the refrigerator.

German Chocolate Cake—an Urban Legend

German chocolate cake is not German. An Englishman, Samuel German, developed a sweet chocolate baking bar for Baker's Chocolate Co. in 1852. The chocolate, which was named in his honor "German's Sweet Chocolate," had been on the market for almost a century before it found fame.

In 1957, a recipe for a rich chocolate cake using German's Sweet Chocolate was published in a Dallas newspaper. Sales of the chocolate bar skyrocketed in Texas, which prompted General Foods, then the owner of Baker's Chocolate Co., to send copies of the recipe and photos of the cake to food editors all over the United States. A smart move, as each time the recipe was published, it triggered an avalanche of reader inquiries on where to buy the chocolate. Within a year, sales rose by 73 percent.

On the way to becoming an American classic, the cake lost the apostrophe and the letter "s," although the name is printed correctly on Baker's German's Sweet Chocolate Bar, now owned by Kraft Foods.

Black Forest Cake

Schwarzwälder Kirschtorte

The most famous of all German cakes was not invented in the Black Forest. Pastry chef Josef Keller came up with this cake in 1927, when he was working at the upscale café Agner in Bad Godesberg, a suburb of Bonn. He was a native of the Lake of Konstanz, so we can assume that this is where the inspiration for the name came from. The kirsch used in this cake is a specialty from the Black Forest. In my family, no holiday went by without my grandmother baking a Black Forest cake. I remember having it ever since I could eat solid food, including the kirsch-infused cherries. Thankfully, none of the adults in my family hesitated to share this alcohol-spiked cake with me in my childhood.

A firmer cake is easier to fill than a freshly baked cake, so I recommend you bake the sponge a day in advance. Steep the cherries in kirsch for at least 4 hours.

Batter:
4 (1-ounce) squares semisweet chocolate
2/3 plus 1/4 cup all-purpose flour
1 teaspoon baking powder
3 tablespoons unsweetened cocoa powder
1 1/4 sticks unsalted butter, softened
3/4 cup sugar
2 teaspoons vanilla extract
4 eggs, separated

1. Preheat the oven to 350 degrees F. Grease a 9-inch springform pan.

2. For the batter: Grate the chocolate in a food processor to a very fine consistency. Mix it with the flour, baking powder, cocoa, and 2 tablespoons water.

3. Beat the butter with the sugar, vanilla, and egg yolks until creamy and pale yellow. Add to the batter.

4. Beat the egg whites until they stand in stiff peaks and fold them into the batter.

5. Pour the batter into the prepared pan and bake for 35 minutes, or until done. Check for doneness with a toothpick. Cool for 5 to 10 minutes. Remove the cake from the pan and cool it completely on a cake rack. Keep in a dry, cool place.

Filling:
1 ($14\frac{1}{2}$-ounce) can red
  tart pitted cherries
$\frac{1}{4}$ cup kirsch
2 tablespoons cornstarch
1 tablespoon sugar
2 cups heavy cream
$\frac{1}{3}$ cup confectioners' sugar
2 teaspoons cherry Jell-O
2 tablespoons boiling water
$\frac{1}{2}$ to 1 (1-ounce) square
  semisweet chocolate for
  garnish

12 to 16 servings

6. For the filling: Strain the cherries and reserve the juice (you should have $\frac{3}{4}$ to 1 cup). Sprinkle the cherries with kirsch, cover, and let stand for a few hours.

7. Dissolve the cornstarch in a few tablespoons of the juice. Heat the juice in a small saucepan and whisk in the cornstarch mixture. Stir vigorously and cook over very low heat until the mixture thickens and becomes clear again. Sweeten with the sugar and add the cherries. Remove from the heat, and cool.

8. Whip the cream with the confectioners' sugar in a chilled bowl until firm but not too stiff. Dissolve the Jell-O in the hot water and set it over a bowl of ice water. Stir continuously until it cools. Blend the Jell-O with the whipped cream.

9. Cut the cake horizontally into 2 layers (to do this in a neat and easy way, see page 183, step 6). Put the bottom layer on a cake plate, cut side up. Spread the cherry mixture evenly on the bottom layer. Top with $\frac{1}{3}$ of the whipped cream mixture. Place the other layer neatly on top. Brush off the crumbs and spread the remaining whipped cream mixture evenly on the entire cake. Finely grate the chocolate over the cake and chill.

Note: Black Forest cake can be kept in the refrigerator for 2 to 3 days. I find that it tastes best the second day.

Quince Almond Tart

Badische Quittentarte

In the early 20th century a quince tree was not an uncommon sight in back-yards in Germany, especially in the south. Quinces then almost disappeared and were forgotten, but in recent years have begun to make a comeback in German restaurants. Because quinces must be cooked to be palatable, they have become an icon of slow food—not only in Germany but also in the United States. If you can get your hands on quince, snap them up! Quince make wonderful jams, jellies, and pies, like this Quince Almond Tart from southwest Germany.

Quince filling:
5 to 6 quinces
Cold water mixed with a few tablespoons lemon juice
2 cups white wine
¾ cup sugar
1 organic lemon, washed and sliced
1 cinnamon stick
1 star anise
2 whole cloves

Dough:
1½ cups all-purpose flour
7 tablespoons cold butter
2 tablespoons sugar
Pinch of salt

Almond paste:
¾ cup blanched almonds
¼ cup sugar
⅛ teaspoon almond extract

½ cup red currant jelly

12 servings

1. For the quince filling: Peel and core the quinces and remove any of the gritty stone cells. Drop the quinces in the lemon water immediately to prevent browning. Bring the wine and 1 cup water to a boil in a pot large enough to hold the quince halves in a single layer. Add the sugar, lemon slices, cinnamon stick, star anise, and cloves. Lower the quinces into the liquid and reduce to a simmer. Cook over low heat for 30 to 40 minutes, until the quinces can be easily pierced with a knife. Remove from the heat and let cool in the cooking liquid.

2. For the dough: Put the flour, butter, sugar, and salt in a food processor and process to a coarse meal. Add 1 tablespoon ice water and pulse until the dough holds together in a ball. Wrap in plastic wrap and refrigerate.

3. For the almond paste: Process the almonds in a food processor with the sugar and almond extract. Add 1 tablespoon water and process until it forms a smooth paste, scraping down the sides of the bowl as needed.

4. Roll the dough on a floured work surface to fit a 10-inch pan plus a 1-inch edge. Grease a 10-inch tart or cake pan. Carefully drop the dough into the pan. Press it against the edges and trim the excess with a sharp knife. Pierce the dough in several places with a fork.

5. Break the almond paste into chunks and distribute it evenly over the dough, pressing it down with your fingers to fill the entire bottom of the pan.

6. Preheat the oven to 350 degrees F.

7. Drain the quinces well, reserving the cooking liquid. Cut each half into a fan shape and arrange the halves decoratively in the pan on top of the almond paste.

8. Measure out ½ cup of the quince cooking liquid and bring it to a boil in a small saucepan. Cook until reduced by about half. Stir in the red currant jelly. Brush the quince with some of this mixture, reserving the rest. Bake in the preheated oven for 34 to 40 minutes.

9. While still hot, brush the tart with the remaining red currant syrup. Cool on a cake rack.

Plum Dumplings

Zwetschgenknödel

German cuisine uses different types of dough for dumplings stuffed with fruit, from yeasted dough to dough made with quark, and potato dough. These dumplings are not very sweet, and so can also be served as a light main course.

Dough:
3 to 4 medium starchy yellow potatoes (about 1½ pounds), washed
1⅔ cups all-purpose flour
¼ teaspoon salt
1 egg

Stuffing:
12 to 15 Italian or Damson plums (depending on size), halved and pitted
12 to 15 sugar cubes

Topping:
¼ cup fine breadcrumbs
1 stick butter
Sugar
Ground cinnamon

4 servings

1. For the dough: Bring salted water to a boil and cook the potatoes in their skins. Peel as soon as they are cool enough to handle and press them through a potato ricer. Mix with the flour, salt, and egg to a smooth dough.

2. Bring water to a boil in a pot large enough for 15 dumplings to float freely. Drop a small piece of dough in the water. If it falls apart, add 1 tablespoon flour at a time to the dough and test another dumpling, until the consistency is right and tested dumpling holds together.

3. For the stuffing: Make an incision in each plum large enough to remove the pit but do not cut all the way through. Remove pits and put 1 sugar cube in the center of each plum and close tightly.

4. Divide the dough into 12 to 15 equal pieces. Shape each piece into dumplings with moistened hands. Place a plum in the center of each dumpling and completely enclose it. Gently lower the dumplings into the simmering water and cook over low heat for 5 to 8 minutes. Remove the dumplings with a slotted spoon and drain. Cover to keep warm.

5. For the topping: Toast the breadcrumbs in an ungreased skillet. Transfer them to a bowl. Melt the butter in the skillet over low-medium heat. Return the breadcrumbs to the skillet and stir. In a small bowl, season some sugar with cinnamon.

6. Serve the warm dumplings topped with the browned butter breadcrumbs and sprinkled with cinnamon sugar.

Hazelnut-Chocolate Cookies with Pistachios

Bayrische Butterbrote

These cute Christmas cookies from Bavaria live up to their German name—the cream-colored topping with chopped pistachios indeed resembles a slice of traditional dark German bread topped with butter (*Butterbrot*)!

Dough:
5 tablespoons unsalted butter
⅔ cup plus 1 tablespoon sugar
¾ teaspoon ground cinnamon
¾ teaspoon ground allspice
1 teaspoon vanilla extract
1 egg plus 1 egg yolk
⅔ cup all-purpose flour
1½ cups whole unpeeled hazelnuts, toasted and ground
4 (1-ounce) squares semi-sweet chocolate, finely grated

Topping:
3 eggs
1 cup confectioners' sugar
Coarsely chopped pistachios

60 pieces

1. For the dough: Cut the butter into small chunks and process in a food processor with the sugar, cinnamon, allspice, vanilla, egg, egg yolk, and flour. Transfer to a bowl and add the hazelnuts and chocolate. Mix well.

2. Transfer the dough to a large sheet of wax paper. In the center of the waxed paper, shape the dough into a log about 12 inches long and 2 inches wide. Fold over the wax paper from both sides and shape dough into a rectangle. Transfer to a platter and place in the freezer for 1 to 2 hours, until hard but not frozen.

3. Preheat the oven to 350 degrees F. Line two baking sheets with parchment paper. Cut the dough log into ¼-inch-thick slices and place on the baking sheets, leaving at least 1 inch between them. Bake one sheet at a time in the preheated oven for 12 minutes. Let the cookies cool slightly, then transfer to a cake rack to cool.

4. For the topping: Boil the eggs for 6 minutes. Shell them and carefully remove the egg yolks, which should still be slightly liquid. Discard the whites, or set aside for another use. Push the yolks through a fine sieve into a bowl. Gradually add the confectioners' sugar and stir vigorously until smooth. Add up to 2 teaspoons water if necessary. Spread a small amount of the glaze on each cookie and sprinkle with chopped pistachios. Let sit until the glaze has hardened. Store in airtight containers.

Apple Strudel Munich–Style

Münchner Apfelstrudel

What sets apart Munich apple strudel from other strudel recipes is that it is basted with milk or cream during baking. This recipe makes two small strudels.

Dough:
1¾ cups plus 1 tablespoon all-purpose flour
1 egg
2 tablespoons plus 2 teaspoons vegetable oil
Pinch of salt
½ cup lukewarm water

Filling:
½ cup raisins, soaked in hot water
6 to 8 tart cooking apples (3¼ pounds), quartered, cored, and thinly sliced
1 teaspoon ground cinnamon
¼ cup lemon juice
Grated zest of 1 organic lemon
⅓ cup sugar
¾ cup sour cream

Basting:
½ stick unsalted butter
½ cup milk

16 servings

1. For the dough: Combine the flour, egg, 2 tablespoons oil, and salt. Knead into a smooth dough, gradually adding the lukewarm water. The dough is sticky at first but becomes smoother the longer you knead it. Grease a bowl with the remaining 2 teaspoons oil, place the dough in it, and turn dough over to coat. Cover and let sit for 30 minutes.

2. For the filling: Drain the raisins and pat them dry. Mix with the apples, cinnamon, lemon juice, lemon zest, and sugar.

3. Place a large clean kitchen towel on the work surface and dust it with flour. Divide the dough in half and cover the second piece with a towel. Roll the first piece on the floured towel as thin as possible with a rolling pin also dusted with flour. Place your hands palms down underneath the dough and gently stretch the dough in all directions, without tearing it.

4. Place the dough on the towel and brush it with half of the sour cream, leaving a 1-inch edge all around. Spread half of the apple filling on top. Fold the edge over the filling and roll up the strudel from the long side, using the towel. Tuck in the ends.

5. Melt the butter for basting and use half to brush a large oblong baking dish. Carefully transfer the strudel into the dish using the towel. Proceed as described to make the second strudel.

6. Preheat the oven to 400 degrees F.

7. Brush the strudels with the remaining butter and pour the milk over them. Bake in the preheated oven for 60 minutes, or until golden brown, basting often. Cool slightly, then dust with confectioners' sugar and serve warm.

Beer with Lemon Soda

Radler

As with many foods and drinks, *Radler* was born out of an emergency. On a hot Saturday in 1922, a large number of bikers stopped at the Kugler-Alm, a popular restaurant 10 miles outside of Munich. The supply of beer was getting short, but lemonade was still available in large quantities. The ingenious owner mixed half beer and half lemon soda and named it *Radler* (biker). He later told the bikers that he created the mixture especially for them so they would not get tipsy from too much beer.

Like all beer in Bavaria, *Radler* is usually served in a large mug that holds about 1 quart (called a *Radlermaß*). Nowadays the drink is popular all over Germany, and you can even buy it ready-made in a bottle or a can. Whether you arrive by foot or bike, there is nothing better than a freshly mixed *Radler* in an outdoor *Biergarten* (beer garden) on a hot summer night.

*2 cups chilled
lemon-flavored soda*
2 cups cold beer

2 servings for thirsty
people or
1 serving for a very
thirsty person
(or a Bavarian)

Pour the soda into a pitcher and slowly add the beer.

White Wine with Seltzer Water

Weinschorle

In German, any drink with the suffix *-schorle* indicates that it is mixed with soda water. Thus *Weinschorle* is a combination of wine (usually white) and soda water.

The alleged origin of this word is a delectable etymologic tidbit. In the nineteenth century, a French officer, stationed in the wine country of Franconia, toasted every glass with the French sentence "Toujours l'amour" (To love every day), which over time became *Schorlemorle*, or just *Schorle*.

The ratio of wine and seltzer water in *Schorle* can vary. The essential thing is that the drink is served very chilled.

½ cup dry white wine
½ cup soda water

Or for a lighter version, use:

⅓ dry white wine
⅔ soda water

1 serving

Mix the wine with the soda water and serve at once.

Potatoes without Prejudice

A common misperception places the Germans inside the "PBS" triangle: potatoes, beer, and sausage. In addition to the idea that Germans consume high daily doses of sausage and beer, one of the most tenacious culinary stereotypes is that they mainly eat potatoes.

Let's get things straight: Germany is, indeed, the largest potato producer in the European Union. However, it's the Irish who have the highest annual average per capita consumption with about 150 pounds per person a year. The Germans eat slightly fewer potatoes than the European average.

In the nineteenth century, the Germans were avid potatoes eaters but not by choice. Around 1770, the Prussian King Frederick the Great ordered the farmers in Pomerania and Silesia in the eastern part of the country to grow potatoes. He gave his subjects detailed instructions on how to store and use potatoes. To the frugal ruler of a country torn by the Seven Years' War, potatoes seemed a good and easy way to feed civilians and soldiers. Yet, it took almost a century before the cultivation of the potato spread widely and potatoes became a staple of German cooking. The twentieth century saw the potato's fall from grace again. Nonetheless, a large variety of potatoes are grown in Germany today; 244 different kinds of potatoes are registered with the German Federal Office for Plant Protection.

One of the reasons potatoes are thought to have such a dominant role in German cuisine might be the tremendous number of potato dishes. Open a classic German cookbook like *Dr. Oetker German Cooking Today*, and you will find it hard to choose between the all-time favorite *Bratkartoffeln* (potatoes fried with onions), potatoes in béchamel sauce, caraway potatoes, potato croquettes, mashed potatoes, potato pancakes, potato dumplings, baked potatoes, and dishes borrowed from neighboring countries such as *Rösti* (Swiss potato cake). Add the large number of regional potato specialties, some of which are included in this book, and you will never run out of ideas. Given this variety, I have never understood the popularity of plain boiled potatoes in Germany. How can you bleed a potato of its entire flavor by peeling and then boiling it for 20 minutes? To some people, it seems too time-consuming to prepare a more elaborate potato dish. I dislike boiled potatoes so much that I have vowed that even in the biggest rush, I would, at a minimum, make *Pellkartoffeln* (potatoes boiled in their skins), or abstain from making potatoes and instead, throw some 3-minute angel hair pasta into boiling water.

The truth about Germans and potatoes is that they eat fewer potatoes than most Europeans. But when Germans eat potatoes, they have a sensational repertoire of traditional recipes to choose from.

Recipe Index

Geographical Index

HUNGARIAN COOKBOOK: OLD WORLD RECIPES FOR NEW WORLD COOKS
Yolanda Nagy Fintor

These Old World recipes were brought to America by the author's grandparents, but they have been updated to accommodate today's faster-paced lifestyle. In many cases, the author presents a New World version of the recipe, in which low-fat and more readily available ingredients are substituted without compromising flavor. Hungarian cuisine is known for generous amounts of paprika, sour cream, bacon and garlic in famous dishes like "Chicken Paprika" and "Hungarian Goulash." This collection includes these classics, and spans the range of home cooking with recipes for "Bean with Sausage Soup," "Stuffed Breast of Veal," "Hungarian Creamed Spinach," and a host of tempting desserts like "Walnut Torte," and "Dilled Cottage Cheese Cake."

This is more than just a collection of 125 enticing Hungarian recipes. Eight chapters also describe the seasonal and ceremonial holidays that Hungarian-Americans celebrate today with special foods: fall grape festivals; Christmas, New Year's and Easter; summer cookouts; weddings and baptisms. The book also includes culinary tips, a glossary of terms and explanations about the Hungarian language.

978-0-7818-1240-5 • $14.95pb

THE BEST OF POLISH COOKING, *Expanded Edition*
Karen West

Now updated with a new chapter on Light Polish Fare!

"Ethnic cuisine at its best."—*The Midwest Book Review*

First published in 1983, this classic resource for Polish cuisine has been a favorite with home chefs for many years. The new edition includes a chapter on Light Polish Fare with ingenious tips for reducing fat, calories and cholesterol, without compromising the flavor of fine Polish cuisine. Fragrant herbal rubs and vinegars add panache without calories. Alternatives and conversion tables for butter, sour cream and milk will help readers lighten other recipes as well.

In an easy-to-use menu format, the author arranges complementary and harmonious foods together—all organized in seasonal cycles. Inside are recipes for "Braised Spring Lamb with Cabbage," "Frosty Artichoke Salad," "Apple Raisin Cake," and "Hunter's Stew." The new Light Polish Fare chapter includes low-fat recipes for treats like "Roasted Garlic and Mushroom Soup" and "Twelve-Fruit Brandied Compote."

0-7818-0826-X • $13.95pb

OLD POLISH TRADITIONS IN THE KITCHEN AND AT THE TABLE

A cookbook and history of Polish culinary customs. Short essays cover subjects like Polish hospitality, holiday traditions, even the exalted status of the mushroom. The recipes are traditional family fare.

0-7818-0488-4 • $14.95pb

THE POLISH COUNTRY KITCHEN COOKBOOK, *Expanded Edition*
Sophie Hodorowicz Knab

This popular cookbook by beloved Polish-American author Sophie Hodorowicz Knab is now updated with a new section on Polish Feasts & Festivals! Arranged according to the cycle of seasons, this cookbook explores life in the Polish countryside through the year, giving readers priceless historical information such as the type of utensils used in Poland at the turn of the century, the meaning behind the Pascal butter lamb, and many other insightful answers to common questions asked by descendants of Polish immigrants.

978-0-7818-1294-8 · $16.95pb

TASTE OF ROMANIA, *Expanded Edition*
Nicolae Klepper

"A brilliant cultural and culinary history . . . a collection of recipes to be treasured, tested and enjoyed."
—George Lang

" . . . dishes like creamy cauliflower soup, sour cream-enriched *mamaliga* (the Romanian polenta), lamb stewed in sauerkraut juice and scallions, and *mititei* (exactly like the ones I tasted so long ago in Bucharest) are simple and appealing . . . Klepper paints a pretty picture of his native country's culinary possibilities."
—Colman Andrews, *Saveur* magazine

A real taste of both Old World and modern Romanian culture. More than

140 recipes, including the specialty dishes of Romania's top chefs, are intermingled with fables, poetry, photos and illustrations in this comprehensive and well-organized guide to Romanian cuisine.

978-0-7818-1264-1 • $16.95pb

THE UKRAINIAN COOKBOOK
Annette Ogrodnik Corona

The New Ukrainian Cookbook introduces readers to the fresh foods, exquisite tastes, hospitality and generous spirit of the Ukrainian table. Scattered amongst the recipes are quotes, poems, historical facts, folklore, and illustrations, making this cookbook not only a culinary adventure but a unique cultural exploration as well.
Includes:

- More than 200 easy-to-follow recipes
- An introduction to Ukraine's history, culture, and cuisine
- Helpful tips and notes with many recipes
- Charming illustrations by renowned Ukrainian-American artist Laurette Kovary

978-0-7818-1287-0 • $29.95hc

Prices subject to change without prior notice. **To purchase Hippocrene Books** contact your local bookstore, visit www.hippocrenebooks.com, call (212) 685-4373, or write to: HIPPOCRENE BOOKS, 171 Madison Avenue, New York, NY 10016.